COLUMBIA CRITICAL GUIDES

T. S. Eliot

The Waste Land

EDITED BY NICK SELBY

Series editor: Richard Beynon

COLUMBIA UNIVERSITY PRESS   NEW YORK

Columbia University Press
Publishers Since 1893
New York
Editor's text copyright © 1999 Nick Selby

First published in the Icon Critical Guides series in 1999 by Icon Books
Ltd.

Library of Congress Cataloging-in-Publication Data

T. S. Eliot : The waste land / edited by Nick Selby.
  p. cm.—(Columbia critical guides)
  ISBN 0–231–12424–4 (cloth)—ISBN 0–231–12425–2 (paper)
   1. Eliot, T. S. (Thomas Stearns), 1888–1965. Waste land.
  2.Eliot, T. S. (Thomas Stearns), 1888–1965—Criticism and
interpretation—History. I. Title: Thomas Stearns Eliot. II Title:
Waste land. III. Selby, Nick. IV. Series.

  PS3509.L13 W3639 2001   2001042378
  812'.912—dc21

Printed in the United States of America

c 10 9 8 7 6 5 4 3 2 1
p 10 9 8 7 6 5 4 3 2 1

Contents

Patterns in Poetry (1934) and demonstrates how the poem has been read through models taken from Jungian psychoanalysis.

New Criticism: Poetry, Literature and Myth

Looks at 'New Critical' readings of the poem, and analyses how Eliot's poetics, and the poem itself, can be seen to have given rise to this highly influential critical practice. An extract from F. O. Matthiessen's *The Achievement of T. S. Eliot* (1935), though not strictly New Criticism, introduces Cleanth Brooks' '*The Waste Land*: Critique of the Myth' (1939), a milestone in New Criticism. Hugh Kenner's analysis of the poem, from his *The Invisible Poet* (1959), and a brief extract from Roy Harvey Pearce's *The Continuity of American Poetry* (1961) close the chapter by demonstrating the continued influence of New Critical modes of thought in readings of the poem up into the 1960s.

Political Readings: Marx, Ideology and Culture

The three extracts in this chapter attempt to get underneath the assumptions about culture and ideology that previous criticism of the poem has fostered. All three essays expose the silent political assumptions on which *The Waste Land*'s modernist ideology can be seen to rest. David Craig's essay 'The Defeatism of *The Waste Land*' (1960) represents the first challenge to orthodox critical ideas about the poem. Craig's Marxist critique of the poem is developed even more vehemently by Terry Eagleton in the next extract, taken from his *Criticism and Ideology* (1976). Michael North's subtle and persuasive political reading of the poem, from his book *The Political Aesthetic of Yeats, Eliot and Pound* (1991), restores some critical decorum to the poem after the onslaught of Eagleton.

Deconstructive Readings: Freud, Feminism and Ideology

Examines the influence of deconstructive critical practice in reading *The Waste Land*. Short extracts from Frank Kermode's 'A Babylonish Dialect' (1966) and Ruth Nevo's '*The Waste Land*: Ur-Text of Deconstruction'

(1982) consider ways of reading the poem deconstructively. Both David Trotter's reading of the poem, from his *The Making of the Reader* (1984) and Maud Ellmann's 'The Waste Land: A Sphinx without a Secret' (1987) use Freudian psychoanalysis to deconstruct the poem. Two of the most brilliant and exciting readings of *The Waste Land*, they show ways forward in contemporary criticism of the poem, not least because they open up this resolutely masculine modernist text to feminist terms of analysis.

CHAPTER SIX   139

Cultural Readings: Modernism, Ideology and Desire

Deals with recent interpretations of *The Waste Land* and their considerations of the operation of a discourse of desire in the text. These readings lead to a reconsideration of the ideology of modernism by examining what the poem hides as much as what it reveals of modern consciousness. The first extract is from Christopher Ricks' book *T.S. Eliot and Prejudice* (1988), one of the first examinations of the complicity of Eliot's poetry with the prejudices of his age. This is followed by Frank Lentricchia's careful and subtle reading of the poem, from his *Modernist Quartet* (1994), which defines the poem's modernity in terms of its desire to escape from modern culture. Harriet Davidson's essay 'Improper Desire: Reading *The Waste Land*' (1994) closes the chapter.

(1982) consider ways of reading the poem deconstructively. Both David Trotter's reading of the poem, from his *The Making of the Reader* (1984) and Maud Ellmann's 'The Waste Land: A Sphinx without a Secret' (1987) use Freudian psychoanalysis to deconstruct the poem. Two of the most brilliant and exciting readings of *The Waste Land*, they show ways forward in contemporary criticism of the poem, not least because they open up this resolutely masculine modernist text to feminist terms of analysis.

Cultural Readings: Modernism, Ideology and Desire

Deals with recent interpretations of *The Waste Land* and their considerations of the operation of a discourse of desire in the text. These readings lead to a reconsideration of the ideology of modernism by examining what the poem hides as much as what it reveals of modern consciousness. The first extract is from Christopher Ricks' book *T.S. Eliot and Prejudice* (1988), one of the first examinations of the complicity of Eliot's poetry with the prejudices of his age. This is followed by Frank Lentricchia's careful and subtle reading of the poem, from his *Modernist Quartet* (1994), which defines the poem's modernity in terms of its desire to escape from modern culture. Harriet Davidson's essay 'Improper Desire: Reading *The Waste Land*' (1994) closes the chapter.

INTRODUCTION

THE YEAR 1922 was a crucial year in the history of modern thought. It was the year that saw the publication of two literary texts that would change the face of twentieth century culture: James Joyce's novel *Ulysses* was published on 2 February (Joyce's fortieth birthday), and T. S. Eliot's poem *The Waste Land* was first published in the October edition of the literary magazine *The Criterion*.[1] Both of these texts are notorious for their many difficulties, for their disdain of literary propriety and for their apparent attack upon cultured sensibilities. They have come to epitomise the high point of an avant-garde literary and artistic movement of the early years of the century. They are commonly thought of as the central, 'classic', texts of modernism. Because modernism can be seen to be a product of *The Waste Land* as much as *The Waste Land* is a product of modernism, any guide to the critical history of Eliot's poem is, to a large extent, an account both of the conditions and constitution of modernism, and of the gradual assimilation of modernism's ideas and practices into critical thought.

What *The Waste Land* and modernism recognise is that traditional notions of culture and society have been – literally and metaphorically – blown apart by recent experiences. Modernism has therefore always been more than just a new literary or artistic movement. At the heart of modernist sensibilities has always been the desire to come to terms with a world whose philosophical certainties, moral codes and aesthetic practices have, under intense interrogation, been brought close to a point of collapse. This experience is witnessed in the desperate sense of incoherence confronting the reader of *The Waste Land*. Its fragmentary form, partial quotations and resolute obscurity make real the struggles of modern consciousness to make sense of a culture in which old ways of seeing and thinking (and even of feeling) now seem partial, fragmented and discredited. Most importantly, the modernist culture that *The Waste Land* engages is a postwar culture. Whether waste land or no-man's land, the poem's imagery of sterility, drought and death is grounded in the trenches and battlefields of the First World War. Its exploded poetic form also seems a delayed effect of the trenches; all that remains of literature and culture is a handful of fragmentary quotations. In this most shell-shocked of poems Eliot seems despairingly to ask: what now, after the war to end all wars?

But the modernity that *The Waste Land* epitomises so powerfully had already had a deep and lasting effect on artistic expression for several years before the war.[2] Eliot's poem, then, can be seen as the culmination of avant-garde aesthetics that had challenged the cultural status quo since, at least, the turn of the century. Famously, the novelist Virginia Woolf noted that 'in or about December 1910, human character changed'.[3] Though she refers specifically to the first exhibition of Post-Impressionist Painting that was held in London's Grafton Galleries in December 1910, her comment also expresses the sense of a general shift in sensibility, one contingent upon the wider conditions of modernity. This changing of human character is, according to Malcolm Bradbury and James McFarlane, crucial to modernism. They note that:

■ Clearly it [modernism] is an art of a rapidly modernizing world, a world of rapid industrial development, advanced technology, urbanization, secularization and mass forms of social life. Clearly, too, it is the art of a world from which many traditional certainties had departed, and a certain sort of Victorian confidence not only in the onward progress of mankind but in the very solidity and visibility of reality itself has evaporated. It contains within itself that tendency, so apparent at the end of the nineteenth century, for knowledge to become both pluralistic and ambiguous, for surface certainties no longer to be taken on trust, for experience to outrun, as it seemed to many to be outrunning, the orderly control of the mind.[4] □

Modernism, then, charts both rapid changes in culture and a discontent that had long been rumbling. The war turned such discontent into disillusioned scepticism and *The Waste Land* was one of its first major articulations.

On one level, modernism can be seen to be based in a radical embracing of the new. Indeed, Ezra Pound, Eliot's great friend, and arguably the most controversial of modernist poets, was especially fond of quoting the motto 'MAKE IT NEW'. However, modernist art is also deeply aware of the break-up of traditional certainties on which it is predicated. In this respect it is highly nostalgic for a language, a history or a sense of self-hood that is unified rather than fragmented, authoritative rather than provisional. One of the key conditions of modernity, then, is a profound sense of loss. In his essay entitled 'Cavalcanti', Ezra Pound had described this sense of loss on which modern consciousness can be seen to rest:

■ We appear to have lost the radiant world where one thought cuts through another with a clean edge, a world of moving energies . . . magnetisms that take form, that are seen, or that border the visible, the matter of Dante's *paradiso*, the glass under water, the form that seems a form seen in a mirror, these realities perceptible to the sense, interacting.[5] □

Such a consciousness of loss typifies the sort of historical yearning that lies underneath *The Waste Land* in particular and modernism in general. Pound's sense of loss is symptomatic of the conditions of modernity: his awareness of chaos leads to a crisis of representation. And it is from such conditions that *The Waste Land* arises.

In the critical essays that Eliot wrote around the same time that he was writing *The Waste Land*, he both examines the conditions of modern consciousness and attempts to articulate a concept of poetry that is adequate to the experience of modernity. These essays have therefore played a crucial role in the critical history of *The Waste Land* by providing its early readers with a conceptual framework for coming to terms with the poem. The three essays that figure most prominently in criticism of *The Waste Land*, and which therefore set the critical terms for reading modernism, are his review of Joyce's *Ulysses*, '*Ulysses*, Order and Myth' (November 1923); perhaps his most famous critical piece, 'Tradition and the Individual Talent' (1919); and his essay 'Hamlet' (1919). Because of the importance of these essays to the critical history of *The Waste Land*, extracts from them are quoted below. In all three pieces Eliot is troubled by the problematic relationship of modernity to a concept of history. How, Eliot asks, is it possible to be modern *and* to preserve the sort of historical consciousness that modernity seems to deny? In providing answers to this question, Eliot sets out the modernist poetics on which *The Waste Land* rests. The three main concepts of such poetics are his idea of 'mythic composition', his doctrine of the impersonality of the artist, and his famous notion of the 'objective correlative'.

The brief extract from '*Ulysses*, Order and Myth' that follows neatly summarises Eliot's idea of mythic composition. This essay suggests that underlying the anarchy of modern history is a deeper, mythic level, one that ultimately gives a shape and order to the chaos of modern consciousness. Eliot's examination of Joyce's novel, then, tests the assertion of its character Stephen Dedalus that 'history . . . is a nightmare', while also setting out some of the major terms for subsequent criticism of his own poem.[6]

■ In using . . . myth, in manipulating a continuous parallel between contemporaneity and antiquity, Mr Joyce is pursuing a method which others must pursue after him. They will not be imitators any more than the scientist who uses the discoveries of Einstein in pursuing his own, independent, further investigations. It is simply a way of controlling, of ordering, of giving a shape and a significance to the immense panorama of futility and anarchy that is contemporary history. . . . It is, I seriously believe, a step toward making the modern world possible for art.[7] □

Clearly, the attempt to manipulate a 'continuous parallel' between modern and historical worlds is crucial to the composition of *The Waste Land*'s attempt to set its lands in some sort of order, and to come to some sort of control over contemporary chaos. The mythic method is therefore the theoretical justification of the poem's desire to overcome futility; it is the means by which Eliot's textual fragments can shore him against his ruins. And, as we shall see in this Guide, it provides the poem's first critics with a clue as to how the poem should be read. Indeed, extended and developed into one of the main doctrines of New Criticism, Eliot's use of mythic composition can be said to have spawned a highly influential school of literary criticism. As the apotheosis of his theories of modernist poetics, then, *The Waste Land* has not only changed the way in which poetry is written in the twentieth century, but also changed the ways in which poetry is read.

One of the most interesting aspects of the previous extract is that it calls upon a scientific example to justify a writer's use of the mythic method. This is the result of Eliot's desire that poetry be seen to be objective and analytic rather than emotional and impressionistic. Modern poetry should, Eliot believed, express – in as disinterested a manner as possible – the modern mind, and not the emotions or personality of the poet. Eliot's essay 'Tradition and the Individual Talent' provides the fullest theoretical exploration of this position. Again, Eliot appeals, in this essay, to scientific examples to demonstrate his doctrine of the impersonality of the poet and his belief that the poem itself is, as it were, a crucial object within an experiment conducted upon modern consciousness. The poet's importance to this experiment, Eliot argues, is like that of a catalyst: it sets things going but plays no actual part in the transformation that occurs. In this model, history and literary tradition are thus vast, impersonal forces. They record the simultaneity of all events, the 'continuous parallel' – as he noted above – 'between contemporaneity and antiquity'. Tradition, therefore, is the record of the relationships between literary works of all ages rather than of the individuality of specific writers. This doctrine of impersonality has had a profound and lasting effect on ways of thinking about literature (and especially poetry) throughout the twentieth century. The next extract, from 'Tradition and the Individual Talent', sets out some of the key elements of this doctrine:

■ Tradition . . . cannot be inherited, and if you want it you must obtain it by great labour. It involves, in the first place, the historical sense, which we may call nearly indispensable to anyone who would continue to be a poet beyond his twenty-fifth year; and the historical sense involves a perception, not only of the pastness of the past, but of its presence; the historical sense compels a man to write not merely with his own generation in his bones, but with a feeling that the whole of the literature of Europe from Homer and within it the whole of the literature of his own country has a simultaneous existence and composes a simultaneous order. This historical sense, which is a sense of the timeless as well as of the temporal and of the timeless and of the temporal together, is what makes a writer traditional. And it is at the same time what makes a writer most acutely conscious of his place in time, of his own contemporaneity.

No poet, no artist of any art, has his complete meaning alone. His significance, his appreciation is the appreciation of his relation to the dead poets and artists. You cannot see him alone; you must set him, for contrast and comparison, among the dead. I mean this as a principle of aesthetic, not merely historical, criticism. . . .

What is to be insisted upon is that the poet must develop or procure the consciousness of the past and that he should continue to develop this consciousness throughout his career.

What happens is a continual surrender of himself as he is at the moment to something which is more valuable. The progress of an artist is continual self-sacrifice, a continual extinction of personality.

There remains to define this process of depersonalization and its relation to the sense of tradition. It is in this depersonalization that art may be said to approach the condition of science. I therefore invite you to consider, as a suggestive analogy, the action which takes place when a bit of finely filiated platinum is introduced into a chamber containing oxygen and sulphur dioxide.

. . . I hinted, by an analogy, that the mind of the mature poet differs from that of the immature one not precisely in any valuation of 'personality', not being necessarily more interesting, or having 'more to say', but rather by being a more finely perfected medium in which special, or very varied, feelings are at liberty to enter into new combinations.

The analogy was that of the catalyst. When the two gases previously mentioned are fixed in the presence of a filament of platinum, they form sulphurous acid. This combination takes place only if the platinum is present; nevertheless the newly formed acid contains no trace of platinum, and the platinum itself is apparently unaffected: has remained inert, neutral, and unchanged. The mind of the poet is the shred of platinum. It may partly or exclusively operate upon the experience of the man himself; but, the more perfect the artist, the more completely separate in him will be the man who suffers and the mind which creates; the more perfectly will the mind digest and transmute the passions which are its material.

The experience, you will notice, the elements which enter the presence of the transforming catalyst, are of two kinds: emotions and feelings. The effect of a work of art upon the person who enjoys it is an experience different in kind from any experience not of art. . . .

The point of view which I am struggling to attack is perhaps related to the metaphysical theory of the substantial unity of the soul: for my meaning is, that the poet has, not a 'personality' to express, but a particular medium, which is only a medium and not a personality, in which impressions and experiences combine in peculiar and unexpected ways. Impressions and experiences which are important for the man may take no place in the poetry, and those which become important in the poetry may play quite a negligible part in the man, the personality.

. . . The business of the poet is not to find new emotions, but to use ordinary ones and, in working them up into poetry, to express feelings which are not in actual emotions at all. . . . There is a great deal, in the writing of poetry, which must be conscious and deliberate. In fact, the bad poet is usually unconscious where he ought to be conscious, and conscious where he ought to be unconscious. Both errors tend to make him 'personal'. Poetry is not a turning loose of emotion, but an escape from emotion; it is not the expression of personality, but an escape from personality. But, of course, only those who have personality and emotions know what it means to want to escape from these things.

. . . The emotion of art is impersonal. And the poet cannot reach this impersonality without surrendering himself wholly to the work to be done. And he is not likely to know what is to be done unless he lives in what is not merely the present, but the present moment of the past, unless he is conscious, not of what is dead, but of what is already living.[8] □

The final, brief, extract of this Introduction is from Eliot's essay 'Hamlet'. Here he explains the vitally important notion of the 'objective correlative'. This concept, like those set out in 'Tradition and the Individual Talent', both helps to explain and illuminate the aims and objectives of *The Waste Land*, and is crucial to critical thought about *The Waste Land*. It develops further the idea of art and poetry as an objective realisation of the artist's special historical sense:

■ The only way of expressing emotion in the form of art is by finding an 'objective correlative'; in other words, a set of objects, a situation, a chain of events which shall be the formula of a *particular* emotion; such that when the external facts, which must terminate in sensory experience, are given, the emotion is immediately evoked.[9] □

In their first readings of *The Waste Land*, Eliot's critics sought to discover and examine how the poem's objective correlatives evoke the experience of modernity. Their examination of the ways in which the poem is both a product of modernism, and a way of reading modernism sets the agenda for the poem's critical history.

As we will see throughout this Critical Guide, criticism of *The Waste Land* was dominated for many years by the concepts of poetry and culture embedded in these, and other, of Eliot's essays from immediately after the war. The poem has, therefore, been read as an exercise in the poetics of mythic composition, impersonality and objectivity. And because of this, critics have read modernism in the same way, believing that such doctrines can distance the artist (and reader) from the harsher realities and emotions of a turbulent culture that is felt to be an 'immense panorama of futility and anarchy'. The critical belief and hope has been that such poetry can redeem the loss felt so searingly by modern culture. Through the course of its critical history, though, critics have gradually prised open these assumptions that have been brought to bear on the poem. What successive generations of its readers have discovered over and over again is that *The Waste Land*'s power lies in its ability to engage our senses of self-hood and identity in their bearing upon the sense (or nonsense) we make of twentieth-century culture.

In later life, Eliot made the following claim about the poem that re-invented poetic culture for modernity:

■ Various critics have done me the honour to interpret the poem in terms of criticism of the contemporary world, have considered it, indeed, as an important bit of social criticism. To me it was only the relief of a personal and wholly insignificant grouse against life; it is just a piece of rhythmical grumbling.[10] □

Finally, though, *The Waste Land* seems more than just rhythmic grumbling. It expresses the turmoil and chaos of a whole culture in transition to modernity. It is a crucial document that marks *and* produces a change in sensibility from unity of thought to a modern – even postmodern – apprehension of the plurality of experience. The critical history of the poem that is charted in this Guide serves merely to emphasise this point.

CHAPTER ONE

The 1920s: Early Reviews

THAT *THE Waste Land* disturbed deeply – if not fully dislodged – the assumptions and commonplaces of literary thought in the 1920s is demonstrated by its initial critical reception. Early reviewers of Eliot's poem exhibit, in pretty much equal measures, scandalised incredulity, rueful bafflement or thankful recognition of a modern poetic 'masterpiece'. Those who enthusiastically heralded the poem were, generally, younger writers, undergraduates and members of the Bloomsbury set who saw it as the exemplary avant-garde text. For them, *The Waste Land* came to be seen as *the* poem of the Jazz Age. The poem's impact on the literary and social scenes of the 1920s, due partly to its power to shock, meant that it sold remarkably well when published by Leonard and Virginia Woolf's Hogarth Press in September 1923.[1]

Those critics and reviewers for whom the poem seemed just too shocking, or too bemusing, dismissed it as the worst kind of modern excess. To them it was a dreadful experiment lacking coherence of theme and structure or any discernible poetic purpose. Worse still for such commentators, *The Waste Land* transgressed poetic decorum: it mixed styles and tones, confused 'high' art with 'popular' culture, and seemed to do away with conventional rhythmic devices. For Charles Powell, writing in the *Manchester Guardian* (31 October 1923), the poem amounted to just 'so much waste paper'. Powell's dismissive tone, which mixes shocked outrage with a perhaps rather too willed bafflement, sets the standard for negative reviews of the poem. While Powell's condemnation of the poem's seeming lack of unity, bookish pedantry and apparent obscurity is typical, the sense of humour with which he delivers his judgement on the poem is not:

■ This poem of 433 lines, with a page of notes to every three pages of text, is not for the ordinary reader. He will make nothing of it. . . . The thing is a mad medley. It has a plan, because its author says so: and presumably it has some meaning, because he speaks of its symbolism; but meaning, plan, and the intention alike are massed behind a smoke-screen of anthropological and literary erudition, and only the pundit, the pedant, or the clairvoyant will be in the least aware of them.[2] □

Clearly attempting to engage *The Waste Land* on its own terms of 'symbolism', and an 'anthropological and literary erudition' that is tempered by clairvoyancy, Powell's dismissal is thus, curiously, one that throws attention back to the poem itself.

Interestingly, the same terms were used to praise the poem. If the poem was felt to be a 'mad medley', then this was precisely because modern life was felt to be fragmented; if reading the poem was an alienating experience then this, too, was because 'the ordinary reader' was alienated by the conditions of modernity. Thus the sorts of worry raised by reviewers such as Powell about the unity or otherwise of the poem, and about how far its obscurities are merely wilful, are taken by favourable reviewers as signs of Eliot's struggle to articulate modern consciousness. This is clear in Gilbert Seldes' review of *The Waste Land*, which appeared in the literary magazine *Nation* on 6 December 1922. Whereas Powell finds it impossible to read *beyond* such worries, Seldes reads *through* them to discover a poem of rare and important power:

■ In essence 'The Waste Land' says something which is not new: that life has become barren and sterile, that man is withering, impotent, and without assurance that the waters which made the land fruitful will ever arise again. . . . The title, the plan, and much of the symbolism of the poem, the author tells us in his 'Notes', was suggested by Miss Weston's remarkable book on the Grail legend, *From Ritual to Romance*; it is only indispensable to know that there exists the legend of a King rendered impotent, and his country sterile, both awaiting deliverance by a knight on his way to seek the Grail; it is interesting to know further that this is part of the Life or Fertility mysteries; but the poem is self-contained. It seems at first sight remarkably disconnected, confused, the emotion seems to disengage itself in spite of the object and events chosen by the poet as the vehicle. . . .

A closer view of the poem does more than illuminate the difficulties; it reveals the hidden form of the work, indicates how each thing falls into place, and to the reader's surprise shows that the emotion which at first seemed to come in spite of the framework and the detail could not otherwise have been communicated. For the theme is not a distaste for life, nor is it a disillusion, a romantic pessimism of any kind. It is specifically concerned with the idea of the Waste Land – that the land was fruitful and now is not, that life had been rich, beautiful, assured, organized, lofty, and now is dragging itself out in a poverty-stricken, and disrupted and ugly tedium, without health, and with no consolation in morality; there may remain for the poet the labor of poetry, but in the poem there remain only 'these fragments I have shored against my ruins' – the broken glimpses of what was. The poem is not an argument and I can only add, to be fair, that it contains no romantic idealization of the past; one feels simply that even in the cruelty and madness which have left their record in history and in art, there was an intensity of life, the germination and fruitfulness, which are now gone, and that even the creative imagination, even hallucination and vision have atrophied, so that water shall never again be struck from a rock in the desert.[3] □

Seldes, then, in keeping with other favourable reviewers of *The Waste Land*, finds in it an emotional intensity that unifies its apparent discontinuities, and illuminates its obscurities. *The Waste Land* is not difficult, such reviewers argue, so much as complex. Its formal and poetic strategies seem chaotic only in so far as contemporary life itself is chaotic. Seldes closes his review by comparing *The Waste Land* with that other great work of high modernism published in 1922, James Joyce's *Ulysses*. Both are texts, he argues, in which 'the theme . . . is seen to have dictated the form'. And *The Waste Land* is, for him, a poem that has 'expressed something of supreme relevance to our present life in the everlasting terms of art'.[4]

We shall see in the following extracts from early reviews of the poem that such manipulating of a parallel between *The Waste Land*'s formal and aesthetic difficulties and the cultural tensions of modernity is particularly marked in the efforts of favourable reviewers and critics to make a case for the status of the poem as an important, indeed crucial, addition to the literary canon. Another feature of such reviews is their recognition of the great emotional trauma and upheaval undergone by the poet, and which gives force and power to the poem. And this is despite the claims for the 'impersonality' of the literary artist made by Eliot in his critical essays of this period. This sort of critical recognition, though, became very quickly unpopular in readings of the poem. As we shall see in the following chapters of this Guide, *The Waste Land* was rapidly elevated to the status of *the* exemplary text of modernist impersonality wherein its causes and effects are universal and mythic, not personal and emotional. The orthodoxies, then, of formalist and New Critical readings of the poem which have dominated the history of *The Waste Land*'s critical reception, and which undoubtedly secured for the poem its central position in twentieth-century letters, have effectively obscured the initial power of its impact as a poem borne out of deep emotional crisis. Only recently have critics returned to the sorts of consideration of the personal grounding of the poem that seemed so apparent to its first readers but were disallowed by subsequent critics.

One thing that does seem clear from *The Waste Land*'s initial critical reception is that much more was felt to be at stake than the place within literary tradition of a fragmentary, avant-garde poem. Here was a poem that seemed to trace the tensions and fault-lines of a world reeling from the impact of the First World War, a world attempting to assess the apparent attack upon sensibility and culture made by modern art. The reviews that follow in this chapter demonstrate how, over the 1920s, a critical consensus began to be formed in which *The Waste Land* was read as a mythic exploration of modern consciousness. And the final two, longer, extracts in this chapter – by Conrad Aiken and I. A. Richards – represent the first major critical readings of the poem. This is because while sharing with its early reviewers a concern with the poem's coherence and obscurity, they also see its use of mythic 'compression' as the key to its explication. In this they prefigure critical readings of the poem that followed over the next forty or fifty years.

The question of the fragmentary nature of *The Waste Land* and whether the poem could be thought, therefore, to display any conceptual coherence was of immediate concern to its first reviewers. The first (and anonymous) review of the poem was published in the *Times Literary Supplement* (26 October 1922). The reviewer here astutely ascribes the poem's disconnected heterogeneity to the perceived mixing of the 'sordid' and the 'beautiful' that goes to make up modern life. In its first review, then, a sense of intriguing doubleness in the poem is remarked. Such a sense has come to characterise ways of reading the poem throughout its critical history – whether that be in the operation of several layers of irony or ambiguity, in the play between mythic and personal histories, or in a questioning of whether the poem represents a radical critique of modern culture or an endorsement of traditionalist values:

■ Mr Eliot's poem is . . . a collection of flashes, but there is no effect of heterogeneity, since all these flashes are relevant to the same thing and together give what seems to be a complete expression of the poet's vision of modern life. We have here range, depth, and beautiful expression. What more is necessary to a great poem? This vision is singularly complex and in all its labyrinths utterly sincere. It is the mystery of life that it shows two faces, and we know of no other modern poet who can more adequately and movingly reveal to us the inextricable tangle of the sordid and the beautiful that make up life.[5] □

Another sense of the poem's doubleness is that of its ability to divide the critical opinions of its first readers. While the *Times Literary Supplement*'s reviewer found it a 'great poem', Louis Untermeyer, writing in the literary magazine *Freeman* (7 January 1923) saw it as 'a pompous parade of erudition . . . a kaleidoscopic movement in which the bright-coloured pieces fail to atone for the absence of an integrated design'.[6] Untermeyer does, if rather grudgingly, concede that the poem has some value as an analysis of contemporary culture. His icy tone, though, allows no misconception of his opinion of the poem's aesthetic value, or indeed of his attitude towards the modern age:

■ As an analyst of desiccated sensations, as a recorder of the nostalgia of this age, Mr Eliot has created something whose value is, at least, documentary. Yet, granting even its occasional felicities, *The Waste Land* is a misleading document.[7] □

Untermeyer's dismissal of the poem, and the ringing endorsement of it in the *Times Literary Supplement* are not, however, as antithetical as they might initially seem. Both reviews see the poem's fragmentary form as crucially important, both see Eliot's method as an attempt to contrast the assumed wholeness and beauty of past culture with the sordidness and sterility of contemporary life, and both recognise that the poem struggles to articulate modern consciousness. Where they depart from each other is in their attitude towards that modernity. For the *Times Literary Supplement*, the poem is movingly revelatory, its complexity finally being the means of redeeming the age. For Untermeyer, on the other hand, the postwar world feels 'desperately insecure': its fears and emotional needs will not be assuaged by this sort of (as he takes it) impoverished poetry.[8]

It is well to remember that the first readers and critics of *The Waste Land* had no 'map' of modern consciousness. In fact, Eliot's poem itself can be seen to have played a major part in shaping that consciousness. The history of the poem's critical reception is, therefore, a history of the attempts of its commentators to examine and explain modernity. The ways in which the poem has been read have determined what we now think of as modernism. Perhaps the most important early critic to see *The Waste Land*'s power both to embody and to produce modernity is Edmund Wilson. For him, the poem exemplifies the sort of desiccated sensibility that Untermeyer found so distasteful in modern life. He sees *The Waste Land* as a necessary reaction to the impoverished conditions of modernity, in which the Waste Land is 'the concrete image of a spiritual drouth'.[9] In such a 'poetry of drouth', as Wilson terms it, it is the age and not the poetry that is sterile. This notion of a 'poetry of drouth' was to become highly influential in later readings of the poem, largely because Wilson's original formulation of it is a compelling account of the power of Eliot's poem to charge the modern world with new meanings and possibilities. Through the dearth of contemporary culture, Eliot sounds, according to Wilson, as 'one of our only authentic poets'.[10] And it is this fact that outweighs objections to the poem in terms of incoherence or intellectual obscurity:

■ It is sure to be objected that Mr Eliot has written a puzzle rather than a poem and that his work can possess no higher interest than a full-rigged ship built in a bottle. It will be said that he depends too much on books and borrows too much from other men . . . [And] it has already been charged against Mr Eliot that he does not feel enough to be a poet and that the emotions of longing and disgust which he does have belong essentially to a delayed adolescence. . . .

Well: all these objections are founded on realities, but they are outweighed by one major factor – the fact that Mr Eliot is a poet. It is true his poems seem the products of a constricted emotional experience and that he appears to have drawn rather heavily on books for the heat he could not derive from life. There is a certain grudging margin, to be sure, about all that Mr Eliot writes – as if he were compensating himself for his limitations by a peevish assumption of superiority. But it is the very acuteness of his suffering from this starvation which gives such poignancy to his art. And, as I say, Mr Eliot is a poet – that is, he feels intensely and with distinction and speaks naturally in beautiful verse – so that, no matter within what walls he lives, he belongs to the divine company. . . . I doubt whether there is a single other poem of equal length by a contemporary American which displays so high and so varied a mastery of English verse. The poem is – in spite of its lack of structural unity – simply one triumph after another . . .

The race of poets – though grown rarer – is not quite dead: there is at least one who, as Mr Pound says, has brought a new personal rhythm into the language and who has lent even to the words of his great predecessors a new music and a new meaning.[11] □

We will return to Edmund Wilson in the following chapter for a longer – and later – critical examination of *The Waste Land*. But it is to the charge, which Wilson doesn't so much answer as side-step, that the poem is wilfully obscure that we turn in the next extracts. Though these next reviewers fail to come up with an image as strangely intriguing as Wilson's one of 'a full-rigged ship built in a bottle', they do react strongly to the curiously frustrating bookish contrivance of the poem.

For F. L. Lucas *The Waste Land* is simply beyond redemption. Lurking beneath his vehement denunciation of the poem's allusiveness is a suggestion that the poem is, in fact, rather 'common'. The grand displays of literary erudition are, to Lucas, the cheap tricks of a decadent and tawdry age. Their appeal is only to a fashionable coterie of ill-educated eccentrics. Lucas' review begins with a charge against the poem's bookishness:

■ Among the maggots that breed in the corruption of poetry one of the commonest is the bookworm.[12] □

He continues by noting that Eliot seems 'harebrained and a little mad', a poet who, in *The Waste Land*, can be seen to be 'sacrificing [his] artistic powers on the altar of some fantastic Mumbo-Jumbo'.[13] To make matters worse, though, Lucas fears that the poem may well remain popular, indeed achieve a dubious status as a 'masterpiece', due to its modish notoriety:

■ Perhaps this unhappy composition should have been left to sink itself: but it is not easy to dismiss in three lines what is being written about as a new masterpiece. For at present it is particularly easy to win the applause of the *blasé* and the young, of the coteries and the eccentrics.[14] □

Hardly less dismissive – though rather more temperate – are the views of J. C. Squire. The poem's continual references to other texts coupled with its formlessness stretch Squire's credulity. He confesses to remaining baffled by the poem, despite (even because of) the notes that had been added to the poem when published in book form on 15 December 1922:

■ I read Mr Eliot's poem several times when it first appeared; I have now read it several times more; I am still unable to make head or tail of it. Passages might easily be extracted from it which would make it look like one of those wantonly affected productions which are written by persons whose one hope of imposing on the credulous lies in the cultivation of a deliberate singularity. It is impossible to feel that when one reads the whole thing: it may bewilder and annoy, but it must leave the impression on any open-minded person that Mr Eliot does mean something by it, has been at great pains to express himself, and believes himself to be exploring a new avenue (though we may think it a dark cul-de-sac) of poetic treatment. The work is now furnished with an extensive apparatus of notes. There are references to Ezekiel, Marvell, 'The Inferno', Ovid, Wagner, St Augustine, Sir James Frazer, and the Grail legend. But though these will tell those who do not know where Mr Eliot got his quotations and symbolism from, they do not explain what these allusions are here for. The legend about the Cumaean Sibyl . . . combined with the title and one casual reference, suggest that Mr Eliot believes the poem to be about the decay of Western civilisation and his own utter sickness with life. But even with this knowledge I confess that I do not see where it comes in.[15] □

Squire, at least, seems willing to allow that Eliot is attempting something new and struggling to express some deeply felt emotion. The poem fails, he implies, because Eliot is too weighed down by literary conceit to say what he really means.

Gorham B. Munson's 1924 review of *The Waste Land* begins by dismissing the poem for its particular sort of 'esotericism', an 'esotericism' that is 'deliberate mystification'.[16] His critique of the poem continues by leading away from aesthetic considerations and on to questions of the moral and the cultural. This shift is managed deftly by claiming that the poem's obscurity acts as a 'mask' worn by Eliot in order for him to avoid having to 'communicate his suffering to the general reader'.[17] Munson then uses this image of Eliot hiding behind the mask of his own erudition as a means of describing how the poem itself seems to hide from the cultural circumstances of its production. Munson's strategy prefigures, quite startlingly, much more recent readings of *The Waste Land* – especially Marxist and feminist readings – which seek to make apparent the ideological and cultural assumptions out of which the poem arises, and which its modernist strategies seem wilfully to cover over. By the close of his review, Munson reads *The Waste Land* as a means of measuring the differences between European and American sensibilities. For him, *The Waste Land* expresses the mind of Europe, a mind of long and enervated tradition which, like the Cumaean Sibyl who provides Eliot with the epigraph for his poem, 'wants only to die'. This is contrasted with America to whom, he declares, 'the future belongs'.[18] This may seem a rather perverse way of thinking about an iconoclastic poetic experiment by an American *émigré*, yet the assumption that *The Waste Land*, as a modern masterpiece, traces the death throes of a moribund Europe rather than the efforts of a new American literary sensibility to assert itself, is one shared by nearly all major critical readings of *The Waste Land*.[19] And, indeed, reading *The Waste Land* today it is difficult not to feel that it is a very different experiment in modernism from the work of American modernists such as Hart Crane, Marianne Moore, William Carlos Williams, even Ezra Pound. Quite obviously this results from the themes, materials and focus of Eliot's poem, but equally it results from the ways in which the poem's commentators have enlisted the poem in their efforts to define and evaluate European modernism.

As a corrective to these rather negative evaluations of *The Waste Land* this chapter will close with two slightly longer readings of the poem – the first by Conrad Aiken and the second by the established critic I. A. Richards. Both of these readings were essential to the propagation of an emerging critical consensus about the poem – namely that its fragmentary nature and its obscurities are deliberately employed in an examination of modern culture, and that its power as a literary masterpiece stems from the conflict it exposes between the personal and the cultural. In contrast, then, to Munson's view earlier – that Eliot's masking of his emotions lessens the power of the poem – both Aiken and Richards see Eliot's literary masks as necessary to the poem's compression and complexity of feeling. In this they follow the argument of two other important early reviewers of *The Waste Land*, Elinor Wylie and Edgell Rickword. Wylie, writing in January 1923, hailed the poem as a classic, charged with emotional power:

■ The power of suggesting intolerable tragedy at the heart of the trivial or the sordid is used with a skill little less than miraculous in *The Waste Land*.[20] □

And Rickword, in one of the most perceptive of early studies of the poem, one that sees it as an exciting but not fully successful experiment, describes how Eliot's emotional reticence produces a poem that is like a 'magic-lantern show'. Rickword notes that Eliot:

■ . . . being too reserved to expose in public the impressions stamped on his soul by the journey through the Waste Land . . . employs the slides made by others.[21] □

That the emotional content of the poem – and its masking – was troubling to Eliot's friend from their Harvard days, Conrad Aiken, is clear from a note he wrote in 1958 about his 1923 review of *The Waste Land*. At the time of the original review he had previously seen, as separate poems, some of the sections that eventually appeared in *The Waste Land*. He notes, though, that to have acknowledged this would have been to make 'of private knowledge, a betrayal'.[22] We must assume that this is because the passages he refers to are ones that seem to portray Eliot's disastrous first marriage.

As well as sharing with Rickword the image of *The Waste Land* as a magic-lantern show, Aiken also finds the literary allusions and incoherence of the poem troublesome. However, he argues that the poem succeeds, by virtue of such troublesomeness, in expressing the modern condition. The dualities from which he sees the poem generated are ones that he feels to be at the heart of modern consciousness: is it revolutionary or traditional? Coherent or incoherent? Meaningful or meaningless? Personal or symbolic? Aiken's is the first review that attempts a sustained and consistent reading of *The Waste Land* in the light of such concerns:

■ Mr T.S. Eliot is one of the most individual of contemporary poets, and at the same time, anomalously, one of the most 'traditional'. . . . in *The Waste Land*, Mr Eliot's sense of the literary past has become so overmastering as almost to constitute the motive of the work. It is as if, in conjunction with the Mr Pound of the *Cantos*, he wanted to make a 'literature of literature' – a poetry actuated not more by life itself than by poetry; as if he had concluded that the characteristic awareness of a poet of the twentieth century must inevitably, or ideally, be a very complex and very literary awareness, able to speak only, or best, in terms of the literary past, the terms which had molded its tongue. This involves a kind of idolatry of literature with which it is a little difficult to sympathize. In positing, as it seems to, that there is nothing left for literature to do but become a kind of parasitic growth on literature, a sort of mistletoe, it involves, I think, a definite astigmatism – a distortion. But the theory is interesting if only because it has colored an important and brilliant piece of work.

The Waste Land is unquestionably important, unquestionably brilliant. It is important partly because its 433 lines summarize Mr Eliot, for the moment, and demonstrate that he is an even better poet than most had thought; and partly because it embodies the theory . . . of the 'allusive' method in poetry. *The Waste Land* is, indeed, a poem of allusion all compact. It purports to be symbolical; most of its symbols are drawn from literature or legend; and Mr Eliot has thought it necessary to supply, in notes, a list of the many quotations, references, and translations with which it bristles. He observes candidly that the poem presents 'difficulties', and requires 'elucidation'. This serves to raise, at once, the question whether these difficulties, in which perhaps Mr

Eliot takes a little pride, are so much the result of complexity, a fine elaborateness, as of confusion. The poem has been compared, by one reviewer, to a 'full-rigged ship built in a bottle',[23] the suggestion being that it is a perfect piece of construction. But is it a perfect piece of construction? Is the complex material mastered, and made coherent? Or, if the poem is not successful in that way, in what way is it successful? Has it the formal and intellectual complex unity of a microscopic *Divine Comedy*; or is its unity – supposing it to have one – of another sort?

If we leave aside for the moment all other consideration and read the poem solely with the intention of understanding, with the aid of notes, the symbolism; of making out what it is that is symbolized, and how these symbolized feelings are brought into relation with each other and with other matters in the poem; I think we must, with reservations, and with no invidiousness, conclude that the poem is not, in any formal sense, coherent. We cannot feel that all the symbolisms belong quite inevitably where they have been put; that the order of the parts is an inevitable order; that there is anything more than a rudimentary progress from one theme to another; nor that the relation between the more symbolic parts and the less is always as definite as it should be. What we feel is that Mr Eliot has not wholly annealed the allusive matter, has left it unabsorbed, lodged in gleaming fragments amid material alien to it. Again, there is a distinct weakness consequent on the use of allusions which may have both intellectual and emotional value for Mr Eliot, but (even with the notes) none for us. The 'Waste Land' of the Grail Legend might be a good symbol, if it were something with which we were sufficiently familiar. But it can never, even when explained, be a good symbol, simply because it has no immediate associations for us. It might, of course, be a good *theme*. In that case it would be given us. But Mr Eliot uses it for purposes of overtone; he refers to it; and as overtone it quite clearly fails. He gives us, superbly, *a* waste land – not *the* waste land. Why, then, refer to the latter at all – if he is not, in the poem, really going to use it? Hyacinth fails in the same way. So does the Fisher King. So does the Hanged Man, which Mr Eliot tells us he associates with Frazer's Hanged God – we take his word for it. But if the precise association is worth anything, it is worth putting into the poem; otherwise there can be no purpose in mentioning it. Why, again, Datta, Dayadhvam, Damyata? Or Shantih? Do they not say a good deal less for us than 'Give: sympathize: control' or 'Peace'? Of course; but Mr Eliot replies that he wants them not merely to mean those particular things, but also to mean them in a particular way – that is, to be remembered in connection with an Upanishad. Unfortunately, we have none of us this memory, nor can he give it to us; and in the upshot he gives us only a series of agreeable sounds which might as well have been nonsense. What we get at, and I think it is important, is that in none of these particular cases does the reference, the allusion, justify itself intrinsically, make itself felt. When we are aware of these references at all (sometimes they are unidentifiable) we are aware of them simply as something unintelligible but suggestive. When they have been explained, we are aware of the material referred to, the fact (for instance, a vegetation ceremony), as something useless for our enjoyment or understanding of the poem, something distinctly 'dragged in', and only, perhaps, of interest as having suggested a pleasantly ambiguous line. For unless an allusion is made to live identifiably, to flower where transplanted, it is otiose. We admit the beauty of the implicational or allusive method; but the key to an implication should be in the implication itself, not outside of it. We admit the value of the esoteric pattern; but the pattern should disclose its secret, should not be dependent on a cypher. Mr Eliot assumes for his allusions, and for the fact that they actually allude to something, an importance which the allusions themselves do not, as expressed, aesthetically command, nor, as explained, logically command; which is pretentious. He is a little pretentious, too, in his 'plan' – *qui pourtant n'existe pas*. If it is a plan, then its principle is oddly akin to planlessness. Here and there, in the wilderness, a broken finger-post.

I enumerate these objections not, I must emphasize, in derogation of the poem, but to dispel, if possible, an illusion as to its nature. It is perhaps important to note that Mr Eliot, with his comment on the 'plan', and several critics, with their admiration of the poem's woven complexity, minister to the idea that *The Waste Land* is, precisely, a kind of epic in a walnut shell: elaborate, ordered, unfolded with a logic at every joint discernible; but it is also important to note that this idea is false. With or without the notes the poem belongs rather to that symbolical order in which one may justly say that the 'meaning' is not explicitly, or exactly, worked out. Mr Eliot's net is wide, its meshes are small; and he catches a good deal more – thank heaven – than he pretends to. . . . Thus the poem has an emotional value far clearer and richer than its arbitrary and rather unworkable logical value. One might assume that it originally consisted of a number of separate poems which have been telescoped – given a kind of forced unity. The Waste Land conception offered itself as a generous net which would, if not unify, at any rate contain these varied elements. We are aware of this superficial 'binding' – we observe the anticipation and repetition of themes, motifs; 'Fear death by water' anticipates the episode of

Phlebas, the cry of the nightingale is repeated; but these are pretty flimsy links, and do not genuinely bind because they do not reappear naturally, but arbitrarily. This suggests, indeed, that Mr Eliot is perhaps attempting a kind of program music in words, endeavoring to rule out 'emotional accidents' by supplying his readers, in notes, with only those associations which are correct. He himself hints at the musical analogy when he observes that 'In the first part of Part V three themes are employed'.

I think, therefore, that the poem must be taken – most invitingly offers itself – as a brilliant and kaleidoscopic confusion; as a series of sharp, discrete, slightly related perceptions and feelings, dramatically and lyrically presented, and violently juxtaposed (for effect of dissonance), so as to give us an impression of an intensely modern, intensely literary consciousness which perceives itself to be not a unit but a chance correlation or conglomerate of mutually discolorative fragments. We are invited into a mind, a world, which is a 'broken bundle of mirrors', a 'heap of broken images'. Isn't it that Mr Eliot, finding it 'impossible to say just what he means'. . . has emulated the 'magic lantern' that throws 'the nerves in pattern on a screen'? If we perceive the poem in this light, as a series of brilliant, brief, unrelated or dimly related pictures by which a consciousness empties itself of its characteristic contents, then we also perceive that, anomalously, though the dropping out of any one picture would not in the least affect the logic or 'meaning' of the whole, it would seriously detract from the value of the portrait. The 'plan' of the poem would not greatly suffer, one makes bold to assert, by the elimination of 'April is the cruellest month' or Phlebas, or the Thames daughters, or Sosostris or 'You gave me hyacinths' or 'A woman drew her long black hair out tight'; nor would it matter if it did. These things are not important parts of an important or careful intellectual pattern; but they are important parts of an important emotional ensemble. The relations between Tiresias (who is said to unify the poem, in a sense, as spectator) and the Waste Land, or Mr Eugenides, or Hyacinth, or any other fragment, is a dim and tonal one, not exact. It will not bear analysis, it is not always operating, nor can one say with assurance, at any given point, how much it is operating. In this sense *The Waste Land* is a series of separate poems or passages, not perhaps all written at one time or with one aim, to which a spurious but happy sequence has been given. This spurious sequence has a value – it creates the necessary superficial formal unity; but it need not be stressed, as the Notes stress it. Could one not wholly rely for one's unity – as Mr Eliot *has* largely relied – simply on the dim unity of 'personality' which would underlie the detailed contents of a single consciousness? Unless one is going to carry unification very far, weave and interweave very closely, it would perhaps be as well not to unify it at all; to dispense, for example, with arbitrary repetitions.

We reach thus the conclusion that the poem succeeds – as it brilliantly does – by virtue of its incoherence, not of its plan; by virtue of its ambiguities, not of its explanations. Its incoherence is a virtue because its *donnée* is incoherence. Its rich, vivid, crowded use of implication is a virtue, as implication is always a virtue – it shimmers, it suggests, it gives the desired strangeness. But when, as often, Mr Eliot uses an implication beautifully – conveys by means of a picture-symbol or action-symbol a feeling – we do not require to be told that he had in mind a passage in the *Encyclopedia*, or the color of his nursery wall; the information is disquieting, has a sour air of pedantry. We 'accept' the poem as we would accept a powerful, melancholy tone-poem. We do not want to be told what occurs; nor is it more than mildly amusing to know what passages are, in the Straussian manner, echoes or parodies. We cannot believe that every syllable has an algebraic inevitability, nor would we wish it so. We could dispense with the French, Italian, Latin, and Hindu phrases – they are irritating. But when our reservations have all been made, we accept *The Waste Land* as one of the most moving and original poems of our time. It captures us. And we sigh, with a dubious eye on the 'notes' and 'plan', our bewilderment that after so fine a performance Mr Eliot should have thought it an occasion for calling 'Tullia's ape a marmosyte'. Tullia's ape is good enough.[24] □

For Aiken, then, *The Waste Land* succeeds 'brilliantly' because it manages to convey with clarity and richness an 'emotional value' that is not gainsaid by questions of the poem's intellectual or formal coherence.

In 1926 the young Cambridge lecturer I. A. Richards, convinced that *The Waste Land* was a major literary work that expressed the 'plight of a whole generation', added an appendix dealing expressly with Eliot's poem to the second edition of his book *The Principles of Literary Criticism* (originally published in 1924). It is from this that the final extract of this chapter is taken. Richards' essay is an appropriate ending for this chapter as it sums up the preoccupations of the poem's readers in the first years of its critical reception, while also setting the terms for a new phase of critical debate about the poem, the sort of 'archetypal' criticism that dominated readings of the poem in the 1930s, and which is dealt with in the next chapter of this Guide.

Richards' books *The Principles of Literary Criticism* and *Practical Criticism*

(1929) were hugely influential and signalled a new and invigorated sense of the role of literary criticism. With their emphasis on close critical reading that illuminates the nuances and ironies of a text and which is, in turn, underpinned by an assumption of the critic's aesthetic and moral responsibilities, these books were to shape what has come to be known as the 'New Criticism'. Richards' reading of *The Waste Land* is both a conscious attempt to secure for Eliot's poem its place as a literary 'classic', and a working through of some of the principles of his new literary criticism. Throughout the following piece, Richards assumes that there is an ideal reader of the poem, the 'right reader', as he terms it. Such a reader, though, seems both remarkably idealised, and uncannily similar in his (and such an 'ideal reader' is almost certainly male) intellectual, political and cultural concerns to Richards himself. Richards' assumption that a *proper* reading of *The Waste Land* will necessitate knowledge and study of Shakespeare, of Weston's *From Ritual to Romance*, and of Dante's *Commedia*, along with a host of other 'classic' literary texts, while being a fair recognition of some of the poem's difficulties, seems also like a proposal that the only fit readers of it are young, white, upper- or upper-middle-class and – undoubtedly – Cambridge educated.[25] From its earliest days, criticism of *The Waste Land* has struggled with the question of whether the poem is élitist or not.

There are two further instances in which Richards' essay reveals its agenda for promoting Eliot's poem as a modern classic. In both these cases Richards attempts to answer the worries about the poem's formal and thematic coherence, and about its bookish allusiveness, that had troubled its early reviewers. In the first case he takes up the idea proposed by Aiken that the best way to think of the poem's structure is by analogy with musical form. *The Waste Land*, then, is best thought of as a 'music of ideas', a notion that is still – and very usefully – heard in critical readings of the poem. In the second case, Richards initiates one of the most influential ways of dealing with the poem's density of allusion. By seeing it as 'a technical device for compression', he prepares the way for the readings of the poem that follow in the next two chapters of this Guide, readings which 'flesh out' the allusions in order to explicate the underlying myths that are felt to animate the poem. In short, then, Richards urges us to read the poem as a sophisticated aesthetic achievement, a poem whose form and methods successfully engage 'the plight of a whole generation':

■ We too readily forget that, unless something is very wrong with our civilisation, we should be producing three equal poets at least for every poet of high rank in our great-great-grandfathers' day.

Something must indeed be wrong; and since Mr Eliot is one of the very few poets that current conditions have not overcome, the difficulties which he has faced, and the cognate difficulties which his readers encounter, repay study.

Mr Eliot's poetry has occasioned an unusual amount of irritated or enthusiastic bewilderment. The bewilderment has several sources. The most formidable is the unobtrusiveness, in some cases the absence, of any coherent intellectual thread upon which the items of the poem are strung. A reader of 'Gerontion', or of 'Preludes', or of *The Waste Land*, may, if he will, after repeated readings, introduce such a thread. Another reader after much effort may fail to contrive one. But in either case energy will have been misapplied. For the items are united by the accord, contrast, and interaction of their emotional effects, not by an intellectual scheme that analysis must work out. The value lies in the unified response which this interaction creates in the right reader. The only intellectual activity required takes place in the realisation of the separate items. We can, of course, make a 'rationalisation' of the whole experience, as we can of any experience. If we do, we are adding something which does not belong to the poem. Such a logical scheme is, at best, a scaffolding that vanishes when the poem is constructed. But we have so built into our nervous systems a demand for intellectual coherence, even in poetry, that we find a difficulty in doing without it.

This point may be misunderstood, for the charge most usually brought against Mr Eliot's poetry is that it is over-intellectualised. One reason for this is his use of allusion. . . . Allusion in Mr Eliot's hands is a technical device for compression. *The Waste Land* is equivalent in content to an epic. Without this device twelve books would have been needed. But these allusions and the notes in which some of them are elucidated have made many a petulant reader turn down his thumb at once. Such a reader has not begun to understand what it is all about.

This objection is connected with another, that of obscurity. To quote a recent pronouncement upon *The Waste Land* from Mr Middleton Murry: 'The reader is compelled, in the mere effort to understand, to adopt an attitude of intellectual suspicion, which makes impossible the communication of feeling. The work offends against the most elementary canon of good writing: that the immediate effect should be unambiguous.' Consider first this 'canon'. What would happen, if we pressed it, to Shakespeare's greatest sonnets or to *Hamlet*? The truth is that very much of the best poetry is necessarily ambiguous in its immediate effect. Even the most careful and responsive reader must reread and do hard work before the poem forms itself clearly and unambiguously in his mind. An original poem, as much as a new branch of mathematics, compels the mind which receives it to grow, and this takes time. Anyone who upon reflection asserts the contrary for his own case must be either a demigod or dishonest; probably Mr Murry was in haste. His remarks show that he has failed in his attempt to read the poem, and they reveal, in part, the reason for his failure – namely, his own overintellectual approach. To read it successfully he would have to discontinue his present self-mystifications.

The critical question in all cases is whether the poem is worth the trouble it entails. For *The Waste Land* this is considerable. There is Miss Weston's *From Ritual to Romance* to read, and its 'astral' trimmings to be discarded – they have nothing to do with Mr Eliot's poem. There is Canto xxvi of the *Purgatorio* to be studied – the relevance of the close of that canto to the whole of Mr Eliot's work must be insisted upon. It illuminates his persistent concern with sex, the problem of our generation, as religion was the problem of the last. There is the central position of Tiresias in the poem to be puzzled out – the cryptic form of the note which Mr Eliot writes on this point is just a little tiresome. It is a way of underlining the fact that the poem is concerned with many aspects of the one fact of sex, a hint that is perhaps neither indispensable nor entirely successful.

When all this has been done by the reader, when the materials with which the words are to clothe themselves have been collected, the poem still remains to be read. And it is easy to fail in this undertaking. An 'attitude of intellectual suspicion' must certainly be abandoned. But this is not difficult to those who still know how to give their feelings precedence to their thoughts, who can accept and unify an experience without trying to catch it in an intellectual net or to squeeze out a doctrine. One form of this attempt must be mentioned. Some, misled no doubt by its origin in a Mystery, have endeavoured to give the poem a symbolical reading. But its symbols are not mystical but emotional. They stand, that is, not for ineffable objects, but for normal human experience. The poem, in fact, is radically naturalistic; only its compression makes it appear otherwise. And in this it probably comes nearer to the original Mystery which it perpetuates than transcendentalism does.

If it were desired to label in three words the most characteristic feature of Mr Eliot's technique, this might be done by calling his poetry a 'music of ideas'. The ideas are of all kinds: abstract and concrete, general and particular; and, like the musician's phrases, they are arranged, not that they may tell us something, but that their effects in us may combine into a coherent whole of feeling and attitude and produce a peculiar liberation of the will. They are there to be responded to, not to be pondered or worked out. . . .

How this technique lends itself to misunderstandings we have seen. But many readers who have failed in the end to escape bewilderment have begun by finding on almost every line that Mr Eliot has written . . . that personal stamp which is the hardest thing for the craftsman to imitate and perhaps the most certain sign that the experience, good or bad, rendered in the poem is authentic. Only those unfortunate persons who are incapable of reading poetry can resist Mr Eliot's rhythms. The poem as a whole may elude us while every fragment, as a fragment, comes victoriously home. It is difficult to believe that this is Mr Eliot's fault rather than his reader's, because a parallel case of a poet who so constantly achieves the hardest part of his task and yet fails in the easier is not to be found. It is much more likely that we have been trying to put the fragments together on a wrong principle.

Another doubt has been expressed. Mr Eliot repeats himself in two ways. The nightingale, Cleopatra's barge, the rats, and the smoky candle-end, recur and recur. Is this a sign of a poverty of inspiration? A more plausible explanation is that this repetition is in part a consequence of the technique above described, and in part something which many writers who are not accused of poverty also show. Shelley, with his rivers, towers, and stars, Conrad, Hardy, Walt Whitman, and Dostoevski spring to mind. When a writer has found a theme or image which fixes a point of relative stability in the drift of experience, it is not to be expected that he will avoid it. Such themes are a means of orientation. And it is quite true that the central process in all Mr Eliot's best poems is the same: the conjunction of feelings which, though superficially opposed – as squalor, for example, is opposed to grandeur – yet tend as they develop to change places and even to unite. If they do not develop far enough the intention of the poet is missed. Mr Eliot is neither sighing after vanished glories nor holding contemporary experience up to scorn.

Both bitterness and desolation are superficial aspects of his poetry. There are those who think that he merely takes his readers into the Waste Land and leaves them there, that in his last poem he confesses his impotence to release the healing waters. The reply is that some readers find in his poetry not only a clearer, fuller realisation of their plight, the plight of a whole generation, than they find elsewhere, but also through the very energies set free in that realisation a return of the saving passion.[26] □

As a poem of 'saving passion', *The Waste Land*'s central position within critical debate was now firmly established. However, despite this position as poetic masterpiece expressing the plight of a whole generation, it was still read as a curiously ambiguous commentary on modern consciousness. Is it radical and avant-garde? Or is it so imbued with the spirit of literary tradition that its force is essentially conservative? Such questions, which mark considerations over the poem's centrality to modernism, are pursued in readings of the poem across the 1930s, readings that mark the development of 'New Criticism'. It is to such readings that the next two chapters turn.

CHAPTER TWO

The 1930s: Archetypal Criticism

WITH *THE Waste Land*'s status as a modern classic firmly established by the end of the 1920s, criticism of the poem in the 1930s both consolidated its reputation and sought to establish patterns for interpreting the poem that would illuminate its vision of modern life. Many of *The Waste Land*'s initial readers, as seen in the previous chapter, had clung to its emotional or tragic intensity – however masked – as the key to overcoming its difficulties. But with the new decade came more critical distance, and a desire to examine the terms on which its literary power rested. The First World War's tragic disruption of Western culture felt, now, less acute; and, likewise, the shock waves of the poem's initial impact had dispersed.

Over the 1930s, then, critics focused less on the poem's intense articulation of the horrors and fears of a 'lost' generation, than on its struggle to perceive an order and a pattern underlying its model of (literary) culture. Such a shift of attitude towards the poem marks its adoption by the academy. The readings of the poem that follow in this chapter can all be seen as attempts to establish the poem's position as a modern classic by pointing to the intellectual structures which are its underpinning. Like Richards in the previous chapter, they see the poem as worthy of study, something that needs to be worked on in order for its real importance to be made apparent. Such attitudes towards *The Waste Land* still prevail today, and mean that the poem has become a mainstay of school and undergraduate literature teaching. In its relatively short literary history, a history that is, nevertheless, one that encompasses massive changes in attitudes to literature, *The Waste Land* has never been off the curriculum. This is due to a belief, first *fully* articulated in criticism from the 1930s, that the poem's meanings are universal ones. If, that is, the poem can tell us anything about the modern world, then its struggles and difficulties are those of the whole of humanity rather than ones that are specific and local to its immediate historic and personal occasion.

What the three extracts that comprise this chapter share, then, in their ways of reading *The Waste Land* is a belief that the poem exposes underlying, or archetypal, patterns of human culture, and that it is from such archetypes that the poem derives its power and meaning. Whether stated explicitly or not, all three of these essays subscribe to Eliot's concept of 'mythic composition', which he articulated in his essay '*Ulysses*, Order and Myth', and which is discussed in the Introduction to this volume. They all seek to make apparent how the poem shapes, and makes significant, the apparent futility that is modern consciousness, through its manipulation of poetic archetypes. Maud Bodkin, whose reading of the poem comes at the end of this chapter, provides a useful explanation of the Jungian notion of the poetic archetype. Interestingly, this seems very close to Eliot's notion of mythic consciousness in that it allows for the marking – in image and symbol – of a 'continuous parallel between contemporaneity and antiquity'.[1] For Jung, antiquity is the 'collective' or 'tribal' memory that has, through long experience (or, in Eliot's term, 'tradition'), become inscribed in the very structure of the human brain. Bodkin writes:

■ In an article, 'On the relation of analytical psychology to poetic art', Dr C. G. Jung has set forth an hypothesis in regard to the psychological significance of poetry. The special emotional significance possessed by certain poems – a significance going beyond any definite meaning conveyed – he attributes to the stirring in the reader's mind, within or beneath his conscious response, of unconscious forces which he terms 'primordial images', or archetypes. These archetypes he describes as 'psychic residua of numberless experiences of the same type', experiences which have happened not to the individual but to his ancestors, and of which the results are inherited in the structure of the brain, *a priori* determinants of individual experience.[2] □

Bodkin's explanation is helpful in setting out the sorts of pattern of significance that all three extracts in this chapter see in *The Waste Land*. We will see, though, that such models conceal and distort the ideology of modernity just as much as they reveal and discover it in their readings of the poem. However, by seeking to identify such patterns in the poem, these critics are seeking to establish a place for it within literary history as a work whose mixing of memory and desire offers a profound reading of the human condition. In short, though *The Waste Land* may be occasioned by the particular circumstances of postwar culture and by personal feelings of sexual failure, criticism of it in the 1930s begins to articulate a critical language that seems adequate to the experience of modernity. It is in this sense – due in large part to the sorts of readings that follow – that the poem has become *the* model and standard for any examination of 'the modern mind'.

For Edmund Wilson, in the first extract to follow, the richness of myth and symbol in Eliot's poetry is what saves it from the futility and anarchy of modern consciousness. This ability to enrich apparently sterile images by stressing their symbolic resonances has, according to Wilson, been learned by Eliot from his reading of French symbolist writers. *The Waste Land*'s profundity and consequent appeal to universality rests, therefore, in the symbolic meaning of its theme of 'emotional starvation'. F.R. Leavis' piece – which still remains one of the most influential readings of *The Waste Land* – sees the poem as expressing the yearning of modern civilisation to return to a simpler and more integrated culture. For Leavis, the archetypal pattern for human culture is an organic relationship to the very land itself, a sort of agrarian utopia of mutually beneficial production. However idealised this may seem, it contrasts sharply with the vision of the Waste Land, and thus provides a useful myth against which to test the modernity of the poem. And Maud Bodkin's gently eccentric reading of the poem draws upon Jungian notions of the 'collective unconscious', and deploys a broadly Jungian psychoanalytic approach in its discovering of the 'archetypal pattern' upon which the poem is built. But, like the poem itself, such struggles for coherence and underlying pattern are dogged by fears of breakdown and incoherence. And with such fears are exposed different patterns of assumption about literature and literary culture itself. All three critics in this chapter betray, to a greater or lesser extent, a notion of literature as a privileged space, an aesthetic realm that is distinct (if not fully autonomous) from the 'real' world of politics, culture and everyday life. And all are troubled by the sense that *The Waste Land*'s appeal and meaning are available only to a small intellectual élite. The poem's ruptures and breakages, its incoherence and obscurity seem therefore to speak of a breakdown at the heart of modern (British) culture. So, although the poem encourages a critical discourse that is distanced, intellectualised and aesthetically removed from everyday concerns, that very discourse is one in which the poem's power is measured by its ability to highlight the difficulties and struggles of everyday, modern life. Throughout its critical history, readings of *The Waste Land* have been generated out of precisely this sense of ambiguity in the poem's position as both aesthetic object and cultural document.

Edmund Wilson's reading of *The Waste Land*, which follows, is a good example of this ambiguous response to the poem. The extract is taken from Wilson's book *Axel's Castle* (1931), which was one of the earliest – and remains one of the most influential – attempts to delineate and examine modern literary history. The inclusion of an examination of Eliot in this book marks the general acceptance of Eliot as one of the literary 'greats' of modernity. Wilson's sense of the ambiguous and difficult position of modern literature in reflecting modern life is profoundly apparent throughout this book. On the one hand, he sees *The Waste Land* as part of a deep literary tradition, a response in symbolist mode to the powerful hold of the Romantic imagination over modern consciousness. For him, *The Waste Land* finally manages to break free from the 'revolt of the individual', as he terms the Romantic imagination, by producing a poetry that is urbane and intellectually charged, and that, through its 'complicated association of ideas represented by a medley of metaphors', can 'communicate unique personal feelings'.[3] But on the other hand, rather than betraying a highly aestheticised literary sensibility, he sees the poem as documenting a decaying culture of 'shattered institutions, strained nerves and bankrupt ideals'. Wilson's reading, then, develops and expands on his early review of the poem that appears in the previous chapter. For him now, nearly ten years later, *The Waste Land* still depicts a 'poetry of drouth' but it is one of 'emotional starvation'. The emphasis on emotion here is important. It allows Wilson to introduce into his account of the poem a new note and a timely recognition – namely the crucial importance of Eliot's Puritan American family history on the emotional range and resonance of the poem. And despite the fact that the Eliots of St Louis, Missouri can hardly be thought of as New Englanders, Wilson does manage to develop a powerful reading of the poem out of his sense that it arises from 'the peculiar conflicts of the Puritan turned artist'. For Wilson, then, the poem becomes a complicated negotiation of national, cultural and literary identities – a sort of cosmopolitan exercise in modern consciousness:

■ Eliot's most complete expression of [the] theme of emotional starvation is to be found in . . . *The Waste Land* (1922). The Waste Land of the poem is a symbol borrowed from the myth of the Holy Grail: it is a desolate and sterile country ruled by an impotent king, in which not only have the crops ceased to grow and the animals to reproduce, but the very human inhabitants have become incapable of having children. But this sterility we soon identify as the sterility of the Puritan temperament. . . . We recognise throughout *The Waste Land* the peculiar conflicts of the Puritan turned artist: the horror of vulgarity and the shy sympathy with the common life, the ascetic shrinking from sexual experience and the distress at the drying up of the springs of sexual emotion, with the straining after a religious emotion which may be made to take its place.

Yet though Eliot's spiritual and intellectual roots are still more firmly fixed in New England than is, I believe, ordinarily understood, there is in *The Waste Land* a good deal more than the mere gloomy moods of a New Englander regretting an emotionally undernourished youth. The colonisation by the Puritans of New England was merely an incident in that rise of the middle-class which has brought a commercial-industrial civilisation to the European cities as well as to the American ones. T. S. Eliot now lives in London and has become an English citizen; but the desolation, the aesthetic and spiritual drought, of Anglo-Saxon middle-class society oppresses London as well as Boston. The terrible dreariness of the great modern cities is the atmosphere in which *The Waste Land* takes place – amidst this dreariness, brief, vivid images emerge, brief pure moments of feeling are distilled; but all about us we are aware of nameless millions performing barren office routines, wearing down their souls in interminable labours of which the products never bring them profit – people whose pleasures are so sordid and so feeble that they seem almost sadder than their pains. And this Waste Land has another aspect: it is a place not merely of desolation, but of anarchy and doubt. In our post-war world of shattered institutions, strained nerves and bankrupt ideals, life no longer seems serious or coherent – we have no belief in the things we do and consequently we have no heart for them.

The poet of *The Waste Land* is living half the time in the real world of contemporary London and half the time in the haunted wilderness of the medieval legend. The water for which he longs in the twilight desert of his dream is to quench the spiritual thirst which torments him in the London dusk . . . The poet of *The Waste Land* mak[es] water the symbol of all freedom, all fecundity and flowering of the soul, [and] invokes in desperate need the memory of an April shower of his youth, the song of the hermit-thrush with its sound of water dripping and the vision of a drowned Phoenician Sailor, sunk beyond 'the cry of gulls and the deep sea swell', who has at least died by water, not thirst. The poet, who seems now to be travelling in a country cracked by drought, can only feverishly dream of these things. One's head may be well stored with literature, but the heroic prelude of the Elizabethans has ironic echoes in modern London streets and modern London drawing-rooms: lines remembered from Shakespeare turn to jazz or refer themselves to the sound of phonographs. And now it is one's personal regrets again – the girl in the hyacinth-garden – 'the awful daring of a moment's surrender which an age of prudence can never retract' – the key which turned once, and once only, in the prison of inhibition and isolation. Now he stands on the arid plain again, and the dry-rotted world of London seems to be crumbling about him – the poem ends in a medley of quotations from a medley of literatures – like Gérard de Nerval's 'Desdichado', the poet is disinherited; like the author of the 'Pervigilium Veneris', he laments that his song is mute and asks when the spring will come which will set it free like the swallow's; like Arnaut Daniel, in Dante, as he disappears in the refining fire, he begs the world to raise a prayer for his torment. 'These fragments I have shored against my ruins.'

The Waste Land, in method as well as in mood, has left Laforgue far behind. Eliot has developed a new technique, at once laconic, quick, and precise, for representing the transmutations of thought, the interplay of perception and reflection. . . . As May Sinclair has said of Eliot '. . . His thoughts move very rapidly and by astounding cuts. They move not by logical stages and majestic roundings of the full literary curve, but as live thoughts move in live brains.' Let us examine, as an illustration, the lovely nightingale passage . . . Eliot is describing a room in London:

> Above the antique mantel was displayed
> As though a window gave upon the sylvan scene
> The change of Philomel, by the barbarous king
> So rudely forced; yet there the nightingale
> Filled all the desert with inviolable voice
> And still she cried, and still the world pursues,
> 'Jug Jug' to dirty ears.

That is, the poet sees, above the mantel, a picture of Philomela changed to a nightingale, and it gives his mind a moment's swift release. The picture is like a window opening upon Milton's earthly paradise – the 'sylvan scene', as Eliot explains in a note, is a phrase from *Paradise Lost* – and the poet associates his own plight in the modern city . . . with Philomela, raped and mutilated by Tereus. But in the earthly paradise, there had been a nightingale singing: Philomela had wept her woes in song, though the barbarous king had cut out her tongue – her sweet voice had remained inviolable. And with a sudden change of tense, the poet flashes back from the myth to his present situation:

> And still she cried, and still the world pursues,
> 'Jug Jug' to dirty ears.

The song of birds was represented in old English popular poetry by such outlandish syllables as 'Jug Jug' – so Philomela's cry sounds to the vulgar. Eliot has here, in seven lines of extraordinary liquidity and beauty, fused the picture, the passage from Milton and the legend from Ovid, into a single moment of vague poignant longing.

The Waste Land is dedicated to Ezra Pound, to whom Eliot elsewhere acknowledges a debt; and he has here evidently been influenced by Pound's *Cantos*. *The Waste Land* like the *Cantos* is fragmentary in form and packed with literary quotation and allusion. In fact, the passage just discussed above has a resemblance to a passage on the same subject – the Philomela-Procne myth – at the beginning of Pound's Fourth Canto. Eliot and Pound have, in fact, founded a school of poetry which depends on literary quotation and reference to an unprecedented degree . . . in *The Waste Land* [Eliot] carries this tendency to what one must suppose its extreme possible limit: here, in a poem of only four hundred and three lines[4] (to which are added, however, seven pages of notes), he manages to include quotations from, allusions to, or imitations of, at least thirty-five different writers (some of them, such as Shakespeare and Dante, laid under contribution several times) – as well as several popular songs; and to introduce passages in six foreign languages, including Sanskrit. . . . We are always being dismayed, in our general reading, to discover that lines among those which we had believed to represent Eliot's residuum of original invention had been taken over or adapted from other writers . . . One would be inclined *a priori* to assume that all this load of erudition and literature would be enough to sink any writer, and that such a production as *The Waste Land* must be a work of second-hand inspiration. . . . Yet Eliot manages to be most effective precisely – in *The Waste Land* – where he might be expected to be least original – he succeeds in conveying his meaning, in communicating his emotion, in spite of all his learned or mysterious allusions, and whether we understand them or not.

In this respect, there is a curious contrast between Eliot and Ezra Pound. Pound's work has been partially sunk by its cargo of erudition, whereas Eliot, in ten years' time, has left upon English poetry a mark more unmistakable than that of any other poet writing in English. It is, in fact, probably true at the present time that Eliot is being praised too extravagantly and Pound, though he has deeply influenced a few, on the whole unfairly neglected. I should explain Eliot's greater popularity by the fact that, for all his fragmentary method, he possesses a complete literary personality in a way that Pound, for all his integrity, does not.

. . . Eliot has thought persistently and coherently about the relations between the different phases of human experience, and his passion for proportion and order is reflected in his poems. He is, in his way, a complete man, and if it is true, as I believe, that he has . . . brought a new personal rhythm into the language – so that he has been able to lend even to the borrowed rhythms, the quoted words, of his great predecessors a new music and a new meaning – it is the intellectual completeness and soundness which has given his rhythm its special prestige.

Another factor which has probably contributed to Eliot's extraordinary success is the essentially dramatic character of his imagination. . . . Most of the best of Eliot's poems are based on unexpected dramatic contrasts: *The Waste Land* especially . . . owes a large part of its power to its dramatic quality, which makes it peculiarly effective read aloud.

. . . In any case . . . *The Waste Land* . . . enchanted and devastated a whole generation. Attempts have been made to reproduce it . . . at least a dozen times. And as Eliot, lately out of Harvard, assumed the rôle of the middle-aged Prufrock and to-day, at forty, in one of his latest poems, 'The Song of Simeon', speaks in the character of an old man 'with eighty years and no to-morrow' – so 'Gerontion' and *The Waste Land* have made the young poets old before their time. In London, as in New York, and in the universities both here and in England, they for a time took to inhabiting barren beaches, cactus-grown deserts, and dusty attics overrun with rats – the only properties they allowed themselves to work with were a few fragments of old shattered glass or a sparse sprinkling of broken bones. They had purged themselves of Masefield as of Shelley for dry tongues and rheumatic joints. The dry breath of the Waste Land now blighted the most amiable country landscapes; and the sound of jazz, which had formerly seemed jolly, now inspired only horror and despair. But in this case, we may forgive the young for growing prematurely decrepit: where some of even the finest intelligences of the older generation read *The Waste Land* with blankness or laughter, the young had recognised a poet.[5] □

Though Wilson ends here with what seems only a grudging appreciation of the power of Eliot's poem, what he does recognise is its power to change ways of looking at the world. He returns to his first justification of the poem from his review of 1922 – that it cannot be mistaken for anything other than the work of a great poet – while also emphasising its importance to a new generation of young poets and readers. It is just such a recognition which compelled F.R. Leavis to declare that 'in [Eliot's] work by 1920 English poetry had made a new start'.[6]

In the next extract, taken from Leavis' *New Bearings in English Poetry* (1932), we see a more fully worked-out examination of how the poem should be read *as a poem*. Like Wilson, Leavis assumes that *The Waste Land* is a reflection of 'the present state of civilisation', and that Eliot's poem has had a profound affect on the sensibilities of a whole generation. He is, however, much more careful than Wilson to provide a very detailed account of the poem that attempts to gloss many of the poem's obscurities and difficulties. Leavis' reading of *The Waste Land* is one, therefore, that establishes some of the major ways of examining the poem that have dominated the history of its critical reception. Indeed, Leavis' critical practice here is one that establishes a whole new critical practice generally. The way in which he combines a close reading of the text with exegesis of the poem's allusions and references demonstrates the priorities of a newly emerging critical sensibility, what was to become known (especially in America) as 'New Criticism'. Leavis' examination of the poem for details of textual nuance, irony and ambiguity, despite its close attention to the poem *as* poem, is an attempt to wrench both poetry and criticism away from the dead end of ultra-refined aesthetic sensibilities and sententious sentiment that he felt characterised poetry and criticism at the time. Leavis' account of the poem, then, is alive to the radical challenge posed by *The Waste Land*. It represents an attempt to give intellectual credence to the poem by discovering the pattern that underpins its critique of society. So, as with Wilson, Leavis' reading of the poem exhibits a tension between the desire to read the poem as a poem that is unadulterated by any concerns except the aesthetic, and the desire to establish the poem as *the* exemplary text of modernism, one that initiates a wholly new phase in the history of English literature.

The consequence of this way of reading the poem is that it emerges as both a radical and iconoclastic agent of the avant garde, and as that which sustains a nostalgic and conservative vision of human society. This is readily apparent in Leavis' concept, which emerges from his contemplation of *The Waste Land*, of how the modern, 'machine', age has brought about the 'final uprooting of the immemorial ways of life, of life rooted in the soil'. At times, indeed, it does feel as though Leavis manipulates Eliot's radical scepticism about the relationship of tradition and modernity to fit his own politics of nostalgic agrarianism. For, whereas Eliot may well exhibit (as Terry Eagleton has claimed) an aristocratic *hauteur* towards the notion of an organic community that is typical of his upbringing in America, Leavis' sense of a life rooted in the soil seems to derive more from a romanticised version of English feudalism than from any real sense of exactly what sort of land has been laid waste by Eliot's poem.[7]

In Leavis' reading of *The Waste Land*, then, can be detected two rather disdainful attitudes, both of which disclose the snobbery inherent in his conception of a full and great literary culture. The first of these lies in his assumption that for literature to be great it must be English, part of an English tradition, and dealing with matters of concern to English culture. Now, although Eliot himself fully surrendered to the force of Anglicisation that such an attitude registers, it effectively means that Leavis' reading of Eliot's poem can not even acknowledge that some of the poem's difficulties and tensions may result from difficulties and tensions in the relationship between English and American cultures. Such an attitude still prevails in criticism of the poem today, where it is very often described as a turning point in English poetry and much less often seen as a milestone (as the poem undoubtedly has been) in American poetry. And such an attitude has a deep impact on Leavis' view of the radical nature of Eliot's poetry. Given his failure to consider Eliot's Americanness, is it any wonder, then, that Leavis should consider his poetry to be so radical a departure from the rural (and very English) romantic tradition?

■ It is mainly due to him [Eliot] that no serious poet or critic today can fail to realise that English poetry in the future must develop (if at all) along some other line than that running from the Romantics through Tennyson, Swinburne, *A Shropshire Lad*, and Rupert Brooke. He has made a new start, and established new bearings.[8] □

The second charge of snobbery that can be levelled against Leavis is that his conception of what constitutes great poetry is one inextricably bound up with an idea of a cultural élite. According to Leavis, Eliot's finely tuned sensibilities express a culture that is realisable only by a 'tiny minority' of people. In 'Poetry and the Modern World', the introductory essay to *New Bearings in English Poetry*, he writes:

■ Poetry matters because of the kind of poet who is more alive than other people, more alive in his own age. He is, as it were, at the most conscious point of the race in his time. . . . The potentialities of human experience in any age are realised only by a tiny minority, and the important poet is important because he belongs to this (and has, of course, the power of communication). . . . He is unusually sensitive, unusually aware, more sincere and more himself than the ordinary man can be.[9] □

Even leaving aside such questions as how it is possible to be 'more alive' than others, and what exactly is meant by being more oneself 'than the ordinary man can be', Leavis conceives of poetry as, ultimately, a mystery into which only a few initiates will be admitted. Poetry is, therefore, fundamentally conservative, a means of preserving the status quo rather than bringing about a new start or a reassessment of the conditions of modern society. This way of thinking about poetry, wherein the poet's role is to distil and crystallise the most sensitive emotions of the age, means, of course, that little can really be done to 'solve' the obscurities and difficulties of *The Waste Land*. In fact, such difficulties become elevated to an exemplary status: the very obscurity of the poem confirms its greatness. And, although Leavis does directly address the question of the poem's appeal to a 'limited public' towards the end of the piece quoted below, he sees this as a 'symptom of the state of culture that produced the poem'.

This sort of argument closes off any meaningful critical engagement with the text. While asserting that a proper reading of the poem must see it as a product of its culture, it also implies that in order to see the poem in this way, criticism must necessarily acknowledge that the poem can never be fully understood. In his privileging of poetry over his notion of the modern world, Leavis confuses cause and effect, symptom and illness.

Such ways of thinking have meant that criticism of *The Waste Land* has tended to short-circuit its use of the poem to illuminate the conditions of modernity. Since Leavis, readings of the poem have, therefore, tended to see their role as one of initiating readers into the rarefied – and seemingly occult – meanings of the poem, rather than explaining (or even accounting for) the poem's exemplary position within discussions of modernism. Leavis' reading of the poem, then, discovers an appropriate archetype for the poem in the fertility rituals detailed by Jessie L. Weston, but is rather hard put to explain exactly how, or why, 'sex . . . is sterile' in this modern waste land:

■ . . . *The Waste Land* . . . appeared first in the opening numbers of the *Criterion* (October 1922 and January 1923). The title, we know, comes from Miss J.L. Weston's book, *From Ritual to Romance*, the theme of which is anthropological: the Waste Land there has a significance in terms of Fertility Ritual. What is the significance of the modern Waste Land? The answer may be read in what appears as the rich disorganisation of the poem. The seeming disjointedness is intimately related to the erudition that has annoyed so many readers and to the wealth of literary borrowings and allusions. These characteristics reflect the present state of civilisation. The traditions and cultures have mingled, and the historical imagination makes the past contemporary; no one tradition can digest so great a variety of materials, and the result is a break-down of forms and the irrevocable loss of that sense of absoluteness which seems necessary to a robust culture. . . .

In considering our present plight we have also to take account of the incessant rapid change that characterises the Machine Age. The result is breach of continuity and the uprooting of life. This last metaphor has a peculiar aptness, for what we are witnessing today is the final uprooting of the immemorial ways of life, of life rooted in the soil. . . .

The remoteness of the civilisation celebrated in *The Waste Land* from the natural rhythms is brought out, in ironical contrast, by the anthropological theme. Vegetation cults, fertility ritual, with their sympathetic magic, represent a harmony of human culture with the natural environment, and express an extreme sense of the unity of life. In the modern Waste Land:

> April is the cruellest month, breeding
> Lilacs out of the dead land,

but bringing no quickening to the human spirit. Sex here is sterile, breeding not life and fulfilment but disgust, accidia, and unanswerable questions. It is not easy today to accept the perpetuation and multiplication of life as ultimate ends.

But the anthropological background has positive functions. It plays an obvious part in evoking that particular sense of the unity of life which is essential to the poem. It helps to establish the level of experience at which the poem works, the mode of consciousness to which it belongs. In *The Waste Land* the development of impersonality that *Gerontion* shows in comparison with *Prufrock* reaches an extreme limit: it would be difficult to imagine a completer transcendence of the individual self, a completer projection of awareness. . . .

The part that science in general has played in the process of disintegration is matter of commonplace: anthropology is, in the present context, a peculiarly significant expression of the scientific spirit. To the anthropological eye beliefs, religions, and moralities are human habits – in their odd variety too human. Where the anthropological outlook prevails, sanctions wither. In a contemporary consciousness there is inevitably a great deal of the anthropological, and the background of *The Waste Land* is thus seen to have a further significance. To be, then, too much conscious and conscious of too much – that is the plight:

> After such knowledge, what forgiveness?

At this point Mr Eliot's note on Tiresias deserves attention:

> Tiresias, although a mere spectator and not indeed a 'character', is yet the most important personage in the poem, uniting all the rest. Just as the one-eyed merchant, seller of currants, melts into the Phoenician Sailor, and the latter is not wholly distinct from Ferdinand Prince of Naples, so all the women are one woman, and the two sexes meet in Tiresias. What Tiresias *sees*, in fact, is the substance of the poem . . .

If Mr Eliot's readers have a right to a grievance, it is that he has not given this note more salience; for it provides the clue to *The Waste Land*. It indicates plainly enough what the poem is: an effort to focus an inclusive human consciousness. The effort . . . is characteristic of the age; and in an age of psychoanalysis . . . Tiresias . . . presents himself as the appropriate impersonation. A cultivated modern is (or feels himself to be) intimately aware of the experience of the opposite sex.

Such an undertaking offers a difficult problem of organisation, a distinguishing character of the mode of consciousness that promotes it being a lack of organising principle, the absence of any inherent direction. A poem that is to contain all myths cannot construct itself upon one. It is here that *From Ritual to Romance* comes in. It provides a background of reference that makes possible something in the nature of a musical organisation. Let us start by considering the use of the Tarot pack.

Introduced in the first section, suggesting, as it does, destiny, chance, and the eternal mysteries, it at once intimates the scope of the poem, the mode of its contemplation of life. It informs us as to the nature of the characters: we know that they are such as could not have relations with one another in any narrative scheme, and could not be brought together on any stage, no matter what liberties were taken with the Unities. The immediate function of the passage introducing the pack, moreover, is to evoke, in contrast with what has preceded, cosmopolitan 'high life', and the charlatanism that battens upon it:

> Madame Sosostris, famous clairvoyante,
> Had a bad cold, nevertheless
> Is known to be the wisest woman in Europe,
> With a wicked pack of cards.

Mr Eliot can achieve the banality appropriate here, and achieve at the same time, when he wants it, a deep undertone, a resonance, as it were, of fate:

> . . . and this card,
> Which is blank, is something he carries on his back,
> Which I am forbidden to see. I do not find
> The Hanged Man. Fear death by water.
> I see crowds of people, walking round in a ring.

The peculiar menacing undertone of this associates it with a passage in the fifth section:

> Who is the third who walks always beside you?
> When I count, there are only you and I together
> But when I look ahead up the white road
> There is always another one walking beside you
> Gliding wrapt in a brown mantle, hooded
> I do not know whether a man or a woman
> – But who is that on the other side of you?

The association establishes itself without any help from Mr Eliot's note; it is there in any case, as any fit reader of poetry can report; but the note helps us to recognise its significance:

> The Hanged Man, a member of the traditional pack, fits my purpose in two ways: because he is associated in my mind with the Hanged God of Frazer, and because I associate him with the hooded figure in the passage of the disciples to Emmaus in Part V.

The Tarot pack, Miss Weston has established, has affiliations with fertility ritual, and so lends itself peculiarly to Mr Eliot's purpose: the instance before us illustrates admirably how he has used its possibilities. The hooded figure in the passage just quoted is Jesus. Perhaps our being able to say so depends rather too much upon Mr Eliot's note; but the effect of the passage does not depend so much upon the note as might appear. For Christ has figured already in the opening of the section . . . Yet it is not only Christ; it is also the Hanged God and all the sacrificed gods: with the 'thunder of spring' 'Adonis, Attis, Osiris' and all the others of *The Golden Bough* come in. . . .

In *What the Thunder Said* the drouth becomes (among other things) a thirst for the waters of faith and healing, and the specifically religious enters into the orchestration of the poem. But the thunder is 'dry sterile thunder without rain'; there is no resurrection or renewal; and after the opening passage the verse loses all buoyancy, and takes on a dragging, persistent movement as of hopeless exhaustion . . . The ominous tone . . . associates it . . . with the reference to the Hanged Man in the Tarot passage of *The Burial of the Dead*. So Christ becomes the Hanged Man, the Vegetation God; and at the same time the journey through the Waste Land along 'the sandy road' becomes the Journey to Emmaus. . . .

All this illustrates the method of the poem, and the concentration, the depth of orchestration, that Mr Eliot achieves; the way in which the themes move in and out of one another and the predominance shifts from level to level. . . .

The unity of *The Waste Land* is no more 'metaphysical' than it is narrative or dramatic, and to try to elucidate it metaphysically reveals complete misunderstanding. The unity the poem aims at is that of an inclusive consciousness: the organisation it achieves as a work of art is of the kind that has been illustrated, an organisation that may, by analogy, be called musical. It exhibits no progression . . . the thunder brings no rain to revive the Waste Land, and the poem ends where it began.

At this point the criticism has to be met that, while all this may be so, the poem in any case exists, and can exist, only for an extremely limited public equipped with special knowledge. The criticism must be admitted. But that the public for it is limited is one of the symptoms of the state of culture that produced the poem. Works expressing the finest consciousness of the age in which the word 'high-brow' has become current are almost inevitably such as to appeal only to a tiny minority. It is still more serious that this minority should be more and more cut off from the world around it – should, indeed, be aware of a hostile and overwhelming environment. This amounts to an admission that there must be something limited about the kind of artistic achievement possible in our time: even Shakespeare in such conditions could hardly have been the 'universal' genius. And *The Waste Land*, clearly, is not of the order of *The Divine Comedy* or of *Lear*. The important admission, then, is not that *The Waste Land* can be appreciated only by a very small minority (how large in any age has the minority been that has really comprehended the masterpieces?), but that this limitation carries with it limitations in self-sufficiency.

These limitations, however, are easily over-stressed. Most of the 'special knowledge', dependence upon which is urged against *The Waste Land*, can fairly be held to be common to the public that would in any case read modern poetry. . . .

It is a self-subsistent poem, and should be obviously such. The allusions, references, and quotations usually carry their own power with them as well as being justified in the appeal they make to special knowledge. . . . The requisite knowledge of Dante is a fair demand. The knowledge of *Antony and Cleopatra* assumed in the opening of *A Game of Chess*, or of *The Tempest* in various places elsewhere, no one will boggle at. The main references in *The Waste Land* come within the classes represented by these to Dante and Shakespeare; while of the many others most of the essential carry enough of their power with them. By means of such references and quotations Mr Eliot attains a compression, otherwise unattainable, that is essential to his aim; a compression approaching simultaneity – the co-presence in the mind of a number of different orientations, fundamental attitudes, orders of experience.

This compression and the methods it entails do make the poem difficult reading at first, and a full response comes only with familiarity. Yet the complete rout so often reported, or inadvertently revealed – as, for instance, by the critic who assumes that *The Waste Land* is meant to be a 'metaphysical whole' – can be accounted for only by a wrong approach, an approach with inappropriate expectations. For the general nature and method of the poem should be obvious at first reading. . . .

The Waste Land, then, whatever its difficulty, is, or should be, obviously a poem. It is a self-subsistent poem. Indeed, though it would lose if the notes could be suppressed and forgotten, yet the more important criticism might be said to be, not that it depends upon them too much, but rather that without them, and without the support of *From Ritual to Romance*, it would not lose more. It has, that is, certain limitations in any case; limitations inherent in the conditions that produced it. Comprehensiveness, in the very nature of the undertaking, must be in some sense at the cost of structure: absence of direction, of organising principle, in life could hardly be made to subserve the highest kind of organisation in art.

But when all qualifications have been urged, *The Waste Land* remains a great positive achievement, and one of the first importance for English poetry. In it a mind fully alive in the age compels a poetic triumph out of the peculiar difficulties facing a poet in the age. And in solving his own problems as a poet Mr Eliot did more than solve the problem for himself. Even if *The Waste Land* had been, as used to be said, a 'dead end' for him, it would still have been a new start for English poetry.[10] □

The final extract of this chapter, from Maud Bodkin's *Archetypal Patterns in Poetry* (1934), makes a rather different set of claims from Leavis about *The Waste Land*'s 'transcendence of the individual self'. The 'new start for

English poetry' that Leavis detects in *The Waste Land* depends upon such transcendence in order to escape the dominant assumptions of Romanticism which still held sway over the literary assumptions of Eliot's time. For Leavis, then, this means that the poem is a successful exercise in modernist impersonality. Bodkin's reading of the poem, though, based as it is in Jungian psychology, sees it as an exercise in revealing the patterns of meaning – symbol and metaphor – by which the individual's unconscious partakes of the collective unconscious.[11] So, while Leavis' version of modernist sensibility may be characterised as a struggle to escape desperate and sterile solipsism, Bodkin's is more a reaching after connectedness and, as we shall see, ineffable mystery.

Both of these attitudes towards modernity in general, and *The Waste Land* in particular, are based in a sense of the conflict between the historical past and the present moment. The feeling of things falling apart that is captured by the poem's fragmentations and incongruities merely underlines a very modern apprehension that the past offered a fuller and more complete cultural experience. The myths upon which these readings of Eliot's poem are sustained are thus deeply nostalgic. While proclaiming the poem to be challengingly modern, they actually assert its place within a tradition of 'classic' literary texts. This should not, necessarily, be taken as an objection to these critical assessments of the poem. In fact, Bodkin's reading is refreshing in the obvious delight it takes in the experience of the poem itself. As she tells us, she really does *love* the poem, and finds that where it is most challenging and difficult it is also most stimulating. This acts as a useful corrective to the sense of world-weary foreboding that very often creeps into criticism of *The Waste Land*. Bodkin's analysis of the poem manages, with the help of comparisons with Coleridge and Dante, to bring a little light to bear on Eliot's gloomy determinism. Though, for her, *The Waste Land* may enact the loss of hope for the individual in modern society, its appeal to something that lies 'Beyond' also entertains the possibility of redemption for the collective experience that is humanity:

■ To one whose early delight in verse took the bias of the nineteenth century, the poetry of to-day presents an alien air. Jarred by incongruity in the sequence of images and phrases, one is disposed to judge – in the words of Mrs Woolf's *Letter to a Young Poet* – 'instead of acquiring a whole object, rounded and entire, I am left with broken parts in my hands'.

Writing from the psychological standpoint, I intend this statement less as criticism than as recognition of the limitations of the vital perspective present in these essays. In commenting on certain aspects of

T. S. Eliot's poem, *The Waste Land*, I am conscious of this bias and limitation. Though the poem is now to me one of the most satisfying of distinctively modern poems, and parts of it were found beautiful from the first, yet I imagine that a sense of the poem's contemporary importance may have served as 'the wire' sustaining the uncertain growth of my response to the whole, until I could begin to feel value in parts loved less through their relation to those loved more.

The aspect of the poem which I wish to consider here is its character as exemplifying the pattern I have termed Rebirth. Notably the poem accomplishes – in Jung's phrase – 'a translation of the primordial image into the language of the present', through its gathering into simultaneity of impression images from the remote past with incidents and phrases of the everyday present.

It has been observed that the re-entrance into myth and legend achieved through phantasmagoria – the shifting play of figures, as in dream, delirium, or the half-discerned undercurrents of consciousness – is an art-form characteristic both of Eliot's poetry, and of the present day; and this form has been criticized as unsatisfying, shapeless, in comparison with the clear definite outline that current belief and story made possible in the art of other ages. One might test one's own attitude to this criticism by bringing the total impression of *The Waste Land* into relation with that of Dante's *Comedy*. As a slighter illustration of the same kind of contrast, let us consider the way in which the agony of drought is conveyed and used in Eliot's poem, as compared with the communication of the experience in Coleridge's straightforward vivid tale of the Ancient Mariner.

In analysing *The Ancient Mariner*, we commented [earlier] on the relation, within the communicated experience, of the imagined sequence of outer events – the calm, drought, the mariner's prayer, storm, rain, renewed motion – and the inner sequence of pent-up energy, discharge, and relief. We saw how the compelling story of outer events, with its vivid detail, could carry the reader's attention from point to point, while, below the level of conscious attention, emotional forces combined in modes ancient and satisfying.

> The silly buckets on the deck,
> That had so long remained,
> I dreamt that they were filled with dew;
> And when I awoke, it rained.

The single realistic detail of the buckets long unused can carry the whole impression, of the sufferings of the frustrated voyage, on with the rhythm of the simple verse-form into the moment of poignantly experienced relief, physical and spiritual. Compare the lines from *The Waste Land*:

Here is no water but only rock
Rock and no water and the sandy road
The road winding above among the mountains
Which are mountains of rock without water
If there were water we should stop and drink
Amongst the rock one cannot stop or think
Sweat is dry and feet are in the sand
If there were only water amongst the rock
Dead mountain mouth of carious teeth that cannot spit
Here one can neither stand nor lie nor sit
There is not even silence in the mountains
But dry sterile thunder without rain
There is not even solitude in the mountains
But red sullen faces sneer and snarl
From doors of mudcracked houses . . .

One ceases to quote with reluctance; since the cumulative effect of the rhythm and repeated word-sounds is needed before one has a nucleus of experience with which to fuse the wide-ranging associations of the words. Since there is no story, no concrete dramatic situation, to bind associations together, the words within the haunting rhythm must play their part unaided, holding attention while the forces of feeling and attendant imagery negotiate in the antechambers of the mind.

The few powerfully evocative words played upon in the lines quoted create for us the bare form of an emotional situation realizable in any period of history, or pre-history, and multiplied, beyond actual occasions, infinitely, in dream and delirium. The horrible image of the dead mountain mouth – echoed later in 'the decayed hole among the mountains' – the craving for ease, for true silence and solitude, instead of faces that sneer and snarl – echoed, again, by the hooded hordes stumbling in cracked earth – all these are potent elements serving, as in the delirious dream, to express together memories and forces both of the individual and of the collective life.

In the lines that follow the nightmare atmosphere is exchanged for the clear beauty of the image that focuses desire:

If there were the sound of water only
Not the cicada

> And dry grass singing
> But sound of water over a rock
> Where the hermit-thrush sings in the pine trees
> Drip drop drip drop drop drop drop
> But there is no water

The question concerning the poetic effectiveness of the modern vision, as compared with the medieval, might be illustrated from these lines, set beside those from the *Inferno* where Master Adam of Brescia, in the torment of thirst, recalls the streams he knew on earth:

> . . . when alive I had enough of what I wished: and now, alas! I crave one little drop of water. The rivulets that from the verdant hills of Casantino descend into the Arno, making their channels cool and moist, stand ever before me. . . .

In each poem the lovely image gains poignancy from its imagined background of frustration and pain. How far do we feel it a loss that the modern poem has no edifice of accepted tradition within whose ordered structure a distinct incident may hold, like a little darkened separate shrine, the fair image shining with the inner light of desire and hope? Hope, I would say, is present in Dante's image, though shown in Hell; because it is only as a transient episode in Dante's journey, or element deep at the foundation of his heavenly vision, that we find beauty in his descriptions of torment. For our poetic experience today, I have argued, the traditional edifice of imagery that Dante uses can serve to sustain imaginative intuition, only in so far as it has the form of those archetypal patterns that changes of experience and outlook cannot render obsolete.

When I ask myself the question how far in Eliot's poem I miss 'the formal beauty of the medieval vision' of heaven and hell, I find that I care for it very little, when I realize in its stead such nexus of relations as Eliot weaves round the lyric image, within the sustaining pattern present through the whole poem. Let us consider farther this nexus of relations.

The hostile crowds that, in this section, are recalled from the agony in the garden, and seen sneering from mud-cracked houses or stumbling over endless plains, link this passage with that in the earlier division of the poem, where in the fog of winter dawn a crowd flowed over London Bridge. The line there quoted from Dante, 'I had not thought death had undone so many', draws to the surface the underlying relation to the *Inferno*, and hints at the extinction of human fellowship in these self-absorbed figures – recalling the *Inferno*'s terrible note of malice in misery, that is repeated in the snarling faces that break the mountain solitude. The murmur of lamentation that sounds in the air above the stumbling hordes, and, fused with the central experience of drought, recalls those wailings in Eanna, for plants that grow not and perishing children, serves to reinforce the impression of that other ancient memory abruptly introduced in the wintry dawn on London Bridge:

> There I saw one I knew, and stopped him, crying:
>   'Stetson!
> 'You who were with me in the ships at Mylae!
> 'That corpse you planted last year in your garden,
> 'Has it begun to sprout? Will it bloom this year?
> 'Or has the sudden frost disturbed its bed? . . . '

A hazardous stroke, yet to me it seems a triumphant one – to choose that glimpse of unreal crowds in city fog, for the stirring of associations of Osiris and his mysteries: the grain, or corpse, under the huddled earth, with its uncertain hope of resurrection, that frost or rifling beast may destroy.

One could cite many such links and associations. The reader who knows the poem will have found them for himself, and, reconstructing the interwoven tissue, will have realized some degree of unity in what appeared perhaps at first mere juxtaposition of fragments. Within my own experience of growing familiarity with the poem, I have found the reading over of certain of the lines come to seem like a ritual entrancing the mind with ancient memories. . . .

The words of ancient wisdom spoken in the thunder receive significance both from their place in the entire emotional pattern and from their special relations to earlier passages. . . . The vision of self-surrender – related . . . to the angelic power of sympathy, and the divine power of control – occurring in the poem's pattern at the moment of energy-release and revulsion, recalls in contrast the earlier pictures of arid human relations: the joyless embraces, for instance, of the typist and her lover on the squalid divan which Tiresias' vision finds indistinguishable from marriage-beds of royal splendour – while their transactions belong to that realm in which the solicitor and the obituary notice have the final word. It is to a world other and more real than this that we are called by the challenge of the thunder.

> *Damyata*: The boat responded
> Gaily, to the hand expert with sail and oar

> The sea was calm, your heart would have responded
> Gaily, when invited, beating obedient
> To controlling hands

These lines that interpret the divine task of control are of a subtlety, in their relation to an earlier passage, that may well communicate diversity of meanings. Mr H.R. Williamson suggests[12] that the implied renunciation – *would have responded* – is related, through the imagery of the boat, to the 'selfish passion' of Tristan and Isolde. But the lines placed between the quotations that recall the story of those lovers seem to me to convey not so much the selfishness of their passion as its fatality, their helplessness beneath its stroke:

> . . . I could not
> Speak, and my eyes failed, I was neither
> Living nor dead, and I knew nothing,
> Looking into the heart of light, the silence.

The deep-stricken love suggested in these lines, and in the legend of Tristan and Isolde – whether, within love's fatality, its consummation be accepted or renounced – seems associated positively with the Grail symbol, as the less to the greater mystery.

Here . . . the lines of the pattern present the Paradisal love of earth, and urge the imagination beyond it; though it is for each reader to interpret as he may that indication of a Beyond.[13] □

In the following chapter we turn to readings of *The Waste Land* in which 'the pattern' that is discovered in the poem seems to be much more rigidly set by Eliot's own critical pronouncements about poetry. This next group of critical readings have played a very large part in setting the pattern itself by which the poem has subsequently been read. These critics develop ways of thinking about the poem that have been seen in this chapter: they stress analogies between the poem and musical form, continue to assert that the poem's compressed allusiveness lends it literary power, and, most importantly, they read through the poem line by line, detailing closely the process by which it is read. In the increasing attention given to the role of Tiresias, they also sound a new note, one which has had a crucial effect on subsequent ways of reading the poem. The extracts that follow in the next chapter, then, witness the full assimilation of *The Waste Land* into the theories and practices of 'New Criticism'.

CHAPTER THREE

New Criticism: Poetry, Literature and Myth

DURING THE 1930s a re-evaluation of literary criticism took place, one that was to have far-reaching and lasting effects on ways of reading texts. This overhauling of critical values and practices came to be known as 'New Criticism', and its roots are deeply embedded in the critical writings of I. A. Richards (whose work we encountered in chapter one) and, most especially, in the ideas of literature and criticism set out by T. S. Eliot in essays written around the time of the composition of *The Waste Land*. Essays such as 'Tradition and the Individual Talent' (1919), 'Hamlet' (1919), 'The Function of Criticism' (1923), and '*Ulysses*, Order and Myth' (1923) furnished New Criticism with a set of critical doctrines that espoused aesthetic impersonality and objectivity, saw myth as a powerful means of unifying human experience, and which worked from a seemingly de-historicised sense of literary tradition. The four readings of *The Waste Land* in this chapter all spring, in varying degrees, from the assumptions and practices of New Criticism.

New Criticism was particularly dominant in American criticism over the 1940s and 1950s. It represented the attempt of young critics to establish literary criticism as a respectable academic endeavour, one that could be thought of as being intellectually as rigorous and meticulous as research into the sciences. In this sense it still exerts a powerful influence over critical practice. Though fundamentally at odds with each other in terms of basic assumptions about the relationship of literary texts to language, culture and society, New Criticism and 'literary theory' share an attempt to systematise and theorise reading practices. Indeed, New Criticism can be thought of as a precursor to much contemporary critical practice because of the stress it puts upon seeing literary language as socially and culturally determined rather than as a means for the expression of purely personal emotions. This underlining of the social function of language may seem, initially, to contradict a basic tenet of New Criticism – namely that the literary text should be thought of as standing outside social considerations as a unified artistic whole, impervious to the stresses and tensions of mundane experience.

However, New Critics felt that by emphasising the autonomy of the literary text, and by concentrating on its aesthetic unity by a process of close reading that would reveal the delicate balance of ironies and tensions underpinning its formal properties, they would discover far deeper truths about the human condition. They believed that a text was complex and ambiguous, not because the author's own particular emotional experience was necessarily complex and ambiguous, but because the unchanging nature of human experience is one of complexity and ambiguity.[1] Any critical response that tried to deduce the author's state of mind from a text was, they felt, bound to fail; it could only ever amount to a second-guessing of the author's intentions. Such a mistake in critical practice, the 'Intentional Fallacy' as it was named in 1946 by Wimsatt and Beardsley, indulges romantic views of authorship rather than critical and objective criteria of reading. For New Critics, then, a text becomes an aesthetic icon, something that is self-contained and isolated, detached from the world of everyday concerns. The literary text (and for New Critics it was nearly always a poem) was to be seen as a container of mythic truths about human consciousness. It was, as the title of Cleanth Brooks' highly important and influential book of New Criticism has it, a 'Well Wrought Urn'.[2] And it was from such a position, New Critics believed, that the poem was able to comment upon – though remain unaffected by – the real world. So, although it has been noted that 'New Criticism was the ideology of an uprooted, defensive liberal intelligentsia who reinvented in literature what they could not locate in reality', its powerful influence over critical thought has been to focus attention on the text's status and function as an aesthetic object within reality.[3] Whether defensive or not, then, New Criticism's espousal of a doctrine of objectivity and impersonality has exposed some of the contradictions and pressures that operate within any critical practice and which have, themselves, had a profound effect on ways of reading *The Waste Land*.

In one sense, the adoption and deployment of New Critical attitudes represented a radical attack upon what were felt to be outmoded – even Victorian – standards of critical judgement. These new critical standards were, as Catherine Belsey has pointed out, 'one of the most important assaults on the orthodoxy of expressive realism' that dominated literary criticism in the early years of the century.[4] Following the lead of Eliot in both his poetry and criticism, such an assault on orthodoxy rested, then, in its hard-edged seriousness, in its desire for scientific objectivity in dealing with texts and in its deep mistrust of any subjective value judgements. Here it was felt that, at last, criticism could be adequate to the experience of modernity. New Criticism would deliver new ways of reading texts and in so doing it could offer new understandings of the world. Clearly, then, with *The Waste Land* seen as the paradigmatic text of modern consciousness, New Criticism turned to the poem as a means of testing its own theories and of establishing its practices.

In another sense, though, the changes in critical theory and practice represented by New Criticism can be seen to be far less radical than they may at first seem. American New Criticism had its roots in the Southern states, and was formulated in the work of such influential critics as John Crowe Ransom, Cleanth Brooks, W. K. Wimsatt, Allen Tate and R. P. Blackmur, all of whom came from – or spent significant amounts of time in – the South. New Criticism can be seen, therefore, as an intellectual expression of a traditional, and deeply conservative, Southern culture that is embedded in an organic relationship to the land. Its conservatism stems from a culture that feels itself to be alienated from, even antagonistic towards, the mainstream American culture of the north-eastern seaboard. It should not be forgotten that Eliot's early years were spent in this Southern culture. The curious mix, then, of conservatism and radicalism that we encounter in Eliot's writings, and which matches that of New Criticism, is a significant effect of the South's attempts to test the limits of a Liberal democracy, which it felt had been imposed on its own culture by the economically prosperous, industrialised north.[5] This may throw some light on the typical New Critical assertion of the aesthetic autonomy of a text – that its meaning derives from formal and intrinsic properties of its existence as a text rather than from the personal, political or cultural circumstances out of which it is produced – by seeing such an assertion as deriving from a culture desperate to assert its own autonomy. However, it remains based in a reactionary attitude towards literature and culture. Such an attitude precludes any consideration of concerns in the text other than aesthetic ones; it effectively silences the political or cultural responsibilities of the critic by settling for a doctrine of disinterestedness. In its theory and practice, therefore, New Criticism is, in the words of Terry Eagleton, 'a recipe for political inertia and thus for submission to the status quo'.[6]

Such apparently contradictory impulses in New Criticism reflect interestingly onto *The Waste Land*. They lend a sense of critical urgency to the extracts that comprise this chapter and which, despite the fact that they range from the mid-1930s to the early 1960s, all share New Critical assumptions. Given Eliot's crucial influence on the early development of New Criticism, then, the readings of *The Waste Land* that follow represent a 'reading back' into the poem of the critical attitudes it is responsible for having inspired. As we shall see, however, rather than providing (as one might expect) a perfect way of reading the poem, the poem itself actually remains eerily untouched by the attention given it by New Critics. A result of New Critical readings of *The Waste Land* may well be that we know better the theories and myths that sustain the poem, but not the poem itself. Strangely then, and despite the explicatory rhetoric of New Critics, *The Waste Land* still seems a Sibylline riddle, a 'handful of dust' that they never manage fully to grasp.

The first extract in this chapter is taken from F. O. Matthiessen's book *The Achievement of T. S. Eliot* (1935), which was the first major book-length examination of Eliot's poetry. In many ways Matthiessen cannot be seen as a fully fledged New Critic: originally from the West coast, he was fascinated by New England literary sensibilities and saw his role as literary critic as forwarding a radical left-wing political agenda. For him, the act of reading a text represented an engagement and investigation of the culture from which it arose, rather than an aesthetic exercise in the disinterested dissection of literary nuance. However, his reading of *The Waste Land* is typical of what would later become New Critical practice in that it seeks to resolve perceived tensions in the text into a unified and coherent whole. His belief – or at least hope – that Eliot's poem can overcome 'chaos' to deliver a 'sense of the potential unity of life' by asserting a fundamental pattern of myths is one that sets the terms for subsequent New Critical readings of the poem. It is perhaps curious that, at the height of the Great Depression, so politically engaged a critic should have produced a book on Eliot in which he concentrates on the formal properties of the poetry rather than its political ideas.[7] In so doing he reproduces the dualism between art and social action that is so marked in Eliot's critical writings, and thereby makes the way for New Critical readings of *The Waste Land* in which such dualisms are felt to sustain the poem in a delicate and intricate ironic balance. Matthiessen's reading of the poem seems to sit uneasily between admiration for the artistic achievement of Eliot and a suspicion that this is at the expense of 'giving a sense of life' back to its readers. This tension, then, generates a lively response to *The Waste Land* but, ultimately, does little more than provide *ways* of reading the poem rather than a *reading* of the poem:

■ In Eliot's earlier work . . . it at first looked as though he was so absorbed in the splendours of the past that he was capable of expressing only the violent contrast between its remembered beauty and the actual dreary ugliness of contemporary existence . . . But on closer examination it appears that his contrasts are not so clear-cut, that he is not confining himself to voicing anything so essentially limited and shallow as the inferiority of the present to the past. He is keenly aware of our contemporary historical consciousness, and of the problems which it creates. The modern educated man possesses a knowledge of the past to a degree hardly glimpsed a century ago, not only of one segment of the past, but, increasingly, of all pasts. If he is sensitive to what he knows, he can feel, in Eliot's words, 'that the whole of the literature of Europe from Homer . . . has a simultaneous existence'. But also, owing to the self-consciousness which results from so much knowledge (scientific and psychological as well as historical and literary), he will have a sense in any given moment, as Eliot has remarked of Joyce, 'of everything happening at once'.

Such a realization can lead either to chaos or to a sense of the potential unity of life. The difficulty with our knowledge to-day consists in the fact that instead of giving the individual's mind release and freedom, the piling up of so many disparate and seemingly unrelated details can merely oppress him with their bewildering variety, with 'being too conscious and conscious of too much' . . . The problem for the artist is to discover some unified pattern in this variety; and yet, if he believes as Eliot does that poetry should embody a man's reaction to his whole experience, also to present the full sense of its complexity. He can accomplish this double task of accurately recording what he has felt and perceived, and at the same time interpreting it, only if he grasps the similarity that often lies beneath contrasting appearances, and can thus emphasize the essential equivalence of seemingly different experiences. Such understanding and resultant emphasis constitute Eliot's chief reason for introducing so many reminiscences of other poets into the texture of his own verse. In this way he can at once suggest the extensive consciousness of the past that is inevitably possessed by any cultivated reader of to-day, and, more importantly, can greatly increase the implications of his lines by this tacit revelation of the sameness (as well as the contrasts) between the life of the present and that of other ages.

This emphasis is a leading element in the method of *The Waste Land*, whose city . . . is many cities, or rather, certain qualities resulting from a pervasive state of mind bred by mass civilization. But the structure of the poem embraces more than that. In his desire to make available for poetry the multiplicity of the modern world in the only way that the artist can, by giving it order and form, Eliot had discovered a clue in anthropology, in its exploration of ancient myths. It was not accidental or owing to any idiosyncrasy that he was affected profoundly by his reading of such a work as *The Golden Bough*, since the investigations of anthropology along with those of psychology have produced the most fundamental revolutions in contemporary thought and belief. It is noteworthy that Jessie Weston's *From Ritual to Romance* appeared in 1920, at the very time when Eliot was seeking a coherent shape for the mass of intricate material that enters into his poem. For reading that book gave to his mind the very fillip which it needed in order to crystallize. What he learned especially from it was the recurring pattern in various myths, the basic resemblance, for example, between the vegetation myths of the rebirth of the year, the fertility myths of the rebirth of the potency of man, the Christian story of the Resurrection, and the Grail legend of purification. The common source of all these myths lay in the fundamental rhythm of nature – that of the death and rebirth of the year; and their varying symbolism was an effort to explain the origin of life. Such knowledge, along with the researches of psychology, pointed to the close union in all these myths of the physical and spiritual, to the fact that their symbolism was basically sexual – in the Cup and Lance of the Grail legend as well as in the Orpheus cults; pointed, in brief, to the fundamental relation between the well-springs of sex and religion.

. . . In such a perception of the nature of myths, of 'a common principle underlying all manifestations of life',[8] Eliot found a scaffold for his poem, a background of reference that made possible something in the nature of a musical organization. He found the specific clue to the dramatic shaping of his material when he read in Miss Weston of the frequent representation of the mystery of death and rebirth by the story of a kingdom where the forces of the ruler having been weakened or destroyed by sickness, old age, or the ravages of war, 'the land becomes Waste, and the task of the hero is that of restoration',[9] not by pursuing advantages for himself, but by giving himself to the quest of seeking the health and salvation of the land.

The poem thus embodies simultaneously several different planes of experience, for it suggests the likenesses between various waste lands. Its quest for salvation in contemporary London is given greater volume and urgency by the additional presence of the haunted realm of medieval legend. . . .

As a result of this method of compressing into a single moment both the memory and the sameness of other moments, it becomes apparent that in 'The Fire Sermon', the section of the poem which deals in particular with the present and the past of London, no sharply separating contrast is made between them. Squalor pollutes the modern river as it did not in Spenser's 'Prothalamion'; but there are also glimpses of beauty where:

> The river sweats
> Oil and tar
> The barges drift
> With the turning tide
> Red sails
> Wide
> To leeward, swing on the heavy spar.

And, conversely, although mention of Elizabeth and Leicester brings an illusion of glamour, closer thought reveals that the stale pretence of their relationship left it essentially as empty as that between the typist and the clerk.

Use of such widely divergent details in a single poem indicates the special problem of the contemporary artist. Faced with so great a range of knowledge as a part of the modern consciousness, he can bring it to satisfactory expression in one of two ways, either by expansion or compression. It can hardly be a coincidence that each of these ways was carried to its full development at almost the same time, in the years directly following the War. Joyce chose the first alternative for *Ulysses* and devoted more than a quarter of a million words to revealing the complexity involved in the passage of a single ordinary day. In the following year Eliot concentrated an interpretation of a whole condition of society into slightly over four hundred lines. . . .

With the example of the nineteenth century behind him, Eliot naturally felt that, if the long poem was to continue to exist, there must be more to distinguish it than length, that its energy must be increased by the elimination of everything superfluous. To convey in poetry the feeling of the actual passage of life, to bring to expression the varied range and volume of awareness which exists in a moment of consciousness, demanded, in Eliot's view, the strictest condensation. Above all, the impression of a fully packed content should not be weakened through the relaxed connectives of the usual narrative structure. . . . Poetry alone, through its resources of rhythm and sound, can articulate the concentrated essence of experience, and thus come closest to the universal and permanent; but it can do so only through the mastery of a concentrated form. Though he approaches the question with a much broader understanding of all the factors involved than was possessed by the author of 'The Poetic Principle', Eliot is at one with Poe in his insistence on the necessary economy of a work of art, in his belief that a poem should be constructed deliberately with the aim of producing a unified effect. Consequently, after composing the first draft of *The Waste Land*, his revisions shortened it to less than two-thirds of its original length, in order that he might best create a dramatic structure that would possess at the same time a lyrical intensity.[10] . . .

[But] there is always the suspicion lingering in the minds of some readers that his way of giving order to the content of his work is too intellectually controlled and manipulated, that what he says cannot be wholly sincere because it is not sufficiently spontaneous. It may be that the large task which Eliot set himself in *The Waste Land* 'of giving a shape and a significance to the immense panorama of futility and anarchy' of contemporary history, caused some of the experiments he made to gain that end appear too deliberate.[11] Certainly some of his analogies with musical structure, in particular the summation of the themes in the broken ending of the final part, have always seemed to me somewhat forced and over-theoretical. But this is very different from saying that he is a too conscious artist. Indeed, such a charge would overlook the fact that some of the poetry of the past which across the remove of time seems most 'spontaneous', that of Chaucer, for example, was actually a product of long experimentation in poetic theory fully as calculated as Eliot's. . . .

Despite some of the protests of the nineteenth century on behalf of the untutored genius, it still appears that the more conscious the artist the better, if that consciousness implies the degree to which he has mastered the unending subtleties of his craft. But I have mentioned Chaucer also to point a difference in modern art. As my paragraphs on our highly developed historical sense tried to indicate, Eliot as a poet is not only inevitably acquainted with a great range of possible techniques, as all expert poets since the Renaissance have increasingly been; he is, in addition, highly aware of the processes of the mind itself. This particular kind of consciousness is in part what led him to feel the necessity of grounding the structure of his longest poem in something outside himself, in an objective pattern of myths.

. . . And in case there should be some feeling that . . . Eliot has revealed a kind of bookish weakness in turning for his structure to literature rather than to life, it should be recollected that Shakespeare himself created hardly any of his plots, and that by the very fact of taking ready-made the pattern of his characters' actions, he could devote his undivided attention to endowing them with life. It is only an uninformed prejudice which holds that literature must start from actual personal experience. It certainly must end with giving a sense of life; but it is not at all necessary that the poet should have undergone in his own person what he describes. Indeed, the more catholic the range of the artist, the more obviously impossible that would be.

The poet's imagination can work as well on his reading as on the raw material of his senses. It is a mark of human maturity, as Eliot noted in his discussion of the metaphysical poets, that there should not be a separation in an individual's sensibility between reading and experience any more than between emotion and thought.[12] □

Despite the fact that Eliot saw such a division between emotion and thought – the 'dissociation of sensibility' as he termed it – as the major symptom of modernity's ills, when we turn to more rigorously New Critical readings of *The Waste Land* it is hard not to feel that these readings are based in exactly this division.

The following essays by Cleanth Brooks and Hugh Kenner are milestones in criticism of *The Waste Land*. They are learned, witty, packed full of information and pay very close attention to the text itself. They are, in short, exemplary pieces of New Criticism. But their very formality of approach precludes any consideration of the poem's emotional impact. Both Brooks and Kenner (though, for different reasons, as we shall see) privilege thought over emotion. And in both cases this leads to interpretations of the poem that can never resolve its contradictions and complex ambiguities into the sort of unified aesthetic whole that they so desire. What does become evident from such readings, then, is that criticism of *The Waste Land* traces the desires of its critics for order and aesthetic propriety just as much as it discovers the poem's 'meaning'. This is true throughout the history of the poem's critical reception, and helps to explain the continuing fascination of the poem to succeeding generations of readers. Seen in this light, as a tracing of the desires of its various readers, both *The Waste Land* and the interplay of its various critical interpretations articulate the struggle of modern consciousness to come to terms with itself.

The following extracts from Cleanth Brooks' long and highly influential essay '*The Waste Land*: Critique of the Myth' (1939) demonstrate that New Critical approaches to the poem are not fully adequate to this struggle. Brooks' desire to discover the underlying mythical pattern that sustains the poem (and thus modern consciousness) seems based in a reactionary sense of tradition, in the belief that the poem plots the resolve of its protagonist 'to claim his tradition and rehabilitate it'. Leaving aside the question of whether the poem can be thought to have a single protagonist, such a reading assumes that the degree to which it can be seen to be unified is a measure of its success in dealing with literary tradition. This assumption is wildly at odds with the experience of the poem itself with its disjointed and fragmentary lyrical snatches, its historically jarring juxtapositions, and its apparent mistrust of the ability of tradition to deliver anything other than a bundle of fragmentary quotations to shore against ruin. What the poem itself seems to offer is a more radical sense of the discontinuities and disunities which threaten the very idea of tradition.

The opening assertion of Brooks' essay, then, that critics have never properly dealt with the poem 'as a unified whole' is, therefore, immediately contentious. First, this is because it is not at all clear how, or even whether, the poem *can* be seen as a unified whole. And second, it seems unlikely that Brooks' repetition of the poem's structure in his analysis of the poem (he reads through the poem line by line) will throw any more light upon the question of the poem's unity than that already available in the poem itself. Brooks thus finds himself caught in a characteristic double-bind of New Criticism. On the one hand the New Critic is duty-bound to respect the poem's assumed aesthetic autonomy. As a well-wrought work of art, nothing extrinsic to the poem can be seen to disturb the delicate poise of its unity. But, on the other hand, any critical commentary inevitably brings to a consideration of the text materials that are extrinsic to that text. Brooks turns to models of irony and myth as ways of (at least partially) solving this problem in his reading of *The Waste Land*. For him, the ironic imagination that he sees operating in *The Waste Land* can encompass such apparent contradictions because, ultimately, its balancing of textual tensions leads to an understanding of a deeper principle of unity. Crucial to this deeper understanding is the poem's use of myth. The use of myth in the poem, according to Brooks, leads to a highly compressed form of expression, a sort of poetic shorthand through which far more is revealed than is immediately apparent. For Brooks, then, *The Waste Land* reveals rather than imposes a sense of the unity of all periods, and the oneness of experience. He sees his task as critic, then, as one that allows the poem itself to reveal its meaning. In this first extract from his essay this may seem merely to act as justification for Brooks' extensive glossing of Eliot's references and allusions – he is, as it were, filling in the shorthand; however, it provides an admirable model for close, critically attentive reading. It sets the standard for a critical practice that reads *The Waste Land* not to impose meanings upon it but to untangle its complexities:

■ Though much has been written on *The Waste Land*, it will not be difficult to show that most of its critics misconceive entirely the theme and the structure of the poem. There has been little or no attempt to deal with it as a unified whole. . . .

The basic symbol used, that of the waste land, is taken, of course, from Miss Jessie Weston's *From Ritual to Romance*. In the legends which she treats there, the land has been blighted by a curse. The crops do not grow and the animals cannot reproduce. The plight of the land is summed up by, and connected with, the plight of the lord of the land, the Fisher King, who has been rendered impotent by maiming or sickness. The curse can be removed only by the appearance of a knight who will ask the meanings of the various symbols which are displayed to him in the castle. The shift in meaning from physical to spiritual sterility is easily made, and was, as a matter of fact, made in certain of the legends. As Eliot has pointed out, a knowledge of this symbolism is essential for an understanding of the poem.

Of hardly less importance to the reader, however, is a knowledge of Eliot's basic method. *The Waste Land* is built on a major contrast – a device which is a favourite of Eliot's and is to be found in many of his poems, particularly his later poems. The contrast is between two kinds of life and two kinds of death. Life devoid of meaning is death; sacrifice, even the sacrificial death, may be life-giving, an awakening to life. The poem occupies itself to a great extent with this paradox, and with a number of variations upon it. . . .

The first section of 'The Burial of the Dead' develops the theme of the attractiveness of death, or of the difficulty in rousing oneself from the death in life in which the people of the waste land live. Men are afraid to live in reality. April, the month of rebirth, is not the most joyful season but the cruellest. Winter at least kept us warm in forgetful snow. . . .

The first part of 'The Burial of the Dead' introduces this theme through a sort of reverie on the part of the protagonist, a reverie in which speculation on life glides off into memory of an actual conversation in the Hofgarten and back into speculation again. The function of the conversation is to establish the class and character of the protagonist. . . .

The next section of 'The Burial of the Dead', which begins with the scrap of song quoted from Wagner (perhaps another item in the reverie of the protagonist), states the opposite half of the paradox which underlies the poem: namely, that life at its highest moments of meaning and intensity resembles death. The song from Act I of Wagner's *Tristan und Isolde*, '*Frisch weht der Wind*', is sung in the opera by a young sailor aboard the ship which is bringing Isolde to Cornwall. The '*Irisch kind*' of the song does not properly apply to Isolde at all. The song is merely one of happy and naive love. It brings to the mind of the protagonist an experience of love – the vision of the hyacinth girl as she came back from the hyacinth garden. . . . The line which immediately follows this passage, '*Oed' und leer das Meer*', seems at first to be simply an extension of the last figure: that is, 'Empty and wide the sea [of silence]'. But the line, as a matter of fact, makes an ironic contrast; for the line, as it occurs in Act III of the opera, is the reply of the watcher who reports to the wounded Tristan that Isolde's ship is nowhere in sight; the sea is empty. And, though the '*Irisch kind*' of the first quotation is not Isolde, the reader familiar with the opera will apply it to Isolde when he comes to the line '*Oed' und leer das Meer*'. For the question in the song is in essence Tristan's question in Act III: 'My Irish child, where dwellest thou?' The two quotations from the opera which frame the ecstasy-of-love passage thus take on a new meaning in the altered context. In the first, love is happy; the boat rushes on with a fair wind behind it. In the second, love is absent; the sea is wide and empty. And the last quotation reminds us that even love cannot exist in the waste land.

The next passage, that in which Madame Sosostris figures, calls for further reference to Miss Weston's book. As Miss Weston has shown, the Tarot cards were originally used to determine the events of highest importance to the people, the rising of the waters. Madame Sosostris has fallen a long way from the high function of her predecessors. She is engaged merely in vulgar fortune-telling – is merely one item in a generally vulgar civilization. But the symbols of the Tarot pack are still unchanged. The various characters are still inscribed on the cards, and she is reading in reality (though she does not know it) the fortune of the protagonist. She finds that his card is that of the drowned Phoenician Sailor, and so she warns him against death by water, not realizing any more than do the other inhabitants of the modern waste land that the way into life may be by death itself. . . .

After the Madame Sosostris passage, Eliot proceeds to complicate his symbols for the sterility and unreality of the modern waste land by associating it with Baudelaire's '*fourmillante cité*' and with Dante's Limbo. . . .

The references to Dante are most important. The line, 'I had not thought death had undone so many', is taken from the Third Canto of the *Inferno*; the line, 'Sighs, short and infrequent, were exhaled', from the Fourth Canto. . . . the Third Canto deals with Dante's Limbo which is occupied by those who on earth had 'lived without praise or blame'. They share this abode with the angels 'who were not rebels, nor were faithful to God, but were for themselves'. They exemplify almost perfectly the secular attitude which dominates the modern world. . . . The people described in the Fourth Canto are those who lived virtuously, but who died before the proclamation of the Gospel – they are the unbaptized. They form the second of the two classes of people who inhabit the modern waste land: those who are secularized and those who have no knowledge of the faith. Without a faith their life is in reality a death. . . .

The Dante and Baudelaire references, then, come to the same thing as the allusion to the waste land of the medieval legends; and these various allusions, drawn from widely differing sources, enrich the comment on the modern city so that it becomes 'unreal' on a number of levels: as seen through 'the brown fog of a winter dawn'; as the medieval waste land and Dante's Limbo and Baudelaire's Paris are unreal.

The reference to Stetson stresses again the connection between the modern London of the poem and Dante's hell. . . . The protagonist, like Dante, sees among the inhabitants of the contemporary waste land one whom he recognizes. (The name 'Stetson' I take to have no ulterior significance. It is merely an ordinary name such as might be borne by the friend one might see in a crowd in a great city.) Mylae . . . is the name of a battle between the Romans and the Carthaginians in the Punic War. The Punic War was a trade war – might be considered a rather close parallel to our late war. At any rate, it is plain that Eliot in having the protagonist address the friend in a London street as one who was with him in the Punic War rather than as one who was with him in the World War is making the point that all the wars are one war; all experience, one experience. . . . I am not sure that Leavis and Matthiessen are correct in inferring that the line, 'That corpse you planted last year in your garden', refers to the attempt to bury a memory. But whether or not this is true, the line certainly refers also to the buried god of the old fertility rites. . . . This allusion to the buried god will account for the ironical, almost taunting tone of the passage. The burial of the dead is now a sterile planting – without hope. But the advice to 'keep the Dog far hence', in spite of the tone, is, I believe, well taken and serious. The passage in Webster goes as follows:

> But keep the wolf far thence, that's foe to men,
> For with his nails he'll dig them up again.

Why does Eliot turn the wolf into a dog? And why does he reverse the point of importance from the animal's normal hostility to men to its friendliness? If, as some critics have suggested, he is merely interested in making a reference to Webster's darkest play, why alter the line? I am inclined to take the Dog (the capital letter is Eliot's) as Humanitarianism and the related philosophies which, in their concern for man, extirpate the supernatural – dig up the corpse of the buried god and thus prevent the rebirth of life. . . .

If 'The Burial of the Dead' gives the general abstract statement of the situation, the second part of *The Waste Land*, 'A Game of Chess', gives a more concrete illustration. The easiest contrast in this section . . . is the contrast between life in a rich and magnificent setting, and life in the low and vulgar setting of a London pub. But both scenes, however antithetical they may appear superficially, are scenes taken from the contemporary waste land. In both of them life has lost its meaning.

. . . the reference to Philomela [in this section] is particularly important, for Philomela, it seems to me, is one of the major symbols of the poem.

Miss Weston points out (in *The Quest of the Holy Grail*) that a section of one of the Grail manuscripts, which is apparently intended to be a gloss on the Grail story, tells how the court of the rich Fisher King was withdrawn from the knowledge of men when certain of the maidens who frequented the shrine were raped and had their golden cups taken from them. The curse on the land follows from this act. . . . the violation of a woman makes a very good symbol of the process of secularization. . . . Love is the aesthetic of sex; lust is the science. Love implies a deferring of the satisfaction of the desire; it implies a certain asceticism and a ritual. Lust drives forward urgently and scientifically to the immediate extirpation of the desire. Our contemporary waste land is in large part the result of our scientific attitude – of our complete secularization. . . . The portrayal of 'the change of Philomel, by the barbarous king' is a fitting commentary on the scene which it ornaments. The waste land of the legend came in this way; the modern waste land has come in this way.

. . . The Philomela passage has another importance, however. If it is a commentary on how the waste land became waste, it also repeats the theme of the death which is the door to life, the theme of the dying god. The raped woman becomes transformed through suffering into the nightingale; through the violation comes the 'inviolable voice'. The thesis that suffering is action, and that out of suffering comes poetry is a favourite one of Eliot's. . . .

In the latter part of 'A Game of Chess' we are given a picture of spiritual emptiness, but this time, at the other end of the social scale, as reflected in the talk between two Cockney women in a London pub. (It is, perhaps, unnecessary to comment on the relation of their talk about abortion to the theme of sterility and the waste land.)

The account here is straightforward enough, and the only matter which calls for comment is the line spoken by Ophelia in *Hamlet*, which ends the passage. Ophelia, too, was very much concerned about love, the theme of conversation between the women in the pub. As a matter of fact, she was in very much the same position as that of the woman who has been the topic of conversation between the two ladies whom we have just heard. And her poetry, like Philomela's, had come out of suffering. . . .

'The Fire Sermon' makes much use of several of the symbols already developed. The fire is the sterile burning of lust, and the section is a sermon, although a sermon by example only. . . .

Mr Eugenides, the Smyrna merchant, is the one-eyed merchant, mentioned by Madame Sosostris. The fact that the merchant is one-eyed apparently means, in Madame Sosostris' speech, no more than that the merchant's face on the card is shown in profile. But Eliot applies the term to Mr Eugenides for a totally different effect. The defect corresponds somewhat to Madame Sosostris' bad cold. He is a rather battered representative of the fertility cults: the prophet, the *seer*, with only one eye.

The Syrian merchants, we learn from Miss Weston's book, were, along with slaves and soldiers, the principal carriers of the mysteries which lie at the core of the Grail legends. But in the modern world we find both the representatives of the Tarot divining and the mystery cults in decay. What he carries on his back and what the fortune-teller is forbidden to see is evidently the knowledge of the mysteries (although Mr Eugenides himself is hardly likely to be more aware of it than Madame Sosostris is aware of the importance of her function). Mr Eugenides, in terms of his former function, ought to be inviting the protagonist into the esoteric cult which holds the secret of life, but on the realistic surface of the poem, in his invitation to 'a weekend at the Metropole' he is really inviting him to a homosexual debauch. The homosexuality is 'secret' and now a 'cult' but a very different cult from that which Mr Eugenides ought to represent. The end of the new cult is not life, but ironically, sterility.

In the modern waste land, however, even the relation between man and woman is also sterile. The incident between the typist and the carbuncular young man is a picture of 'love' so exclusively and practically pursued that it is not love at all. The tragic chorus to the scene is Tiresias, into whom, perhaps, Mr Eugenides may be said to modulate, Tiresias, the historical 'expert' on the relation between the sexes.

The fact that Tiresias is made the commentator serves a further irony. In *Oedipus Rex*, it is Tiresias who recognizes that the curse which has come upon the Theban land has been caused by the sinful sexual relationship of Oedipus and Jocasta. But Oedipus' sin has been committed in ignorance, and knowledge of it brings horror and remorse. The essential horror of the act which Tiresias witnesses in the poem is that it is not regarded as a sin at all – is perfectly casual, is merely the copulation of beasts.

. . . The moral of all the incidents which we have been witnessing is that there must be an asceticism – something to check the drive of desire. The wisdom of the East and West comes to the same thing on this point. Moreover, the imagery which both St Augustine and Buddha use for lust is fire. What we have witnessed in the various scenes of 'The Fire Sermon' is the sterile burning of lust. Modern man, freed from all restraints, in his cultivation of experience for experience's sake, burns, but not with a 'hard and gemlike flame'. One ought not to pound the point home in this fashion, but to see that the imagery of this section of the poem furnishes illustrations leading up to the Fire Sermon is the necessary requirement for feeling the force of the brief allusions here at the end to Buddha and St Augustine.

. . . Whatever the specific meaning of the symbols, the general function of the section, 'Death by Water', is readily apparent. The section forms a contrast with 'The Fire Sermon' which precedes it – a contrast between the symbolism of fire and that of water. Also readily apparent is its force as a symbol of surrender and relief through surrender.

Some specific connections can be made, however. The drowned Phoenician Sailor recalls the drowned god of the fertility cults. Miss Weston tells that each year at Alexandria an effigy of the head of the god was thrown into the water as a symbol of the death of the powers of nature, and that this head was carried by the current to Byblos where it was taken out of the water and exhibited as a symbol of the reborn god. . . .

. . . one may suggest [therefore] that 'Death by Water' gives an instance of the conquest of death and time . . . through death itself. . . . The reference to the 'torchlight red on sweaty faces' and to the 'frosty silence in the gardens' obviously associates Christ in Gethsemane with the other hanged gods. . . .

The passage on the sterility of the waste land and the lack of water provides for the introduction later of two highly important passages:

> There is not even silence in the mountains
> But dry sterile thunder without rain

lines which look forward to the introduction later of 'what the thunder said' when the thunder, no longer sterile, but bringing rain, speaks.

The second of these passages is 'there is not even solitude in the mountains', which looks forward to the reference to the Journey to Emmaus theme a few lines later: 'Who is the third who walks always beside you?' The god has returned, has risen, but the travellers cannot tell whether it is really he, or mere illusion induced by their delirium.

. . . As Miss Weston has shown, the fertility cults go back to a very early period and are recorded in Sanscrit [sic] legends. Eliot has been continually, in the poem, linking up the Christian doctrine with the beliefs of as many peoples as he can. Here he goes back to the very beginnings of Aryan culture, and tells the rest of the story of the rain's coming not in terms of the setting already developed, but in its earliest form. . . .

The use of Sanscrit in what the thunder says is thus accounted for. In addition, there is of course a more obvious reason for casting what the thunder said into Sanscrit here: onomatopoeia. The comments on the three statements of the thunder imply an acceptance of them. The protagonist answers the first question, 'What have we given?' with the statement:

The awful daring of a moment's surrender
Which an age of prudence can never retract
By this, and this only, we have existed

Here the larger meaning is stated in terms which imply the sexual meaning. Man cannot be absolutely self-regarding. Even the propagation of the race – even mere 'existence' – calls for such a surrender. Living calls for . . . belief in something more than 'life'.

The comment on *dayadhvam* (sympathize) is obviously connected with the foregoing passage. The surrender to something outside the self is an attempt (whether on the sexual level or some other) to transcend one's essential isolation. The passage gathers up the symbols previously developed in the poem just as the foregoing passage reflects, though with a different implication, the numerous references to sex made earlier in the poem. . . .

The third statement made by the thunder, *damyata* (control) follows the condition necessary for control, sympathy. The figure of the boat catches up the figure of control already given in 'Death by Water' – 'O you who turn the wheel and look to windward' – and from 'The Burial of the Dead' the figure of happy love in which the ship rushes on with a fair wind behind it: '*Frisch weht der Wind . . .*'.

I cannot accept Mr Leavis' interpretation of the passage, 'I sat upon the shore/Fishing, with the arid plain behind me' as meaning that the poem 'exhibits no progression'. The comment upon what the thunder says would indicate, if other passages did not, that the poem does 'not end where it began'. It is true that the protagonist does not witness a revival of the waste land; but there are two important relationships involved in his case: a personal one as well as a general one. If secularization has destroyed, or is likely to destroy, modern civilization, the protagonist still has a private obligation to fulfill. Even if the civilization is breaking up – 'London Bridge is falling down falling down falling down' – there remains the personal obligation: 'Shall I at least set my lands in order?' . . .

The bundle of quotations with which the poem ends has a very definite relation to the general theme of the poem and to several of the major symbols used in the poem. Before Arnaut leaps back into the refining fire of Purgatory with joy, he says: 'I am Arnaut who weep and go singing; contrite I see my past folly, and joyful I see before me the day I hope for. Now I pray you by that virtue which guides you to the summit of the stair, at times be mindful of my pain.' This theme is carried forward by the quotation from *Pervigilium Veneris*: 'When shall I be like the swallow.' The allusion is also connected with the Philomela symbol. (Eliot's note on the passage indicates this clearly.) The sister of Philomela was changed into a swallow as Philomela was changed into a nightingale. The protagonist is asking therefore when shall the spring, the time of love, return, but also when will he be reborn out of his sufferings, and – with the special meaning which the symbol takes on from the preceding Dante quotation and from the earlier contexts already discussed – he is asking what is asked at the end of one of the minor poems: 'When will Time flow away?'

The quotation from 'El Desdichado' . . . indicates that the protagonist of the poem has been disinherited, robbed of his tradition. The ruined tower is, perhaps, also the Perilous Chapel . . . and it is also the whole tradition in decay. The protagonist resolves to claim his tradition and rehabilitate it.

The quotation from *The Spanish Tragedy* – 'Why then Ile fit you. Hieronymo's mad againe' – is, perhaps, the most puzzling of all these quotations. It means, I believe, this: The protagonist's acceptance of what is in reality the deepest truth will seem to the present world mere madness. . . . Hieronymo in the play, like Hamlet, was 'mad' for a purpose. The protagonist is conscious of the interpretation which will be placed on the words which follow – words which will seem to many apparently meaningless babble, but which contain the oldest and most permanent truth of the race:

Datta. Dayadhvam. Damyata.

Quotation of the whole context from which the line is taken confirms this interpretation. Hieronymo, asked to write a play for the court's entertainment, replies:

> Why then, I'll fit you; say no more.
> When I was young, I gave my mind
> And plied myself to fruitless poetry;
> Which though it profit the professor naught,
> Yet it is passing pleasing to the world.

He sees that the play will give him the opportunity he has been seeking to avenge his son's murder. Like Hieronymo, the protagonist in the poem has found his theme; what he is about to perform is not 'fruitless'.[13] □

From this act of close textual scrutiny, then, Brooks sees the theme of sterility emerging as the major theme of the poem. This, in turn, is derived from Weston's *From Ritual to Romance*. However, though a unified pattern seems to be becoming apparent from this manner of examining the poem, there are many moments in Brooks' reading of the poem that disrupt such unity, moments that beg questions of the text rather than see it resolving into neatly formulated themes. For instance, how and why Brooks takes Eliot's 'Dog' to signify 'humanitarianism' is baffling in the extreme. Far more serious, though, is his deliberate refusal to talk about the pub scene at the end of 'A Game of Chess'. That he feels the only thing worthy of mention in this scene is its reference to Shakespeare is indicative of the worst kind of literary snobbishness. It also shows how he is prepared *not* to read the poem if what it seems to be saying fails to furnish him with a neat argument. In both this passage and that dealing with Mr Eugenides, Brooks exhibits very clearly his squeamishness when it comes to non-literary sex and sexuality. Finally, to conclude that the Thunder's speech is in Sanskrit because of onomato-poeia seems far too easy a solution to one of the major difficulties of the poem's closing section. As we will see in later criticism, the problematic questioning of the relationship between language, tradition and nation-ality that is encapsulated in the poem's final passages is not so easily resolved as Brooks here implies.

In the closing paragraphs of his essay Brooks attempts to draw together the themes he has teased out of the poem. Perhaps a little sur-prisingly, though fully in accord with what he has already outlined, he concludes that the 'message' of *The Waste Land* is a Christian one. Though filtered through a modern consciousness, it is, finally, a statement of religious beliefs:

■ The basic method used in *The Waste Land* may be described as the application of the principle of complexity. The poet works in terms of surface parallelisms which in reality make ironical contrasts, and in terms of surface contrasts which in reality constitute parallelisms. (The second group sets up effects which may be described as the obverse of irony.) The two aspects taken together give the effect of chaotic experience ordered into a new whole, though the realistic surface of experience is faithfully retained. The complexity of the experience is not violated by the apparent forcing upon it of a predetermined scheme.

The fortune-telling of 'The Burial of the Dead' will illustrate the general method very satisfactorily. On the surface of the poem the poet reproduces the patter of the charlatan, Madame Sosostris, and there is the surface irony: the contrast between the original use of the Tarot cards and the use made by Madame Sosostris. But each of the details . . . assumes a new meaning in the general context of the poem. There is then, in addition to the surface irony, something of a Sophoclean irony too, and the 'fortune-telling', which is taken ironically by a twentieth-century audience, becomes *true* as the poem develops – true in a sense in which Madame Sosostris herself does not think it true. The surface irony is thus reversed and becomes an irony on a deeper level. The items of her speech have only one reference in terms of the context of her speech: the 'man with three staves', the 'one-eyed merchant', the 'crowds of people, walking round in a ring', etc. But transferred to other contexts they become loaded with special meanings. To sum up, all the central symbols of the poem head up here; but here, in the only section in which they are explicitly bound together, the binding is slight and accidental. The deeper lines of association only emerge in terms of the total context as the poem develops – and this is, of course, exactly the effect which the poet intends.

. . . The effect is a sense of the oneness of experience, and of the unity of all periods, and with this, a sense that the general theme of the poem is true. But the theme has not been imposed – it has been revealed.

. . . The poem would undoubtedly be 'clearer' if every symbol had a single, unequivocal meaning; but the poem would be thinner, and less honest. For the poet has not been content to develop a didactic allegory in which the symbols are two-dimensional items adding up directly to the sum of the general scheme. They represent dramatized instances of the theme, embodying in their own nature the fundamental paradox of the theme.

We shall better understand why the form of the poem is right and inevitable if we compare Eliot's theme to Dante's and to Spenser's. Eliot's theme is not the statement of a faith held and agreed upon (Dante's *Divine Comedy*), nor is it the projection of a 'new' system of beliefs (Spenser's *Faerie Queen* [*sic*]). Eliot's theme is the rehabilitation of a system of beliefs, known but now discredited. Dante did not have to 'prove' his statement; he could assume it, and move within it about a poet's business. Eliot does not care, like Spenser, to force the didacticism. He prefers to stick to the poet's business. But, unlike Dante, he cannot assume acceptance of the statement. A direct approach is calculated to elicit powerful 'stock responses' which will prevent the poem's being *read* at all. Consequently, the only method is to work by indirection. The Christian material is at the centre, but the poet never deals with it directly. The theme of resurrection is made on the surface in terms of the fertility rites; the words which the thunder speaks are Sanscrit words.

. . . To put the matter in still other terms: the Christian terminology is for the poet a mass of clichés. However 'true' he may feel the terms to be, he is still sensitive to the fact that they operate superficially as clichés, and his method of necessity must be a process of bringing them to life again. The method adopted in *The Waste Land* is thus violent and radical, but thoroughly necessary. For the renewing and vitalizing symbols which have been crusted over with a distorting familiarity demands the type of organization which we have already commented on in discussing particular passages: the statement of surface similarities which are ironically revealed to be dissimilarities, and the association of apparently obvious dissimilarities which culminates in a later realization that the dissimilarities are only superficial – that the chains of likeness are in reality fundamental. In this way the statement of beliefs emerges *through* confusion and cynicism – not in spite of them.[14] □

We turn in the next extract to a rather later reading of *The Waste Land*. This is taken from Hugh Kenner's very important book *The Invisible Poet: T.S. Eliot* (1959), and it shares with Brooks' analysis a method of close-reading and textual exegesis. As the title of this book indicates, Kenner's starting point is Eliot's doctrine of the impersonality of the artist, the poet's invisibility within a text. So, while for Brooks the exercising of critical intelligence upon *The Waste Land* allows a 'statement of beliefs' to emerge, for Kenner the poem demands high intellectual resources of its readers precisely because it is an exercise in critical intelligence. It is as divorced from the feeling and emotions of its author as possible. The poem, Kenner asserts, does not betray Eliot's mind but 'the mind of Europe', its modernist consciousness is not that of an individual but of a culture pushed to its limits. Indeed, the chapter from which this extract is taken is entitled 'The Mind of Europe'. Given Kenner's pre-eminent status as a commentator on modernism, his authoritative reading of *The Waste Land* sees it fully assimilated into a European literary tradition.

In keeping with Kenner's other examinations of modernist writers (he has written major critical works on Ezra Pound, James Joyce, Wyndham Lewis and Samuel Beckett), his analysis of Eliot is an exciting and idiosyncratic mix of acute critical insights and scholarly knowledge. His style seems at times a little eccentric, but it is nevertheless the perfect vehicle for his infectious enthusiasm for getting to the heart of a text. It is because of this that his reading of *The Waste Land* opens up new critical ground in thinking about the poem. Kenner, through the very force of his critical intelligence, pushes beyond the stuffiness in which some New Critical ways of tackling the poem get stuck. For him the poem is much less of a closed form than for earlier New Critics such as Richards, Matthiessen and Brooks. While these earlier critics saw the poem's 'ironic contrasts' as crucial indicators of its underlying formal unity, Kenner reads the poem's ironies as an index of the restless multiplicity of modern consciousness.

Kenner's reading of *The Waste Land* emphasises this sense of multiplicity by focusing on the three different mythical roles of Tiresias (which derive from *Oedipus Rex*, the *Odyssey*, and the *Metamorphoses* respectively). This, in turn, brings about an important change in ways of looking at the poem. Effectively it draws new critical attention to the passage in which Tiresias appears, that which tells of the seduction of the typist by the young man, and which Kenner calls the 'great tour de force of the poem'. Neglected by previous critics largely from a sense of sexual squeamishness similar to that displayed in Brooks' essay, this passage now becomes absolutely central to readings of the poem. One reason for this is Eliot's own note about the passage, which states:

■ Tiresias, although a mere spectator and not indeed a 'character', is yet the most important personage in the poem, uniting all the rest. Just as the one-eyed merchant, seller of currants, melts into the Phoenician Sailor, and the latter is not wholly distinct from Ferdinand

Prince of Naples, so all the women are one woman, and the two sexes meet in Tiresias. What Tiresias *sees*, in fact, is the substance of the poem.[15] ☐

To see Tiresias as the guiding principle of unity in the poem, then, does seem to have Eliot's sanction. Another reason, and one that has become even more important in recent criticism, is that analysis of Tiresias' role in the poem has allowed a more thorough deconstruction of assumptions held by Eliot (and modernity in general) about sex, gender and the social hierarchy. So, Kenner's placing of Tiresias centrally in the critical debate heralds a vital development in examinations of the poem. His reading is innovative in another sense as well. Before Kenner, critics tended to attempt to 'solve' the mysteries of the poem; this meant that a great deal of critical energy was expended in glossing references, and explaining allusions. With much of this initial 'spadework' having been done, Kenner was able to initiate a new phase in the poem's critical history, that of bringing this critical intelligence to bear on the reading of the poem. The myth of the Grail Legend, always acknowledged as fundamental to the poem, is thus seen by Kenner in a new relation to the poem. In the legend what brings fertility back to the waste land is not the actual knowledge that the quester gains at the Chapel Perilous, but the very act of asking for that knowledge, of asking the right questions. Such an act of intellectual curiosity, Kenner argues, is all-important to *The Waste Land*. If the culture so blown apart by the experience of modernity is to be revived, then, we must ask the right questions of the fragments that have been shored against ruin. His reading starts asking some of those questions:

■ 'A Game of Chess' is a convenient place to start our investigations. Chess is played with Queens and Pawns: the set of pieces mimics a social hierarchy, running from 'The Chair she sat in, like a burnished throne', to 'Goonight Bill. Goonight Lou. Goonight May. Goonight'. It is a silent unnerving warfare . . . in which everything hinges on the welfare of the King, the weakest piece on the board, and in this section of the poem invisible (though a 'barbarous king' once forced Philomel). Our attention is focused on the Queen. . . . The woman at the dressing table in *The Waste Land*, implied but never named or attended to, is not like [Pope's] Belinda the moral centre of an innocent dislocation of values but simply the implied sensibility in which . . . multifarious effects dissolve and find congruence. All things deny nature; the fruited vines are carved, the Cupidons golden, the light not of the sun, the perfumes synthetic, the candelabra (seven-branched, as for an altar) devoted to no rite, the very colour of the firelight perverted by sodium and copper salts. The dolphin is carved, and swims in a 'sad light' . . .

No will to exploit new sensations is present; the will has long ago died; this opulent ambience is neither chosen nor questioned. The 'sylvan scene' is not Eden nor a window but a painting, and a painting of an unnatural event:

> The change of Philomel, by the barbarous king
> So rudely forced; yet there the nightingale
> Filled all the desert with inviolable voice
> And still she cried, and still the world pursues,
> 'Jug Jug' to dirty ears.

Her voice alone, like the voice that modulates the thick fluid of this sentence, is 'inviolable'; like Tiresias in Thebes, she is prevented from identifying the criminal whom only she can name. . . .

If we move from the queens to the pawns, we find lowlife no more free or natural, equally obsessed with the denial of nature, artificial teeth, chemically procured abortions, the speaker and her interlocutor battening fascinated at secondhand on the life of Lil and her Albert, Lil and Albert interested only in spurious ideal images of one another. . . . And this point – nature everywhere denied, its ceremonies simplified to the brutal abstractions of a chess game . . . – this point is made implicitly by . . . the juxtaposition without comment or copula of two levels of sensibility: . . . the world of the inquiring wind and the sense drowned in odours with the world of ivory teeth and hot gammon. In Lil and Albert's milieu there is fertility, in the milieu where golden Cupidons peep out there is not; but Lil and Albert's breeding betokens not a harmony of wills but only Albert's improvident refusal to leave Lil alone. The chemist with commercial impartiality supplies one woman with 'strange synthetic perfumes' and the other with 'them pills I took, to bring it off', aphrodisiacs and abortifacients; he is the tutelary deity, uniting the offices of Cupid and Hymen, of a world which is under a universal curse.

From this vantage point we can survey the methods of the first section, which opens with a denial of Chaucer. . . . In the twentieth-century version we have a prayer book heading, 'The Burial of the Dead', with its implied ceremonial of dust thrown and of souls reborn; . . . No 'vertu' is engendered amid this apprehensive reaching forward of participles, and instead of pilgrimages we have European tours. . . . Up out of the incantation breaks a woman's voice, giving tongue to the ethnological confusions of the new Europe, the subservience of *patria* to whim of statesmen, the interplay of immutable fact and national pride:

Bin gar keine Russin, stamm' aus Litauen, echt deutsch.

– a mixing of memory and desire. Another voice evokes the vanished Austro-Hungarian Empire, the inbred malaise of . . . objectless travels. . . . 'In the mountains, there you feel free'. We have only to delete 'there' to observe the collapse of more than a rhythm: to observe how the line's exact mimicry of a fatigue which supposes it has reached some ultimate perception can telescope spiritual bankruptcy, deracinated ardour, and an illusion of liberty which is no more than impatience with human society and relief at a temporary change. It was a restless, pointless world that collapsed during the war, agitated out of habit but tired beyond coherence, on the move to avoid itself. . . .

The plight of the Sibyl in the epigraph rhymes with that of Marie; the terrible thing is to be compelled to stay alive. . . . The Sibyl in her better days answered questions by flinging from her cave handfuls of leaves bearing letters which the postulant was required to arrange in a suitable order; the wind commonly blew half of them away. Like Tiresias, like Philomel, like the modern poet, she divulged forbidden knowledge only in riddles, fitfully. . . . *The Waste Land* is suffused with a functional obscurity, sibylline fragments so disposed as to yield the utmost in connotative power, embracing the fragmented present and reaching back to 'that vanished mind of which our mind is a continuation'. As for the Sibyl's present exhaustion, she had foolishly asked Apollo for as many years as the grains of sand in her hand; which is one layer in the multilayered line, 'I will show you fear in a handful of dust'. She is the prophetic power, no longer consulted by heroes but tormented by curious boys, still answering because she must; she is Madame Sosostris, consulted by dear Mrs Equitone and harried by police . . .; she is the image of the late phase of Roman civilization, now vanished; she is also 'the mind of Europe', a mind more important than one's own private mind, a mind which changes but abandons nothing en route, not superannuating either Shakespeare, or Homer, or the rock drawing of the Magdalenian draughtsmen; but now very nearly exhausted by the effort to stay interested in its own contents.

Which brings us to the 'heap of broken images': not only desert ruins of some past from which life was withdrawn with the failure of the water supply, like the Roman cities in North Africa, or Augustine's Carthage, but also the manner in which Shakespeare, Homer, and the drawings of Michelangelo, Raphael, and the Magdalenian draughts-men coexist in the contemporary cultivated consciousness: fragments, familiar quotations. . . . For one man who knows *The Tempest* inti-mately there are a thousand who can identify the lines about the cloud-capp'd towers; painting is a miscellany of reproductions, litera-ture a potpourri of quotations, history a chaos of theories and postures . . . A desert wind has blown half the leaves away; disuse and vandals have broken the monuments. . . . Cities are built out of the ruins of previous cities, as *The Waste Land* is built out of the remains of older poems. But at this stage no building is yet in question; the 'Son of man' (a portentously generalizing phrase) is moving tirelessly east-ward, when the speaker accosts him with a sinister '(Come in under the shadow of this red rock)', and offers to show him not merely hor-ror and desolation but something older and deeper: fear.

Hence the hyacinth girl, who speaks with urgent hurt simplicity, like the mad Ophelia:

> 'You gave me hyacinths first a year ago;
> 'They called me the hyacinth girl.'

They are childlike words, self-pitying, spoken perhaps in memory, perhaps by a ghost, perhaps by a wistful woman now out of her mind. . . .

Five pages later 'A Game of Chess' ends with Ophelia's words before her death; Ophelia gathered flowers before she tumbled into the stream, then lay and chanted snatches of old tunes . . . while her clothes and hair spread out on the waters. 'The Burial of the Dead' ends with a sinister dialogue about a corpse in the garden . . . [and] 'The Fire Sermon' opens with despairing fingers clutching and sink-ing into a wet bank; it closes with Thames-daughters singing from beneath the oily waves. The drowned Phlebas in Section IV varies this theme; and at the close of the poem the response to the last challenge of the thunder alludes to something that happened in a boat . . . but what in fact did happen we are not told . . .

In *The Waste Land* . . . the guilt of the protagonist seems coupled with his perhaps imagined responsibility for the fate of a perhaps ideally drowned woman. . . .

Part Two, 'A Game of Chess' revolves around perverted nature, denied or murdered offspring; Part Three, 'The Fire Sermon', the most explicit of the five sections, surveys with grave denunciatory candour a world of automatic lust, in which those barriers between person and person which so troubled Prufrock are dissolved by the suppression of the person and the transposition of all human needs and desires to a plane of genital gratification. . . .

The typist passage is the great tour de force of the poem; its gentle lyric melancholy, its repeatedly disrupted rhythms, the automatism of its cadences, in alternate lines aspiring and failing nervelessly . . . constitute Eliot's most perfect liaison between the self-sustaining gesture of the verse and the presented fact. Some twenty-five lines in flawlessly traditional iambic pentameter, alternately rhymed, sustain with their cadenced gravity a moral context in which the dreary business is played out; the texture is lyric rather than dramatic because there is neither doing nor suffering here but rather the mutual compliance of a ritual scene. . . . In [this passage] the speaker for the first time in the poem identifies himself as Tiresias:

> I Tiresias, though blind, throbbing between two lives,
> Old man with wrinkled female breasts, can see

There are three principal stories about Tiresias, all of them relevant. In *Oedipus Rex*, sitting 'by Thebes below the wall' he knew why, and as a consequence of what violent death and what illicit amour, the pestilence had fallen on the unreal city, but declined to tell. In the *Odyssey* he 'walked among the lowest of the dead' and evaded predicting Odysseus' death by water; the encounter was somehow necessary to Odysseus' homecoming, and Odysseus was somehow satisfied with it, and did get home, for a while. In the *Metamorphoses* he underwent a change of sex for watching the coupling of snakes: presumably the occasion on which he 'foresuffered' what is tonight 'enacted on this same divan or bed'. He is often the prophet who knows but withholds his knowledge, just as Hieronymo, who is mentioned at the close of the poem, knew how the tree he had planted in his garden came to bear his dead son, but was compelled to withhold that knowledge until he could write a play which, like *The Waste Land*, employs several languages and a framework of allusions impenetrable to anyone but the 'hypocrite lecteur'. It is an inescapable shared guilt that makes us so intimate with the contents of this strange poem; it is also, in an age that has eaten of the tree of the knowledge of psychology and anthropology . . . an inescapable morbid sympathy with everyone else, very destructive to the coherent personality, that (like Tiresias' years as a woman) enables us to join with him in 'foresuffering all'. . . . [Throughout this passage] some transfiguring word touches with glory line after line:

> He, the young man carbuncular, arrives,

If he existed, and if he read those words, how must he have marvelled at the alchemical power of language over his inflamed skin! As their weary ritual commences, the diction alters; it moves to a plane of Johnsonian dignity without losing touch with them . . .

'Endeavours to engage her in caresses' is out of touch with the small house agent's clerk's speech, but it is such a sentence as he might *write*; Eliot has noted elsewhere how 'an artisan who can talk the English language beautifully while about his work or in a public bar, may compose a letter painfully written in a dead language bearing some resemblance to a newspaper leader and decorated with words like "maelstrom" and "pandemonium"'. So it is with the diction of this passage: it reflects the words with which the participants might clothe, during recollection in tranquillity, their own notion of what they have been about, presuming them capable of such self-analysis; and it maintains simultaneously Tiresias' fastidious impersonality. . . .

The opulent Wagnerian pathos, with its harmonic rather than linear development and its trick of entrancing the attention with leitmotifs, is never unrelated to the methods of *The Waste Land* . . . for Wagner had more than a bag of orchestral tricks and a corrupt taste for mythologies, he had also an indispensable sense of his own age, something that partly sustains and justifies his methods.

. . . Wagner, more than Frazer or Miss Weston, presides over the introduction into *The Waste Land* of the Grail motif. In Wagner's opera, the Sangreal quest is embedded in an opulent and depraved religiosity . . .

So in Part V of *The Waste Land* the journey eastward among the red rocks and heaps of broken images is fused with the journey to Emmaus ('He who was living is now dead. We who were living are now dying') and the approach to the Chapel Perilous.

The quester arrived at the Chapel Perilous had only to ask the meaning of the things that were shown him. Until he has asked their meaning, they have none; after he has asked, the king's wound is healed and the waters commence again to flow. So in a civilization reduced to 'a heap of broken images' all that is requisite is sufficient curiosity; the man who asks what one or another of these fragments means – seeking, for instance, 'a first-hand opinion about Shakespeare' – may be the agent of regeneration. The past exists in fragments precisely because nobody cares what it meant; it will unite itself and come alive in the mind of anyone who succeeds in caring, who is unwilling that Shakespeare shall remain the name attached only to a few tags everyone half-remembers . . .

Eliot develops the nightmare journey with consummate skill and then manoeuvres the reader into the position of the quester, presented with a terminal heap of fragments which it is his business to inquire about. The protagonist in the poem perhaps does not inquire; they are fragments he has shored against his ruins. Or perhaps he does inquire; he has at least begun to put them to use, and the 'arid plain' is at length behind him.

The journey is prepared for by two images of asceticism: the brand plucked from the burning, and the annihilation of Phlebas the Phoenician. 'The Fire Sermon', which opens by Thames water, closes with a burning, a burning that images the restless lusts of the nymphs, the heirs of city directors, Mr Eugenides, the typist and the young man carbuncular, the Thames-daughters. They are unaware that they burn. . . . They burn nevertheless, as the protagonist cannot help noticing when he shifts his attention from commercial London to commercial Carthage (which stood on the North African shore, and is now utterly destroyed). There human sacrifices were dropped into the furnaces of Moloch, in a frantic gesture of appeasement. There Augustine burned with sensual fires: 'a cauldron of unholy loves sang all about mine ears'; and he cried, 'O Lord, Thou pluckest me out'. The Buddhist ascetic on the other hand does not ask to be plucked out; he simply turns away from the senses because (as the Buddhist Fire Sermon states) they are each of them on fire. . . .

Part V opens, then, in Gethsemane, carries us rapidly to Golgotha, and then leaves us to pursue a nightmare journey in a world now apparently deprived of meaning . . . where towers hang 'upside down in air' [and] stability is imaged by a deserted chapel among the mountains, another place from which the life has gone but in which the meaning is latent, awaiting only a pilgrim's advent. The cock crows as it did when Peter wept tears of penitence . . . There the activity of the protagonist ends. Some forty remaining lines in the past tense recapitulate the poem in terms of the oldest wisdom accessible to the West. The thunder's DA is one of those primordial Indo-European roots that recur in the *Oxford Dictionary*, a random leaf of the Sibyl's to which a thousand derivative words, now automatic currency, were in their origins so many explicit glosses. If the race's most permanent wisdom is its oldest, then DA, the voice of the thunder and of the Hindu sages, is the cosmic voice not yet dissociated into echoes. It underlies the Latin infinitive 'dare', and all its Romance derivatives; by a sound change, the Germanic 'geben', the English 'give'. It is the root of 'datta', 'dayadhvam', 'damyata': give, sympathize, control: three sorts of giving. To sympathize is to give oneself; to control is to give governance.

Then spoke the thunder
DA
Datta: what have we given?
My friend, blood shaking my heart
The awful daring of a moment's surrender
Which an age of prudence can never retract
By this, and this only, we have existed

The first surrender was our parents' sexual consent; and when we are born again it is by a new surrender . . . The thunder is telling us what Tiresias did not dare tell Oedipus, the reason for the universal curse: 'What have we given?' As for 'Dayadhvam', 'sympathize':

DA
Dayadhvam: I have heard the key
Turn in the door once and turn once only
We think of the key, each in his prison
Thinking of the key, each confirms a prison

– a prison of inviolate honour, self-sufficiency . . .

DA
Damyata: The boat responded
Gaily, to the hand expert with sail and oar
The sea was calm, your heart would have responded
Gaily, when invited, beating obedient
To controlling hands

Unlike the rider, who may dominate his horse, the sailor survives and moves by cooperation with a nature that cannot be forced; and this directing, sensitive hand, feeling on the sheet the pulsation of the wind and on the rudder the momentary thrust of waves, becomes the imagined instrument of a comparably sensitive human relationship. If dominance compels response, control invites it; and the response comes 'gaily'. But – 'would have': the right relationship was never attempted.

> I sat upon the shore
> Fishing, with the arid plain behind me

The journey eastward across the desert is finished; though the king's lands are waste, he has arrived at the sea.

Shall I at least set my lands in order?

Isaiah bade King Hezekiah set his lands in order because he was destined not to live; but Candide resolved to cultivate his own garden as a way of living. We cannot set the whole world in order; we can rectify ourselves. And we are destined to die, but such order as lies in our power is nevertheless desirable.

London Bridge is falling down falling down falling down
Poi s'ascose nel foco che gli affina
Quando fiam uti chelidon – O swallow swallow
Le Prince d'Aquitaine à la tour abolie
These fragments I have shored against my ruins

An English nursery rhyme, a line of Dante's, a scrap of the late Latin *Pervigilium Veneris*, a phrase of Tennyson's ('O swallow, swallow, could I but follow') linked to the fate of Philomel, an image from a pioneer nineteenth-century French visionary who hanged himself on a freezing January morning: 'a heap of broken images', and a fragmentary conspectus of the mind of Europe. Like the Knight in the Chapel Perilous, we are to ask what these relics mean; and the answers will lead us into far recesses of tradition.

. . . These fragments I have shored against my ruins
Why then Ile fit you. Hieronymo's mad againe.

Here Eliot provides us with a final image for all that he has done: his poem is like Hieronymo's revenge play. Hieronymo's enemies – the public for the poet in our time – commission an entertainment . . . Hieronymo . . . [specifies]:

Each one of us
Must act his part in unknown languages,
That it may breed the more variety:
As you, my Lord, in Latin, in Greek,
You in Italian, and for because I know
That Bellimperia hath practised the French,
In courtly French shall all her phrases be.

Each of these languages occurs in *The Waste Land*; all but Greek, in the list of shored fragments. Balthasar responds, like a critic in *The New Statesman*,

> But this will be a mere confusion,
> And hardly shall we all be understood.

Hieronymo, however, is master of his method:

> It must be so: for the conclusion
> Shall prove the invention and all was good.

Hieronymo's madness, in the context provided by Eliot, is that of Platonic bard. If we are to take the last two lines of *The Waste Land* as the substance of what the bard in his sibylline trance has to say, then the old man's macaronic tragedy appears transmuted into the thunder's three injunctions, Give, Sympathize, Control, and a triple 'Peace', 'repeated as here', says the note, 'a formal ending to an Upanishad'.[16] □

To close this chapter we turn to a brief extract from the book *The Continuity of American Poetry* (1961) by Roy Harvey Pearce. As with the other pieces in this chapter, Pearce sees *The Waste Land* as an exercise in 'mythic composition'. But the myth is, for Pearce, very different. In his hands Eliot's poem is a deliberate assault upon American poetic sensibilities, an answer to the idea of a mythical America that is proposed in the work of a poet such as Walt Whitman. Pearce's book is one of the first to attempt a systematised theory of American poetry. It argues that American poetry has a continuity of tradition and of theme, and that the major constituent of this continuity is what it terms the 'Adamic poem'. The biblical myth of Adam creating a new world in Eden, is, for Pearce, *the* basic myth underpinning American consciousness.[17] The notion of an Adamic poem, then, is one that is based in this myth and which sees language itself as essentially creative, a poem that realises, as Pearce puts it, the 'fecundative power of language'.[18] Because his reading of *The Waste Land* sees it sitting in an uncomfortable relationship to this notion of a continuous American poetic tradition it acts as a very useful corrective to the excessively Eurocentric readings of the poem practised by New Critics. While Kenner claims (as we have just seen) that the poem is an expression of 'the mind of Europe', for Pearce it displays the troubled mind of America. Pearce's consideration of Eliot's poem, then, raises questions about the cultural and ideological force of both the poem and critical readings of the poem, questions which are pursued further in the next chapter:

■ Eliot's is *the* poetics of the counter-current. It constitutes a theory of the mythic poem; and a considerable portion of its force as theory is the product of a certain over-determination in the sensibility of its originator and those for whom he speaks. For the mythic poem – like its counterpart, the Adamic poem – is an over-determined poem. It asks too much of both its protagonists and its readers; for it asks them that they reject utterly the principle of personality (to recall the social scientist's terms) and as utterly opt for the principle of culture. It boldly faces the possibility (for by the time of the First World War it surely was at least a possibility) that the life-style projected by the Adamic poem might not be capable of coming to grips with the problems set for it by history, tradition, and orthodoxy. . . . Now, in all his agony, modern man might see how the very loss of that continuity argued all the more for the need for its recovery. The only means, a means which Eliot quite frankly realized was extreme, was that surrender of the self whereby the hope for an immanent narrative was resigned in favor of a hope for a transcendent myth. Thus over-determination was quite consciously acknowledged to be the price for making the modern world possible for art.

. . . *The Waste Land* has become such an assured part of the twentieth-century consciousness, one of the major vehicles for its sensibility, that we easily forget the transformation it worked. . . .

The disparate materials of which *The Waste Land* is composed are designed to lose their disparateness in the composing. Tiresias, the Fisher King, Phlebas, the Thames maidens, and the rest – each participates in the life of the other, and so contributes to the single-minded effect of the poem: not because of what he is but because of what he manifests, negatively or positively, for good or for bad. Even the reader is made out to be one of the poem's *personae*. *The Waste Land*, in so far as it succeeds in its intention, offers us everything – locales, *personae*, motifs, structure – everything but a poet assured in his ability to make a poem. Certainly the poet *is* there, as his wit, intelligence, and imagination are there. But he can *pretend* not to be, except as he is but one bootless protagonist among many such. This, in any case, is a principal attribute of his particular kind of make-believe: that the poet is there only so that he may compose a poem which, in the light of his ultimate vision, will make his existence unnecessary.

He makes Tiresias, his principal protagonist, into a shape-shifter, unstable, uncertain of the powers of his own sense and sensibility, his creativity lying in his wise passiveness. Tiresias is not at the center of the history which the poem epitomizes; he does not have the power to be at the center of anything. . . . The poem, taken as a pronouncement on the nature of man, argues against the possibility of . . . authentic autobiography. For such a possibility would inevitably argue the significance of the existence of the poet as a radically free self. The development of *The Waste Land* is such as theoretically to do away with that self, actually to put it in its place, low in the scale of things. The poet ostentatiously removes himself from his poem. . . .

Eliot's method in *The Waste Land* is constantly to define the persons in the poem in terms of that which they are not. They cannot even directly conceive of that which they are not; they do not have the power to set going within themselves that process of action and reaction whereby they may begin to establish their own identity. . . . *The Waste Land*, thus, cannot be self-contained. For if it were, it would *a fortiori* argue for the possibility that somehow one or another of its protagonists might in and of himself do or make something. That enormous range of allusiveness which has set so many exegetes to work is accordingly the central technique of the poem, as it is the means of preventing the self-containment which any single poem, written by any single man, might achieve merely by virtue of its singleness. . . .

Strictly speaking, there is no individual action which can be *imitated* in this mythic poem. There is potentially a communal action, a ritual, but it is as yet one which can only be observed. . . .

Such ritual, not directly participated in because considered as an historical-cultural rather than a theological fact, becomes explicitly the technique of *The Waste Land* in the final part of the concluding section, 'What the Thunder Said'. There are the ritual words, listened to from afar and registered in a 'dead' language: *Datta, Dayadhvam, Damyata – Give, Sympathize, Control.* (True enough, these words are proved not *really* to be dead, for they have much to signify for us. The point, however, is that Eliot cannot find the properly ritualistic words in the language of any culture presently 'alive'.) *Make*, much less *Create*, is not part of the poet's vocabulary. He has only the fragments which he has shored against his ruins, the materials out of a world now known to be mythic, trans-historical.[19] □

CHAPTER FOUR

Political Readings: Marx, Ideology and Culture

THE CRITICAL pieces that make up this chapter all demonstrate (indeed all derive from) the realisation that despite the best efforts of earlier critics to render *The Waste Land* unified, coherent and unproblematic, the poem still remains deeply problematic and troublesome. Most particularly, what David Craig, Terry Eagleton and Michael North share in their analyses of the poem is a conviction that *The Waste Land's* difficulties are an index of its problematic politics. For them, previous critical assessments of the poem have smoothed out the poem's difficulties in their desire to see it as a unified artistic whole. In so doing, they argue, such analyses of the poem have disguised a political agenda of radical conservatism that characterises not just the poem in particular, but modernist aesthetics in general. What emerges from the extracts in this chapter, then, is a very different critical version of *The Waste Land*. Both the poem itself and the critical act of reading the poem are seen to be tools of a coercive and all-pervading ideology of modernity – namely late-capitalism. The three essays that follow represent an attempt to read against the grain of established critical opinions on *The Waste Land* by seeing it in the light of a broadly Marxist analysis of the culture and ideology of modernity.

In their attempts to get beneath the surface of underlying assumptions about poetics and culture that have, perhaps, been suppressed by the poem and its critics these readings certainly signal a new direction in critical thought about *The Waste Land*. In fact, it is very difficult to imagine how more recent commentaries on the poem could have emerged without the work, carried out by David Craig and Terry Eagleton, of making the poem seem, once more, deeply problematic. However, such a new direction is not as new as it may at first seem. As we have already seen in chapter one, when *The Waste Land* was first published it received favourable attention from both left-wing *and* conservative literary critics. Both groups took the poem to exemplify their respective aesthetic and cultural positions. Whether radically iconoclastic or radically conservative, though, the fact that the poem was felt to occupy such apparently contradictory positions is indicative of the contradictory impulses from which it is produced, and which, in large part, have been responsible for the intensity of the critical debate that has surrounded it from the outset. In short, then, *The Waste Land* has always been felt to be ideologically troublesome and politically contentious; it has always been read as a model of a culture in crisis and interpretations of it have always betrayed the ideological dispositions of its critics. Michael North (whose reading of *The Waste Land* comprises the final extract in this chapter) is well aware of the political stakes that have been in play in criticism of *The Waste Land* since its first publication. He notes that many early enthusiasts for the poem – such as A. L. Morton, Edgell Rickword and John Cornford – were communists who saw the poem's assault upon poetic sensibilities as an assault upon the evil of capitalism. They felt the poem to be an expression of the political despair of the working classes, one that was witnessed in its depiction of the sterile lives of the 'carbuncular' young man and the typist. Such readers were, according to North, 'shocked and disappointed when Eliot announced his conversion to the Anglican church just when they were expecting him to embrace Marxism'.[1] He continues by arguing that this is precisely why the poem's critical history is so interesting: its apparently contradictory political impulses have led to an opening up of the ideological conditions of the culture from which it was produced. Crucial to *The Waste Land*'s importance, to its powerful hold over successive generations of readers, North notes, is the very fact of its ability 'to suggest a politics so wildly at odds with what eventually emerged' in Eliot's life.[2]

Such a realisation about the poem indicates a new willingness in Eliot criticism to read beyond the doctrines of impersonality and aesthetic autonomy that had, up to the 1960s, dominated ways of reading *The Waste Land*. The pieces in this chapter chart an increasing desire to locate the text back in the ideology of modernity. They see the poem, therefore, as the exemplary product of a postwar culture of anxiety and debate about urbanisation, the technologisation of labour and class relations in their relationship to artistic production, rather than as a disinterested poetic icon. This means that not only *The Waste Land* itself, but also the dominant ways of reading it, come under intense scrutiny. These readings look to the poem as a means of examining the process by which poetry and criticism produce their own particular idea of culture and the poet live in. That is the kind of assumption, and the pessimistic thought behind it, which I wish to challenge.

The technique of *The Waste Land* is very various; it gives the impression (compared with, say, Pound's *Cantos*) of rich, or intensely felt, resources both of literature and of life direct. But one method stands out: that way of running on, with no marked break and therefore with a deadpan ironical effect, from one area of experience, one place or time or speech or social class, to another. Section II, 'A Game of Chess', throws shifting lights on the woman protagonist by changes of style. At first Cleopatra is present, but a Cleopatra who lives in an indoor, lifelessly ornate setting:

> The Chair she sat in, like a burnished throne,
> Glowed on the marble, where the glass
> Held up by standards wrought with fruited vines
> From which a golden Cupidon peeped out
> (Another hid his eyes behind his wing)
> Doubled the flames of sevenbranched candelabra
> Reflecting light upon the table as
> The glitter of her jewels rose to meet it . . .

By this point she has become Belinda from *The Rape of the Lock*, living in a world of 'things', make-up, dress, *bijouterie* – in Veblen's phrase, conspicuous consumption. But the modern poet does not have a mocking relish for the woman, as did Pope. . . . In *The Waste Land*, the woman is not even Belinda, moving with assurance in her idle, expensive world. She is a neurotic who cannot stand being alone with her own thoughts . . . The change is given in the shift from a quite richly 'literary' diction . . .

> Under the firelight, under the brush, her hair
> Spread out in fiery points
> Glowed into words, then would be savagely still.

. . . to a bitty, comparatively unshaped, modern spoken English (though the repetitiveness is cunningly stylized):

> 'My nerves are bad to-night. Yes, bad. Stay with me.
> 'Speak to me. Why do you never speak. Speak.
> 'What are you thinking of? What thinking? What?
> 'I never know what you are thinking. Think.'

and ideology – one, moreover, that they feel to be partial and politically suspect. What version of modernity, they ask, are we being given as a result of following Eliot's notions of mythic consciousness, impersonality and the individual talent within literary tradition? And why? By opening up such questions in relation to the poem, criticism of *The Waste Land* can be seen to have entered a new phase.

In effect, the poem is still seen to be vitally important to modern consciousness – not, however, because it expresses the hopes and fears of the postwar generation, but because it allows for (maybe even insists upon) an examination of the root causes of the anxieties of modernity. New priorities are thus set for the critical examination of the poem: these critical readings of it tend to look outwards from it to the culture from which it is produced, rather than inwards to a central meaning within it that is validated artistically by a unifying theme or subject. This, in turn, means that critical attention is given to passages in the poem that had been avoided, by and large, in earlier criticism. Here, now, in attending to Albert, Lil and the others in the pub scene, and to the typist's drearily fumbled sexual encounter, critics attend to the implicit class struggle on which they see the poem to be structured. This struggle is not, they argue, an occasion for discussion of the poem's ironic manipulations, more a means of entering into debate about the sort of cultural and ideological assumptions with which the poem colludes. In the first two extracts of this chapter we shall see that David Craig and Terry Eagleton are deeply suspicious of the poem's ideological collusion; indeed, their determination to disturb critical complacencies about the poem and to stir up critical debate leads to essays that are deliberately polemical. They may, initially, seem rather dismissive of the poem. For example, Eagleton seems scandalised by the very fact that the poem exists at all. He writes:

■ Cultures collapse, but Culture survives, and its form is *The Waste Land*: this is the ideological gesture of the text, inscribed in the scandalous fact of its very existence.[3] □

However, the point of contention is not so much the 'scandalous fact' of the poem's existence as *what* it inscribes. What fascinates all three critics whose essays are included in this chapter is the notion of culture that *The Waste Land* inscribes, the ideological gesture that it encodes.

The readings of *The Waste Land* that follow are all attempts to free the poem from what the cultural theorist Louis Althusser has called 'the grip of ideology'.[4] Indeed Althusser's notion of ideology adds a useful gloss on the ways in which the critical pieces of this chapter read how the poem inscribes its particular ideological gesture. For Althusser, ideology is:

■ . . . the representation of the subject's *Imaginary* relationship to his or her *Real* conditions of existence.[5] □

Within this concept of ideology, then, what we believe our social and political relationships to be as subjects within a particular culture, and what they actually are, become divorced from each other. Ideology, according to Althusser and other Marxist critics following his lead, performs a crucial political function of disguising and deterring a full understanding of the conditions of our existence by providing a convenient set of beliefs that *seem* (but only seem) to explain those conditions.[6] It is to the ways in which *The Waste Land* carries out this act of disguising and deterring that the critical pieces in this chapter pay attention. And in this sense, by asking what version of culture is disguised within the poem's difficulties and evasions, they represent the first critical attempts to 'deconstruct' both the poem and the culture from which it arose.

In the essay that follows, 'The Defeatism of *The Waste Land*' (1960), David Craig is the first critic seriously to attempt to read the poem in terms other than those 'sanctioned', as it were, by Eliot himself. It offers a deliberately contentious, and therefore very refreshing, reading of the poem. His essay asks us to reassess both our relationship to the poem, and our responsibility – as readers who are complicit in its ideological gestures – to the poem itself and to modern culture in general. By challenging the whole notion that Eliot himself fostered of the impersonality of the poet Craig turns the poem back on itself to suggest that, in fact, it portrays a deep personal depression, one that stems from a 'defeatist' sense of the failure of modern culture and subjectivity. The poem, he argues, has a powerful hold over readers and critics precisely because it is predicated on an act of masking its true feelings. Its ideological weight seems to derive, therefore, from the way it disguises its cultural agenda. This is borne out, according to Craig, by the way in which earlier criticism of *The Waste Land* can be read as having furthered the cultural assumptions and ideological imperatives from which the poem is constituted. An example of this can be found in Craig's attitude towards the poem's use of irony, or at least towards the way in which critics such as F.R. Leavis and Cleanth Brooks use a notion of irony in their analyses of the poem.

Such critics, Craig insists, prize the poem's irony so highly because they feel it reveals the poet's finer sensibilities. However, Craig finds such irony to be 'no finer than ordinary sarcasm', and at the expense of the working classes. He sees the poem and critical accounts of the poem,

therefore, as exercises in evasion. If the poem disguises an ideological function, then for Craig this happens because of – in the poem and in criticism on the poem – on a notion of sonality of the poet. What Craig's reading brings to the poe understanding of how it deliberately masks what it most wa So, while his analysis of the poem returns to the sorts of que its obscurity and élitism that troubled its very first readers, he very different set of conclusions about why the poem exerts su ful influence over those seeking to define the conditions of His reading is crucially important in the history of criticism *Land* because it is the first to articulate a sense of the disgu that operate through the poem. It initiates, therefore, not ju of reading the poem but of reading modernism:

■ T.S. Eliot's *The Waste Land* is one of the outstanding case times of a work which projects an almost defeatist perso sion in the guise of a full, impersonal picture of society. *Women in Love* is a much more substantial case of the sam the response it demands is much less easy. Both, how experience, encourage in readers, especially young studer superior cynicism which flatters the educated man by lett that he is left as the sole bearer of a fine culture which the barbarians have spurned and spoiled. Eliot has characteri out of responsibility in the matter by means of his rem *Waste Land* pleased people because of 'their own illusion c illusioned'.[7] But, I suggest, the essential (and very origina his poem and the peculiar sense of life which it mediates a they invite that very response – and get it from the most c critics as well as from young cynics.

Before considering *The Waste Land* itself, it will be as w a case of that view of the modern 'plight' which the poem I or seemed sufficient grounds for. Summing up the so affairs which he sees as the basis for the poem's 'rich diso F.R. Leavis writes: 'The traditions and cultures have ming historical imagination makes the past contemporary; no c can digest so great a variety of materials, and the break-down of forms and the irrevocable loss of th absoluteness which seems necessary to a robust culture'.[8] gestive, and 'that sense of absoluteness' implies a more what modern rapid change has done to us than is usual in 'the organic community'. . . . Dr Leavis considers the expe *Waste Land* a self-evident, perfectly acceptable version of th

The effect is of landing up with final disenchantment face to face with the unpleasant reality of life today.

There is then, in mid-section, a change of social class, from wealthy life ('The hot water at ten./And if it rains, a closed car at four.') to ordinary ('When Lil's husband got demobbed, I said – '). But life is fruitless here, too, and the poet's aloof revulsion is conveyed by similar means. The working-class women in the pub talk about false teeth, abortions, promiscuous sexual rivalry between the wives of Great War soldiers, in a lingo which sprawls over any kind of formal elegance of metre or rhyme; and the poet does not intrude on the common speech until the closing line:

> Goonight Bill. Goonight Lou. Goonight May.
>   Goonight.
> Ta ta. Goonight. Goonight.
> Good night, ladies, good night, sweet ladies, good
>   night, good night.

'Sweet ladies' – the irony is, to say the least, obvious. As well as the effect of 'sweet' there is the reminiscence of the innocently hearty student song (this seems more relevant than Ophelia's mad snatch in *Hamlet*). The effect is identical with what he does by incorporating Goldsmith's ditty ['When lovely woman stoops to folly . . . '] from *The Vicar of Wakefield* at the end of the typist's dreary seduction in 'The Fire Sermon'. . . . This technique, which is typical of the transitions of tone and of the collocation of two cultures which occur throughout the poem, seems to me unsatisfactory in two ways. The irony is no finer than ordinary sarcasm – the simple juxtaposing of messy reality and flattering description (as in a common phrase like 'You're a pretty sight'). The pub women and the typist have been made so utterly sour and unlovely that the poet's innuendo, being unnecessary, does no more than hint at his own superior qualities. Secondly, using earlier literature to embody the better way of life which is the poet's ideal depends on a view of the past which is not made good in the poem (it hardly could be) and which the reader may well not share – unless he is pessimistic. . . .

This is an absurdly partial outlook on culture – groundlessly idealizing about the old and warped in its revulsion from the modern. If magnificence is desired, modern life can supply it well enough, whether the show of royalty or big-business ostentation. And if one thinks of the filth, poverty, superstition, and brutal knock-about life invariable in town or country four centuries ago, one realizes how fatuous it is to make flat contrasts between then and now. History, reality, are being manipulated to fit an escapist kind of prejudice, however detached the writer may feel himself to be.

As one would expect, the cultural warp has as strong an equivalent in the poet's way of presenting personal experience. Consider the attitudes implied in the seduction of the typist. In this most cunningly managed episode, one is induced to feel, by means of the fastidiously detached diction and movement, that a scene part commonplace, part debased, is altogether unpleasant. The experience is a more intimate meeting between people than Eliot deals with directly anywhere else in his work, but here is the style he finds for it:

> He, the young man carbuncular, arrives,
> A small house agent's clerk, with one bold stare,
> One of the low on whom assurance sits
> As a silk hat on a Bradford millionaire.
> The time is now propitious, as he guesses,
> The meal is ended, she is bored and tired,
> Endeavours to engage her in caresses
> Which still are unreproved, if undesired.
> Flushed and decided, he assaults at once;
> Exploring hands encounter no defence;
> His vanity requires no response,
> And makes a welcome of indifference.

The unfeeling grossness of the experience is held off at the fingertips by the analytic, unphysical diction – 'Endeavours to engage her in caresses' – and by the movement, whose even run is not interrupted by the violence of what is 'going on'. The neat assimilation of such life to a formal verse paragraph recalls Augustan modes. But if one thinks of the sexual passage concerning the 'Imperial Whore' in Dryden's translation of Juvenal's sixth Satire, or even the one concerning the unfeeling Chlöe in Pope's *Moral Essay* 'Of the Characters of Women', one realizes that the Augustans did not stand off from the physical with anything like Eliot's distaste. Eliot's style is carefully impersonal; it enumerates with fastidious care the sordid details:

> On the divan are piled (at night her bed)
> Stockings, slippers, camisoles, and stays.

But here one has doubts. This is given as a typically comfortless modern apartment, suggesting a life which lacks the right pace, the right sociableness, the right instinctive decency for it to merit the name of civilization . . . But the touch in the second line feels uncertain: is the heavily careful art with which the line is built up not too contrived for the rather ordinary modern habit it is meant to satirize? When we come to 'carbuncular' – an adjective which, placed after the noun and resounding in its slow movement and almost ornamental air, is deliberately out of key with the commonplace life around it – I think we begin to feel that Eliot's conscious literariness is working, whatever his intention, more to hold at arm's length something which he personally shudders at than to convey a poised criticism of behaviour. There is a shudder in 'carbuncular'; it is disdainful, but the dislike is disproportionately strong for its object; queasy emotions of the writer's seem to be at work . . . and we are also left wondering what warrant the poet has for uniting himself with some class finer, it seems, than the provincial bourgeoisie. And the passage ends with the snatch of Goldsmith, 'When lovely woman stoops to folly':

> She smooths her hair with automatic hand
> And puts a record on the gramophone.

Here the nerveless movement and the ordinariness of the detail are deftly managed. And the human poverty of the scene has never been in doubt. But the writer's means of conveying his valuation of it are surely objectionable. One may agree or not that modern civilization has its own kind of health; one may agree or not that the petty bourgeoisie are a decent class. But one must surely take exception to a method which seeks its effects through an irony which is no more than smart sarcasm. It is amazing that Dr Leavis should speak of 'delicate collocations',[9] when the contrasts are regularly so facile in their selection of old grandeur and modern squalor.

. . . *The Waste Land*, then, seems to me to work essentially against life, for the range of options it mobilizes, that come welling up in response to it, are negative. In the final section Eliot uses the philosophy of F. H. Bradley. The lines . . .

> I have heard the key
> Turn in the door once and turn once only
> We think of the key, each in his prison
> Thinking of the key, each confirms a prison

. . . he himself glosses from Bradley's *Appearance and Reality*:

My external sensations are no less private to myself than are my thoughts or my feelings. In either case my experience falls within my own circle, a circle closed on the outside; and, with all its elements alike, every sphere is opaque to the others which surround it . . . In brief, regarded as an existence which appears in a soul, the whole world for each is peculiar and private to that soul.

This thought of Bradley's has led on to [a] barren line of philosophy. . . . To say what must suffice here: if our sensations, thoughts, and feelings are perfectly private and the sphere of each person's life 'opaque', how is it that speech and literature themselves are intelligible – and intelligible so fully and intimately that to reach understanding with a person or appreciate a piece of writing can seem to take us inside another existence? That the question of whether one mind can get through to another should even have arisen seems to me a perversion of thought. (Historically, it is perhaps a cast from the anti-co-operative state of existence brought about by entrepreneur capitalism. It seems similar to the helplessly solipsistic 'denial of objective truth' which Lenin refutes in *Materialism and Empirio-Criticism*. In each case the individual ego relies less and less on anything outside itself.)

The obscurity of *The Waste Land* is significant likewise, for though the trained reader no longer jibs at it, it is certainly impossible that it should ever become popular reading as did earlier important literature (Burns, Byron, George Eliot, D. H. Lawrence). Dr Leavis writes on the issue of 'minority culture' which this raises, 'that the public for it is limited is one of the symptoms of the state of culture which produced the poem. Works expressing the finest consciousness of the age in which the word "high-brow" has become current are almost inevitably such as to appeal only to a tiny minority.'[10]

The argument that follows is dubious at a number of points. In the first place, Lawrence expressed many sides of the 'finest consciousness of the age' and he has been read in cheap editions by the millions. . . . The usual obstinately pessimistic reply is that 'they only read Lawrence for the sex, or the love story'. But this is only reaching for another stick to beat the times, for is it not good that a major writer should have devoted himself to the universal subject of love and sex? Dr Leavis goes on to say that the idea that the poem's obscurity is symptomatic of our cultural condition 'amounts to an admission that there must be something limited about the kind of artistic achievement possible in our time'. But if this were so, how account for the work of Lawrence and of the many other considerable novelists of our time? Finally his question 'How large in any age has the minority been that has really comprehended the masterpieces?' contains an equivocation – 'really'. If one sets the highest standard, of course 'real' (that is, full) comprehension is attained by few; but if the numbers of even the *total* public reached are small, as has happened with *The Waste Land*, then there is indeed a significant difference between its meaningfulness and appeal for readers and that which the major novelists have regularly achieved. . . . *The Waste Land*, in short, is not the representative work of the present age, and to make it so implies that pessimistic view of the present age which I have already challenged.[11] □

If David Craig's essay sets up the terms for a critique of what he calls the poem's 'absurdly partial outlook on culture', then it is Terry Eagleton, in the following extract, who leads the main assault. Interestingly, both Craig and Eagleton take issue with what they see as the poem's nostalgic yearning for a lost social order that is depicted in its imagining of an organic society. For Craig this nostalgia becomes the ground of the poem's pessimism (which, being anti-progressive therefore denies the possibility of revolution). And for Eagleton, as we shall shortly see, such nostalgia performs an ideological function by silencing any sense of *real* social relations and replacing them with a set of *imaginary* relationships. Eagleton's critique thus delivers a new way of thinking about the old problem of the poem's obscurity. To be baffled by the poem, says Eagleton, is exactly the point, that *is* the poem's ultimate meaning. The poem's inscription of such bafflement is the means by which it maintains the social order and contains any threat to the 'closed, coherent, [and] authoritative discourse of the mythologies which frame it'.

As with Craig's essay, Eagleton's reading of *The Waste Land* is a reply to earlier criticism of the poem as much as it is an explication of the poem itself. What he attempts to make explicit are the silent assumptions that have operated throughout the critical history of the poem. Most especially he seeks to dislodge F. R. Leavis' interpretation of the poem from its pre-eminent and highly influential position. Leavis' reading of *The Waste Land*, which promotes a disillusioned organicist conception of society, has, according to Eagleton, silenced other ways of reading the poem by making it seem culturally neutral where, in fact, it is highly charged with cultural and political meaning. By seeking to expose what *The Waste Land* and its critics tacitly endorse, Eagleton can be seen to be working within a model of literary criticism that is suggested by another Marxist critic, Pierre Macherey. For Macherey, criticism can get beneath the surface of a text's ideological assumptions by asking of that text what it does not say. Indeed, this process of exposing a text's silences and evasions is necessary to the process of political critique. The translation of Macherey's *Pour Une Théorie de la Production Littéraire* (1966) describes this process in the following terms:

■ The speech of a book comes from a certain silence, a matter which it endows with form, a ground on which it traces a figure. Thus, the book is not self-sufficient; it is necessarily accompanied by a *certain absence*, without which it would not exist. A knowledge of the book must include a consideration of this absence.

This is why it seems useful and legitimate to ask of every production what it tacitly implies, what it does not say.[12] □

What Macherey provides here is the theory that legitimates the sort of political reading practice that we encounter in Eagleton's essay on *The Waste Land*. Despite the poem's overtly avant-garde poetics it covertly inscribes, according to Eagleton, a conservative politics. For him, its silences, gaps and ellipses both trace and produce its repressive ideology.

■ Henry James' successor as a conservative American expatriate was T. S. Eliot, son of an 'aristocratic' St Louis family. The social and intellectual hegemony of the Eliots had been traumatically undermined in the early years of this century by revelations of the corrupt, boss-ridden system of St Louis – a corruption in which the Eliots were apparently implicated. Spiritually disinherited like James by industrial capitalist America, able later to discover in America the 'blood', breeding and 'organic' regionalism he valued only in such phenomena as the right-wing neo-agrarian movement in Virginia, Eliot came to Europe with the historic mission of redefining the organic unity of its cultural traditions, and reinserting a culturally provincial England into that totality. He was, indeed, to become himself the focal point of the organic consciousness of the 'European mind', that rich, unruptured entity mystically inherent in its complex simultanity in every artist nourished by it. English literary culture, still in the grip of ideologically exhausted forms of liberal humanism and late Romanticism, was to be radically reconstructed into a classicism which would eradicate the last vestiges of 'Whiggism' (protestantism, liberalism, Romanticism, humanism). It would do so in the name of a higher, corporate ideological formation, defined by the surrender of 'personality' to order, reason, authority and tradition.

The wholesale demolition and salvage job which it was Eliot's historical task to carry out in the aesthetic region of English ideology was one for which he was historically peculiarly well-equipped, as an expatriate with a privileged, panoramic vantage-point on that area. He was sufficiently internal to it as a New Englander to judge 'authoritatively', yet as a 'European' American sufficiently external to identify its parochial limitations. Eliot's own description of his function is characteristically sham-casual: 'From time to time, every hundred years or so, it is desirable that a critic shall appear to review the past of our literature, and set the poets and the poem in a new order. This task is not one of revolution but of readjustment'.[13] It seems a modest description of what Graham Martin has rightly termed 'the most ambitious feat of cultural imperialism the century seems likely to produce';[14] but the bland unalarmist, evolutionary stress of Eliot's formulation is central to his project. Confronted with world imperialist crisis, severe economic depression and intensifying working-class militancy, English society in the early years of Eliot's career as poet and critic stood in urgent ideological need of precisely the values his literary classicism encapsulated. Yet the ideological potency of that classicism rested in its refusal of static, rationalist forms for an empiricist, historicist mould – rested, indeed, in the production of a classicism contradictorily united with the evolutionary organicism of the Romantic tradition. Eliot's 'Tradition' is a labile, self-transformative organism extended in space and time, constantly reorganised by the present; but this radical historical relativism is then endowed with the status of absolute classical authority. What Eliot does, in fact, is to adopt the aesthetics of a late phase of Romanticism (symbolism), with its view of the individual artefact as organic, impersonal and autonomous, and then project this doctrine into an authoritarian cultural ideology.[15]

By framing his classicist doctrine in the organicist terms of the Romantic tradition, Eliot is able to combine an idealist totality with the sensuous empiricism which is its other aspect. If the aesthetic region of ideology is to be effectively refashioned, poetic language must clutch and penetrate the turbulent, fragmentary character of contemporary experience, sinking its tentacular roots into the primordial structures of the collective unconsciousness. As such, poetry offers a paradigm of ideological affectivity in general: Eliot's ideal of the organic society is one in which a finely conscious élite transmits its values through rhythm, habit and resonance to the largely unconscious masses, infiltrating the nervous system rather than engaging the mind.[16] Hence the radical anti-intellectualism of the scholarly, esoteric Eliot: the nervous distrust of abstract ideas, the insistence on the poetic transmutation of thought into sense-experience, the imagist emphasis on the hard, precise image as 'containing' its concept, yoked to the symbolist preoccupation with poetry as music.

There is, however, a latent contradiction between Eliot's concern for art as organic order and his insistence on the sensuously mimetic properties of poetic language. The Olympian pontificator of *Tradition and the Individual Talent*, with his values of order and impersonality, is also the poet of *The Love-Song of J. Alfred Prufrock*, with its restlessly subjective universe of doomed emotions and discrete objects. Eliot attempts to surmount this contradiction in his recourse to the Metaphysical poets: . . . Donne creates organic wholes from experience while enacting its actual fragmentation; and this, presumably, is also the intention of *The Waste Land*. Yet the 'form' of that poem is in contradiction with its 'content': *The Waste Land*'s fragmentary content listlessly mimes the experience of cultural disintegration, while its totalising mythological forms silently allude to a transcendence of such collapse. The poem is opaque both because of its verbal complicity in that collapse, and in the esoteric allusions which attempt to construct an ideal order across it.

It is possible to trace in this aesthetic dissonance something of Eliot's own ambiguous relationship to the crisis of European bourgeois society which *The Waste Land* records. Indeed, the question of where Eliot stands in relation to the poem becomes the question of where he stands in relation to his adopted society. As an 'aristocratic' American expatriate preoccupied in the first place with a vision of organic cultural unity, Eliot's idealism partly dissevers him from the historical reality of the crisis he confronts. Yet the cosmopolitan avant-garde poet of the early work is also the industrious servant of Lloyd's bank, necessarily supporting the economic system which practically ensures, even while it 'spiritually' threatens, the conditions of élitist culture. It is in the blank space between the 'form' and 'content' of *The Waste Land*, between its cosmic detachment and guilty collusion, that the ideology which produces it is most visibly inscribed.

Yet *The Waste Land* produces an ideology, as well as being produced by one. It is not in the first place an ideology of 'cultural disintegration'; it is an ideology of *cultural knowledge*. What the poem signifies, indeed, is not 'the decay of Europe' or fertility cults but its own elaborate display of esoteric allusion – a display *enabled* by such arcane or panoramic motifs. The reader who finds his or her access to the poem's 'meaning' baulked by its inscrutable gesturing off-stage is already in possession of that 'meaning' without knowing it. Cultures collapse, but Culture survives, and its form is *The Waste Land*: this is the ideological gesture of the text, inscribed in the scandalous fact of its very existence. It is in this sense that the poem's signifying codes contradict their signifieds: for if history is indeed sterility then the work itself could not come into being, and if the work exists then it does so only as an implicit denial of its 'content'. The self-cancelling status of *The Waste Land* is the index of an ideological riddle of origins to which there is no material answer: if history is futile and exhausted, where does Culture come from? One may rephrase the riddle differently: if poetic signs have ideological potency only by virtue of being crammed with sensory experience, how are they to fulfil the ideologically vital role of *commenting* on the experience they enact? It is the same question in a different guise: where within the sphere of experience is the source of the discourse (Culture, ideology) needed to redeem it? It cannot be inside that sphere, for this would be to level its transcendental status; but it cannot be outside of it either, for this would be to rob it of 'experiential' force, rendering it as impotent as the spectatorial Tiresias. If, then, positive value can lie neither inside nor outside the poem, it must reside instead in the very limits of the text itself – in that which gives it its form. It must lie in that which can be shown but not spoken, which is nothing less than the 'fact' of the poem itself. The 'fact' of the poem is constituted by a set of 'progressive' devices which articulate discourse with discourse, refusing the allure of organic closure; the text's partial dissolution of its signs to its fragmentary situations, its mimetic denial of a 'totalising' overview, is its ideological affectivity. Such partial dissolution, however, is in no sense a 'naturalising' of the sign: in its articulated discourses, the poem parades itself as a thoroughly constructed text, tempting a 'representational' reading which it simultaneously subverts by its exposed productive mechanisms. Yet this subversion turns out to be merely phenomenal: for behind the back of this ruptured, radically decentred poem runs an alternative text which is nothing less than the closed, coherent, authoritative discourse of the mythologies which frame it. The phenomenal text, to use one of Eliot's own metaphors, is merely the meat with which the burglar distracts the guard-dog while he proceeds with his stealthy business. The ideology of the text lies in the distance between these two discourses – in the fact that the 'phenomenal' text is able to 'show', but not *speak of*, the covert coherence which sustains it. For if that coherence is directly articulated, an ideological impact gained only through indirection is lost; yet it is important, none the less, that such impact should not be wholly dispersed to its phenomenal effects. It is for this reason that at the end of the poem the 'covert' text does, for once, speak, in the cryptic imperatives delivered by the voice of the thunder. It is not T. S. Eliot, or a character, or the 'phenomenal' text who speaks; it can only be an anonymous, conveniently hypostasised absolute. What the thunder enunciates is a withdrawn ascetic wisdom whose ideological implications are at odds with the 'progressive', pioneering, typographically conscious forms of the poem itself; but it is precisely in this conjuncture of 'progressive form' and 'reactionary content' that the ideology of *The Waste Land* inheres. Both elements are united by a certain 'élitism': the 'avant-garde' experiments of a literary côterie match the conservative values of a ruling minority. The purpose of those experiments is precisely to put such values 'in train'; yet the effect of this is nothing less than a questioning of their efficacy, as the thunder's Olympian *fiats* are shown up for the hollow booming they are.[17] □

Eagleton's deep suspicion of the political consequences of *The Waste Land* means that he sees it, pretty much, as a cultural dead-end. For Michael North, from whose book *The Political Aesthetic of Yeats, Eliot and Pound* (1991) the final extract of this chapter is taken, however, the poem presents not so much a dead-end as a challenge to critical thought. To some extent, North returns to older critical models for reading the poem in that he sees its power stemming from its portrayal of the 'paradoxical condition' of modern consciousness. But he strikes a new note in his examination of the poem by arguing that the very difficulty with which the poem asserts an idea of aesthetic unity is the key to understanding what it tacitly implies. His use of notions of unity, irony and ambiguity, then, far from returning to 'New Critical' or formalist ways of reading the poem, is a means of opening it up to further critical debate. He questions the very terms upon which our understanding of the poem has been founded. Like Eagleton and Craig before him, then, North seeks to uncover *The Waste Land*'s ideological underpinnings and to deconstruct their political consequences.

Perhaps the most important element in North's examination of *The Waste Land* is his use of it to highlight the plight of the worker within modern society. In this sense he deploys a broadly Marxist analysis of the conditions of a workforce alienated from the means of production in order to throw fresh light on the poem. The poem's sense of alienation – present even in its earliest drafts – can thus be seen to be both an effect of modernity and a poetic means of producing a model of modern consciousness. In fact, North sees this way in which the poem mobilises *specific* poetic effects in order to produce a *general* model of modern society as one of the poem's key ideological gestures. In focusing on how the poem moves between particulars and generalities, North is therefore able to deconstruct the sets of opposites upon which he sees the poem depending. As *The Waste Land* swings between 'high' and 'low' cultures, between the individual and the crowd, or (in Marxist terms) base and superstructure, it reveals its hidden political agenda. Or rather, it elicits in its readers a response that is, perhaps, at odds with its seeming favouring of artistic disinterestedness over political responsibility. North's reading, then, re-radicalises the poem by showing how it reveals the alienated condition of modern consciousness. This is most clearly the case in his detailed, subtle and highly convincing analysis of Eliot's depictions of the typist and Tiresias. One of the high points in criticism of the poem, North's reading touches on sympathies that the poem itself disallows and reveals the sexual politics that underpin the poem's pervasive imagery of cultural sterility. It exemplifies, therefore, some of the ways in which a new generation of critics have striven to re-engage the poem by reading against the grain of long established critical assumptions about it:

■ Essays like 'Tradition and the Individual Talent' and 'The Metaphysical Poets' promise so much that they impose insupportable burdens on the poetry to follow. To announce an aesthetic modernism that will resolve the contradictions of political and social modernism is one thing; to actually provide it, quite another. In order to succeed, Eliot would have to do much more than simply find a form for the fragmented materials of the present, a task *The Waste Land* is traditionally held to have accomplished. Instead, he would have to find a form that could be distinguished from the false, repressive unity that is the counterpart of modern fragmentation. Few modern poems succeed as well as *The Waste Land* at depicting this necessary connection between the isolated worker and the anonymous crowd . . . But having painted such a vivid picture of this social contradiction seems to make it all the more difficult to resolve aesthetically. Though a number of contemporary critics feel that Eliot has succeeded in doing just this, it might be more accurate to say that *The Waste Land* vividly illustrates the difference between the necessary connection of opposites like worker and crowd, fragment and form, and a reconciliation of them.

According to Ronald Bush, Eliot began serious work on *The Waste Land* by taking up a fragment he had written several years before:

London, the swarming life you kill and breed,
Huddled between the concrete and the sky;
Responsive to the momentary need,
Vibrates unconscious to its formal destiny . . . [18]

Though this passage was eventually dropped from 'The Fire Sermon' at Pound's suggestion, it serves as a remarkably compact introduction to the entire poem. In this quatrain, London appears as an early version of the force that swarms and breeds at the beginning of the final text. But the city inspires such horror because it breeds *and* kills . . .

[The passage reveals] the spatio-temporal nightmare behind *The Waste Land*. The picture of the London crowd huddled between concrete and sky is a physical realization of a modern plight: Human beings are held in utter subjection to the immediate, their noses in the very concrete, as it were, *and* to vast impersonal forces they cannot perceive. The passage portrays a kind of post-Kantian hell where humanity is fastened by iron links to empirical facts and is also shadowed by immaterial forms. The urban crowd is itself a physical embodiment of this condition, because it piles individuals up into 'swarms', vast forms without perceptible character, beyond the ken of the individual, but also prunes humanity back, so that each individual is a barely surviving remnant of the whole.

Accurately portraying this paradoxical condition is the poetic problem of *The Waste Land*, as Eliot conceives it in this early version. This early passage introduces all the major formal problems Eliot was to encounter in composing his poem, problems that have survived as critical controversies. How does the poet portray immediate, contemporary reality and also the 'formal destiny' behind it? How does he relate the present moment to the totality of history? What is the relationship between the perceiving consciousness, both the poet and the character fitfully visible within the poem, and the crowd?

Because Eliot began with a collection of loosely related poetic fragments, what he later called 'a sprawling, chaotic poem', that all too accurately reflected the social chaos of its subject, the problem facing him was to find the 'formal destiny' that animated and unified his collection of scraps. But the real difficulty was to find a form that would not reproduce on an aesthetic level the formal terrorism that had beaten the crowd into a featureless mass. . . .

It is clear that at one point Eliot hoped that the figure of Tiresias might solve his aesthetic difficulties. In the drafts of *The Waste Land*, Tiresias appears just after the passage on London's 'swarming life'. . . . At one point in the draft, Tiresias announces that having 'perceived the scene' he knows 'the manner of these crawling bugs'. Pound thought this 'too easy' and removed it, but it revealed a dangerous possibility that remains in the final text, that Tiresias will unify the London crowd only by diminishing its individual members. Of course, to do so would be to recapitulate and reinforce the horror that afflicts the crowd, not to alleviate it. . . .

In any case, to understand the relationship of particular to general in *The Waste Land* we must, as Levenson says, confront 'what comes to the same thing, the problem of Tiresias'.[19] After Pound's work, what remained of the crucial London episode that introduces Tiresias was the dramatic scene that begins:

> At the violet hour, when the eyes and back
> Turn upward from the desk, when the human engine
>   waits
> Like a taxi throbbing waiting, . . .

The physical metonyms constitute a mild, rather conventional, critique of the division of labor. Because the worker is tied to the desk, he or she becomes part of a machine, a 'human engine'. At the same time, the definite articles suggest that this is just one set of human components from among an infinite number of sets. The human subject is both fragmented and generalized at the same time. The feeling given is one of infinite, simultaneous repetitions of a single gesture in which isolated body parts detach themselves from the work that has both held and dispersed them. Here the figure of metonymy is used polemically to depict a metonymized society in which individuals are both dismembered and standardized.

The typist who appears next in the passage is a worker named metonymically for the machine she tends, so merged with it, in fact, that she is called a 'typist' even at home. In *The Education*, Henry Adams proclaims his astonishment at the denizens of the new American cities: 'new types, – or type-writers, – telephone and telegraph-girls, shop-clerks, factory hands, running into millions on millions . . . '.[20] Eliot's point here seems very close to Adams's. Eliot's woman is also a 'type', identified with her type-writer so thoroughly she becomes it. She is a machine, acting as she does with 'automatic hand'. The typist is horrifying both because she is reduced by the conditions of labor to a mere part and because she is infinitely multiple. In fact, her very status as a 'type' is dependent on a prior reduction from whole to part. She can become one member of Adams's faceless crowd only by being first reduced to a 'hand'.

The typist is the very type of metonymy, of the social system that accumulates its members by mere aggregation. Yet this 'type' is linked syntactically to Tiresias as well. In fact, the sentence surrenders its nominal subject, Tiresias, in favor of her. The evening hour 'strives/ Homeward, and brings the sailor home from sea,/The typist home at teatime, clears her breakfast, lights/Her stove, and lays out food in tins.' The typist shifts in mid-line from object to subject, from passive to active. Does the evening hour clear her breakfast, or should the reader search even farther back for an appropriate subject, to Tiresias himself? Though this would hardly clarify the syntax, Tiresias could function logically as both subject and object, seen and seer, because, as the notes tell us, he is the typist: 'all the women are one woman, and the two sexes meet in Tiresias.' The confused syntax represents this process of identification, erasing ordinary boundaries between active and passive, subject and object.

On what basis can the typist merge with all other men and women to become part of Tiresias? In other words, what is the figurative relationship between the whole he represents and the part acted by the typist? . . . His gift of prophecy, however, depends on the supposition that human behaviour is repetitive, that 'all' is in fact the mere repetition of a single act into infinity, enacted 'on this same divan or bed'. What, therefore, is the real difference between the industrial system, in which 'all the women are one woman' and the identification represented by Tiresias? In which case is the typist less of a type?

The poem itself suggests that there may be no difference because Tiresias and the 'human engine' are one and the same:

> . . . when the human engine
>   waits
> Like a taxi throbbing waiting,
> I Tiresias, though blind, throbbing between two lives, . . .

By means of this intricate chiasmus, Eliot links the human engine that waits to Tiresias who throbs through the middle term of the taxi, which both waits and throbs. In so doing, Eliot suggests a link between the reduced conditions of the modern worker and the mythical hermaphrodite who includes all experience. The passage contains within itself a representation of this link in Tiresias's throbbing 'between two lives'. Tiresias appears here almost as a metaphor for metaphor, throbbing between two lives as the common term that joins them. But the activity of joining, the throbbing that seems to evoke human longing, is in fact the noise of the taxi engine, the drumming of its pistons a travesty of human sexual activity. In this way, the passage mocks its own insertion of Tiresias between two lives by positioning the taxi as the true medium between individual and race, present and eternity. Even stylistically, the passage undermines its own assertion of metaphorical identification by merely juxtaposing the two elements that both terms share: There is no 'between' between throbbing and waiting, no comma or other punctuation, and yet this is where the all important connection between Tiresias and the modern worker is accomplished. Read in this way, the passage suggests that the process by which Tiresias represents all men and women is no different from the process by which the modern industrial machine conglomerates them into one mass, that what looks like metaphorical representation is but the additive accumulation typical of industrialism.

The typist, that is to say, is just as much a type within the 'inclusive human consciousness' represented by Tiresias as she is within the routines of her office. The same thing is true of the typist's lover. Tiresias is able to understand the young man carbuncular, 'one of the low', because he has 'walked among the lowest of the dead'. He is able to understand human beings, in other words, only insofar as they are types. . . .

Such an interpretation of Tiresias's role in *The Waste Land* calls into question a common idea about the poem first suggested by Eliot himself. In '*Ulysses*, Order and Myth', Eliot describes the famous 'mythical method' by which the disorder of contemporary reality is to be gathered up into a coherent aesthetic form. Thus *The Waste Land* is often read as backing its apparent disorder with some image of an ultimate historical order. . . . In other words, tradition, like Tiresias in the conventional interpretation of him, is a normative whole made up out of the resemblances between particular historical times. In this way, criticism provides the resolution Eliot so devoutly wished for when he began his poem, a resolution in which the particular and the general would shake off their modern, contradictory relationship and assume a new one of organic reciprocity. But this norm, this fruitful interpenetration of temporal particularity and eternity, is precisely what Eliot does not provide.

The opening lines of 'The Fire Sermon' might be taken as a representative example:

Sweet Thames, run softly, till I end my song.
The river bears no empty bottles, sandwich papers,
Silk handkerchiefs, cardboard boxes, cigarette ends
Or other testimony of summer nights. The nymphs are
    departed.

Eliot's vision superimposes the vividly realized trash of the modern Thames onto the absence of such trash from Spenser's river. The past, we understand this passage to say, was full, whole, unbesmirched by the detritus of the present. Yet such fullness appears in the poem only as an absence, whereas the emptiness of the present seems sharp and real. The present is represented metonymically as parts of parts, each one of which figures the incompleteness of the modern world. But the purely additive nature of the metonymic list also makes it impossible to definitively stop adding to it. The river fills with these absent items and thus serves as a figure for the negative plenitude, the empty totality, of the modern age.

The river's barrenness, the fact that it does not 'bear' the freight of modern trash, signifies its purity, but also, perversely, its fullness. The more it does not bear, the more beautiful it seems in contrast. Its refusal of the present preserves a continuity the modern world destroys. On the other hand, the plenitude of modern times, its sheer industrial productivity, appears as a paradoxical emptiness. Within such tortured paradoxes how to distinguish the past's fruitful barrenness from the present's barren fruitfulness? Tradition appears in the form of the contradictory force Eliot confronted at the very beginning of his work on *The Waste Land*, a force that is at once barren and oppressively fruitful, that both breeds and kills. Tradition, in other words, suffers from the same paradoxes that fracture present-day London itself. . . .

Eliot's essays of this period seem to promise a poetry in which present and past, modernity and tradition, will seamlessly join with one another, resolving modern contradictions by dissolving the modern into tradition and vice versa. But *The Waste Land* actually portrays a relationship in which tradition resembles modernity only in reproducing its contradictions. Tradition itself is just as paradoxically blighting and smothering as the contemporary London that had once begun the poem. There is no whole that can be distinguished from the repressive, false whole of contemporary reality.

. . . Whatever promise might be contained in 'What the Thunder Said' is inextricably involved with the most extreme negativity it depicts. The last section of *The Waste Land* begins by considering the crucifixion as a finality, not as a prelude to resurrection: 'He who was living is now dead'. Yet, after a long exilic passage through many lines of dry rock without water, the reader emerges onto the road to Emmaus, where the risen Christ is truly, though ambiguously, present: 'Who is the third who walks always beside you?' Eliot suggests by his use of this particular part of the resurrection story that Christ is present in our very doubts and confusions about him; he is the third who insists on being counted even though it throws off the total. The fact that experience does not add up, these lines suggest, is our best evidence of the hand of God, not the symmetry and order of the cosmos but its excess over human forms of order.

The figure of the risen Christ is, moreover, 'hooded' and sexually ambiguous. The hood recurs a few lines later in a passage that seems to recoil from the waves of communist revolution then washing over Europe, a passage in which 'maternal lamentation' merges with 'hooded hordes' swarming over the dry earth. If the 'maternal lamentation' is that of the Virgin Mary, in her well-known pose over the body of Christ, and if the hood is the same that so recently hid the risen Christ, are the 'hordes' somehow to be associated with the resurrection? Is Eliot somehow drawing from his most gruesome representation of social disorder a promise of spiritual rebirth? The rest of this section is littered with 'empty cisterns and exhausted wells', dried-up sources of water that are clearly parallel to the 'empty chapel' bereft of its god. But just these exhausted sources give rise to 'voices singing out', to lightning and finally to rain. In other words, *The Waste Land* does not include any hints of salvation until the very bottom has been reached, and then it seems to suggest that salvation comes only out of the very exhaustion of the negative. It seems as though Eliot can logically conceive of only one absolute, the negative, but that the very existence of an absolute in any form suggests the possibility of something beyond mere chaos.

There is some reason to believe that Eliot had something like this in mind at the end of *The Waste Land*. The long drought is ended by 'a damp gust/Bringing rain', and yet two lines later the leaves still 'Waited for rain'. There is a voice from heaven, yet at the end of its statement, the human protagonist still sits on the shore waiting for answers. The last section builds to an obvious climax that it refuses to accept. Indeed, it reopens matters with a last verse paragraph of startling disorder. It may be, however, that such disorder contains an answer of greater validity than those given by the voice of thunder. The final word, 'shantih', is, by definition, beyond understanding, ineffable. Its meaning seems to exist, in fact, only in contradistinction to the wild cacophony of languages and styles preceding it. . . . It is as if Eliot could only approach peace through conflict, as if he could only grasp linguistic unity as an implication of linguistic disorder, and, finally, as if he could imagine social solidarity only by extension of social chaos. Disorder thus becomes not a fault to be overcome, but a necessary moment in the process of arriving at order.

. . . The original ambition of *The Waste Land*, to reconcile the contradictions of London life by assuming a position outside it, is therefore doomed to failure. The individual cannot, by any expenditure of might and main, think his way out of the society that contains him. Only irony can suggest what cannot really be achieved. The relationship of part to whole in *The Waste Land* is therefore not metaphorical but ironic, because the reconciliation of part and whole, like that of individual and community or concrete fact and 'formal destiny', is only an impossibility implied by the mutual exclusiveness of the two terms of the relationship.

The most obvious objection to this solution is that it merely justifies a complete abdication. . . . The obscurity of the poem has also seemed to some a retreat into an elite enclave. But the original readers of the poem reacted somewhat differently. A. L. Morton and other young communists like Edgell Rickword were thrilled by the 'strange and unexpected transitions of the poem, even by its obscurity; it was in this sense "a liberating experience"'. For such readers, Eliot was 'a standard, around which certain forces of revolt gathered'.[21] Morton's opinion is not particularly idiosyncratic. . . . In *Contemporary Techniques of Poetry*, Robert Graves places Eliot's work with that of left-wing writers committed to revolution.[22]

Stylistic disorientation did, in such readings, figure political freedom. But readers like John Cornford, who joined the Communist Party after reading *The Waste Land*, were not responding to a theory of individual freedom. The thrill felt by Cornford, Morton, and Rickword must have come in part from the dialectical process Adorno describes in defending modernist literature from Lukács: 'loneliness will turn into its opposite: the solitary consciousness potentially destroys and transcends itself by revealing itself in works of art as the hidden truth common to all Men'.[23] Morton and Rickword recognize in the isolated lives of the typist and the young man a common fate and thus make solidarity out of fragmentation. In the same way, stylistic discontinuity can become a 'standard' around which people might 'gather', a disunity that paradoxically brings about unity.[24] □

In their efforts to read *The Waste Land* for the 'hidden truth' that it reveals but cannot acknowledge, all the extracts in this chapter have sought to expose what the poem tacitly implies. In so doing they can be seen to have sounded a new note in criticism of the poem. The next chapter details this development further by turning to readings of the poem that see it as inscribing not just a political ideology, but also one of selfhood and subjectivity as well. They are based, therefore, in psychoanalytic reading practices.

CHAPTER FIVE

Deconstructive Readings: Freud, Feminism and Ideology

THE FINAL two chapters of this Critical Guide explore further the ideo-logical implications of both *The Waste Land* and its critical history. They map, therefore, some of the new directions taken by criticism of the poem since the early-1980s and bring its critical history up to date. Still regarded as a modern classic, *The Waste Land* emerges from these recent readings as a poem that is both fascinating *and* deeply suspect precisely because of its inscription of a particular set of assumptions about mod-ernist ideology and culture. Such criticism attempts to interrogate the text in order to explore the conditions and meanings of modernity. In this sense, then, these new readings of *The Waste Land* offer up a 'post-modern' version of the poem: one that deconstructs the text, opens up to investigation its ideological gestures, and sees it as an inevitable product of the cultural materials of the early years of this century.

The essays in the following chapter all attempt to get beneath, as it were, Eliot's mask of impersonality. By reading the poem in the light of new biographical information about Eliot, they illuminate how the workings of prejudice, anti-Semitism and frustrated sexual desire in Eliot's own life can be seen to run throughout modernism in general. And the pieces in this chapter can be seen to set the terms for such broadly deconstructive and cultural materialist approaches to *The Waste Land* in their use of Freudian psychoanalysis and feminist critiques to open up new interpretive possibilities in the text. The essays in this chap-ter, then, profoundly challenge the reliance of earlier critical readings of the poem upon ideas of poetic impersonality, mythic consciousness and aesthetic autonomy. In challenging such ideas – dominant in criticism of the poem because they seem sanctioned by Eliot himself – the essays in this chapter strive to demonstrate the poem's susceptibility to reading strategies that unpick rather than reinforce the poem's cultural assumptions. These final two chapters chart a profound change of direction, both in criticism of *The Waste Land* and in critical practice generally, towards reading practices that are ideologically aware and which acknowledge that no act of textual criticism is culturally innocent.

What emerges most strongly from the readings that comprise this chapter is a sense that the modernist moment from which *The Waste Land* is generated is a moment of personal and cultural crisis – one, moreover, that is grounded in a profound sense of loss. The modernism that they see the poem enacting is one that announces the fragmentation and loss of 'master-narratives' that had previously seemed to lend coherent meaning and significance to life. In this version of modernity, traditional ways of thinking about history, religion, language or even selfhood can no longer be relied on to deliver a unified, fixed and thus authoritative standard by which to measure culture and consciousness. All such organising structures are felt to be under challenge, and consequently the poem's fragmented heterogeneity is read by this new generation of critics as an index of the impossibility of construing a single meaning for either the poem or for the experience of modernity. Thus, whereas previous critics had looked to the poem as a means of shoring up culture against loss, these essays examine the experience of loss itself and the poem's articulation of that loss.

Throughout this chapter, then, *The Waste Land* is seen as important because of the way in which the loss of a single coherent meaning is staged in its dispersal of many different (and sometimes contradictory) meanings. As a result of this, the following essays can be seen to employ, broadly speaking, 'deconstructive' reading practices. They share a concern with language and ideology as a system of power, one that can be dismantled through an examination of *The Waste Land*. The sort of deconstructive critical practice that operates, to a greater or lesser degree, in these essays is perhaps best summed up by Jonathan Culler in his book *On Deconstruction* (1983). Culler writes that:

■ . . . to deconstruct a discourse is to show how it undermines the philosophy it asserts, or the hierarchical oppositions on which it relies, by identifying in the text the rhetorical operations that produce the supposed ground of argument, the key concept or premise.[1] □

In the critical extracts that follow, we witness how *The Waste Land* undermines the ideological ground of modernism even as it produces its terms and conditions. Its poetics may be one of fragmentation and discontinuity, but its anxious philosophy is one of wholeness and coherence snatched from chaos. If the poem can be seen to rescue modern consciousness from its overwhelming sense of loss, then these readings stress that such an act of rescue is only imaginary, part and parcel of the rhetorical operation of modernity.

Perhaps the earliest recognition of the potential of deconstructive reading practices to unpick *The Waste Land*'s ideological assertions is Frank Kermode's essay 'A Babylonish Dialect' (1966). This appeared in the issue of *Sewanee Review* that was published in memory of Eliot who had died early in the previous year (4 January 1965). In this essay, from which a brief extract follows, Kermode sees the poem as depicting the loss of civilisation in its imagery of 'imperial catastrophe'.[2] For Kermode, the cities that Eliot's poem precariously inhabits are, like the biblical city of Babylon, cities on the brink of collapse. Their very inscription in the poem signals the loss and destruction that they struggle to withstand. In its poetic shoring of fragments, then, Kermode argues that the poem grounds itself, necessarily, upon ruin. This poetic act, in which the poem animates the loss that it most wants to overcome, is, according to Kermode, crucial to the poem's place within modernity, while it also demonstrates the way in which it deconstructs its own rhetoric of cultural salvation. Writing before the term deconstruction was used to describe such an effect in a text, Kermode calls this an act of 'decreation':

■ [The] imperialistic Eliot is the poet of the urbs *aeterna*, of the transmitted but corrupted dignity of Rome. Hence his veneration not only for Baudelaire (where his Symbolist predecessors would have agreed) but for Virgil (where they would not). The other side of this city is the Babylon of *Apocalypse*, and when the *imperium* is threadbare and the end approaches of that which Virgil called endless, this is the city we see. . . . Here is the imagery of sea and imperial city, the city which is the whore and the mother of harlots, with Mystery on her forehead: Mme Sosostris and the bejewelled lady of the game of chess – diminished as the sailors and merchants have dwindled to Phlebas, the sea swallowing his concern for profit and loss, and to Mr Eugenides, his pocket full of currants (base Levantine trade) and his heart set on metropolitan whoring. This is the London of *The Waste Land*, the City by the sea with its remaining flashes of inexplicable imperial splendor: the Unreal City, the *urbs aeterna* declined into *l'immonde cité*. . . .

No one has better stated the chief characteristics of [the modernist] epoch than the late R.P. Blackmur in a little book of lectures, *Anni Mirabiles* 1921–1925 . . . We live, wrote Blackmur, in the first age that has been 'fully self-conscious of its fictions' – in a way, Nietzsche has sunk in at last; and in these conditions we are more than ever dependent on what he calls, perhaps not quite satisfactorily, 'bourgeois human-ism' – 'the residue of reason in relation to the madness of the senses'. Without it we cannot have 'creation in honesty', only 'assertion in des-peration'. But in its operation this residual humanism can only deny the validity of our frames of reference and make 'an irregular meta-physic for the control of man's irrational powers'. So this kind of art is a new kind of creation, harsh, medicinal, remaking reality 'in rivalry with our own wishes', denying us the consolations of predictable form but showing us the forces of our world, which we may have to control by other means. And the great works in this new and neces-sary manner were the product of the 'wonderful years' – in English, two notable examples are *Ulysses* and *The Waste Land*.

The function of such a work, one has to see, is what Simone Weil called *decreation* . . . [She] explains the difference from destruction: decreation is not a change from the created to nothingness, but from the created to the uncreated. . . .

This seems to me a useful instrument for the discrimination of modernisms. The form in which Simone Weil expresses it is rather obscure, though she is quite clear that 'destruction' is 'a blameworthy substitute for decreation'. The latter depends upon an act of renuncia-tion, considered as a creative act like that of God. 'God could create only by hiding himself. Otherwise there would be nothing but him-self.' She means that decreation, for men, implies the deliberate repudiation (not simply the destruction) of the naturally human and so naturally false 'set' of the world: 'we participate in the creation of the world by decreating ourselves.' Now the poets of the *anni mirabiles* also desired to create a world by decreasing the self in suffering; to purge what, in being merely natural and human, was also false.[3] □

While Kermode offers here an early deconstructive model for reading *The Waste Land* he attempts, also, to accommodate Eliot's poetic ideal of impersonality to this model. This attempt is not entirely successful. On the one hand it implies a strategy for reading beneath the poem's assumptions about poetry and culture – one that is, as it were, 'fully self-conscious of its fictions'. On the other hand, however, Kermode reads the poem as able, finally, to transcend the conditions from which it was produced by 'decreasing the self in suffering'.

Once again, then, *The Waste Land* is called upon to bolster a sensibil-ity that is highly aestheticised and therefore deeply suspicious of what it terms the '*merely* natural and human'. The problem here – as indeed throughout the whole of its critical history – seems to lie in the poem's conception of selfhood, consciousness and identity. Though *The Waste*

Land's modernist methodology of fragmentary allusion promises a radically decentered subjectivity, what the jostling voices of its poetic materials actually deliver is a text in which subjectivity is central to its meaning. Read in this way, the poem charts the struggle of modern consciousness to find a single legitimating voice for itself. Far from deconstructing the poem's ideological gestures, then, such critiques merely reinscribe them in their own reading practice. Kermode's essay is fascinating precisely because it acknowledges this as the contradictory position in which critical readings of the poem find themselves. The importance of his essay, therefore, lies in its implicit call for a critical model for reading *The Waste Land* that is more adequate to the deconstructive task which the poem itself seems to demand.

Writing in 1982, Ruth Nevo attempted to set down the deconstructive terms with which she felt *The Waste Land* could adequately be read. Hers is the first essay seriously to suggest that the seminal poem of modernity should be read as a manifesto of postmodernity. Unfortunately, the reading of the poem that comprises the main substance of her essay is, given the apparent extremity of the assumptions she brings to bear on the poem, rather tame and unadventurous. The short extract that follows from her essay details the terms (rather than the substance) of her argument for seeing the poem as a precursor of deconstruction, its 'Ur-Text':

■ . . . it is my thesis at present that *The Waste Land*, that seminal modernist poem of 1922, can now be read as a postmodernist poem of 1982: as a deconstructionist Ur-text, even as a Deconstructionist Manifesto. . . .

It is my objective in this paper to show that . . . disunification, or desedimentation, or dissemination (to use Derridean terminology) is the *raison d'être* of the poem; that in it the strategies of self-consumption, *mise en abyme*, and influence anxiety can be inspected at large; and that if one wanted a concise account of it, one could not do better than to quote Derrida himself on his own practice: it exhibits throughout 'a certain strategic arrangement, which, within the field and its own powers, turn[s] against itself its own stratagems, producing a force of dislocation which spreads itself through the whole system, splitting it in all directions and delimiting it through and through.'[4]

Let us begin with deconstructive strategies of the simpler kind: in *The Waste Land* the fundamental categories of literary discourse are dismantled or simply abandoned. There is no narrative, there is no time, though there are 'withered stumps of time', and no place – or rather there is no single time or place but a constant, bewildering shifting and disarray of times and places; there is no unifying central character either speaking or spoken about, no protagonist or antagonist, no drama, no epic, no lyric, though there are moments suggestive of all these generic constellations. . . .

Beyond this *mise en abyme* of seers, or ventriloquism of voices, there is no one point of view, no single style, idiom, register, or recurrent and therefore linking linguistic device which could define a subject, in the sense of a dominant speaking or projecting persona. The 'poet's mind' for which we are accustomed to seek is indeterminately catalyser and/or catalysed. Nor, similarly, can we differentiate a subject in the sense of an overall subject matter, or argument, or myth, or theme for the poem to be unequivocally about or to embody. I say nothing of the absence of obvious conventional poetic features such as meter, rhyme, stanza, or any regularity or recurrence or set of symmetries which could constitute formal pattern in any classical sense at all. It is totally, radically nonintegrative and antidiscursive, its parts connected by neither causes, effects, parallelism, nor antithesis. It is a cinematographic mélange or montage of glimpses, gestures, images, echoes, voices, phrases, memories, fragments of speech, song, quotation, appearances, and disappearances. It consists of a plethora of signifiers in complete discomplementarity with any set or sequence of recognizably related signifieds in a represented world. It is an apogee of fragmentation and discontinuity, referring, if at all, only to itself. But this self that it is is constituted by what it is not, its presence is made up of its absences, its gaps and ellipses are the fountainheads of its significance, its disorder its order. . . .

An irreducible plurality of meaning, of course, is no news to literary critics, and would not in itself justify the title of this paper. If, however, deconstruction has been no more than the valorizing of plurality to a point where no vestige of embarrassment stemming from the rationalist, universalist traditions of thought is left, even that would bring *The Waste Land*, with its extremist aesthetic of irrationality and the infinite regress of its discontinuities, firmly into the orbit. But I believe there is more to it than this. T. S. Eliot's own 'mythical method', which he attributed to Joyce and Yeats as initiators – the manipulation of a continuous parallel between contemporaneity and antiquity, which made, he said, the modern world possible in art – is the identical twin to Harari's account of Derrida's deconstruction: 'The tracing of a path among textual strata in order to stir up and expose forgotten and dormant sediments of meaning.'[5] And if, according to Derrida, 'a text is a text only if it conceals, from the first glance, from the first comer, the law of its composition and the rules of its game,' then Eliot's text positively out-Herods Herod. . . .

The final deconstructive act of *The Waste Land* deconstructs distinctions between critic and author, 'fiction' and 'fact', presentation and representation, origin and supplement. These are the classic, central deconstructionist themes. Deconstructionists will know better than I what profit they may derive from this Ur-text of their creed. But at least we may all feel freed at last in our readings of a superimposed message, an indoctrination, an obligation to the definitive.[6] □

Nevo's final sense, that a deconstructive reading of *The Waste Land* will free us from the indoctrinations and obligations of prior interpretations of the poem, is an important one. It indicates the sorts of direction taken by contemporary critical practice in reading *The Waste Land*. Following on from Nevo's testing of the deconstructive waters in criticism of the poem, the most important of recent readings of the text have striven to examine the ways in which the poem's rhetorical strategies can be seen, in a particularly Derridean manner, to 'stir up and expose forgotten and dormant sediments of meaning' in the culture of modernity from which the poem is produced.

The next two critical pieces – by David Trotter and Maud Ellmann – use Freudian psychoanalysis to perform this deconstructive act of stirring up and exposing the limits of modernist ideology. Both Trotter's and Ellmann's excellent analyses of the poem are exercises in what might be termed cultural materialist reading practices. They both argue that the poem, far from being an aesthetically autonomous object, is inescapably a product of its culture. To analyse the poem is to open up the culture of modernity to investigation. Both critics, then, use their deconstructive readings of the poem to lever open the systems of social, cultural and political power which they see operating in Europe in the early years of this century. In a sense, therefore, their deployment of psychoanalytic strategies allows them to read anew not just the poem but also modern consciousness. They set out to psychoanalyse modern culture, taking *The Waste Land* as the text of its neuroses. And like Freud before them, they focus especially on the neurotic role of women within such a culture. Their examinations of the poem are vitally important in turning the poem back in on itself in order both to assess the force of its ideological assertions and to suggest ways in which the recalcitrantly masculine discourse of the poem may be deconstructed as part of a feminist critique of modernism.

David Trotter's critique of *The Waste Land*, from which the following extract is taken, begins by examining attitudes towards women that were prevalent in the culture that gave rise to the poem. Women, especially society women, were felt to represent a threat to society, their 'seductive languor' betokening – as is seen in other Eliot poems such as 'The Love Song of J. Alfred Prufrock' and 'Portrait of a Lady' – the collapse of civilisation into degenerate *ennui*. According to Trotter, this attitude is fundamental to *The Waste Land*'s overarching sense of sexual frustration and cultural sterility. It is an attitude that reaches beyond the poem's depictions of upper- and middle-class women to include all classes of women, from Marie in the Hofgarten to the typist in her apartment and Lil in the London pub. The poem's anxieties are therefore seen as those of a society in crisis, a crisis of national, cultural and (most crucially) sexual identity that reflects the breaking up of Victorian values within the crucible of modernity.

Trotter's mobilisation of Freud in his deconstruction of such attitudes is a stunning piece of literary criticism. His psychoanalytic approach allows him a double perspective, one in which both the individual and the culture are examined at the same time, and which is therefore necessary to his reading of the poem's struggles with subjectivity as symptoms of a malaise affecting society at large. It is via Freud that Trotter is able to expand upon Kermode's argument that the poem inscribes the loss it desires so strongly to overcome. While this loss is deeply personal, it also articulates the sense of loss that lies at the heart of modern culture. Trotter's reading of *The Waste Land* therefore sees it revealing the unconscious drives of modernist ideology. In the example from Freud's *Beyond the Pleasure Principle* (1920), which Trotter cites (and to which we shall return when considering Maud Ellmann's analysis of the poem), the child's game in which the loss and retrieval of its toy is staged becomes the means for the child of overcoming its sense of helpless passivity when faced with the real world. From being a passive spectator, the child becomes an active participant; after all, the child does control the game. However, the child's sense of loss can only be compensated for by an *imaginary* retrieval, a game. And Trotter sees *The Waste Land* caught in a similar double-bind: its poetic language can only stage a partial and imaginary retrieval from its overwhelming sense of loss. It would seem, Trotter argues further, that part of modernism's coercive ideology, and one highly evident in *The Waste Land*, is that it allows its readers to imagine that their passive position is in fact an active one of participation in the poem's subjective rituals. The poem, therefore, reasserts the hierarchy of power that it seems to oppose: women seem dangerous in their sexual passivity, the reader remains subject to the poem's rhetoric of obscurity, which cannot but repeat modernity's obsessive rituals.

■ *The Waste Land* attempts a rite of passage, a rite which will reconstitute subjectivity in a realm beyond social structure. It is dogged by an awareness that little separates religious from neurotic ceremonial, and that the schematisms imposed on us by society run deep and dividingly. For Eliot's thinking had by this time become genuinely social in scope, even if its codes and gestures remained defiantly personal. I want now to draw attention to that scope.

The second section of the poem, 'A Game of Chess', is as confessional as anything Eliot ever wrote. It alludes to his disastrous first marriage, and he gave it the interim title of 'In the Cage'. But cages often have people outside them looking in, and anyone peering through these particular bars in 1922 might well have recognised the captives.

For Eliot certainly wasn't the only writer to deplore the neurotic behaviour of society-women like the one portrayed in the opening passage of 'A Game of Chess'. Julien Benda's *Belphégor* (1918), which Eliot considered a model of the new 'classical' consciousness, managed to reveal an entire Decline of the West in their seductive languor. Benda thought that there were two types of sensibility, 'plastic' and 'musical', the one poised and compact, the other dizzy and diffuse. Women, it turns out, were mostly 'musical', and Benda cited the example of a young countess whose 'whole process of thought is an orgy of disconnected somersaults, her reasoning a cyclone of impressions, her opinion a jingle of images' . . . [7]

Max Nordau was another pundit who wandered through fashionable boudoirs denouncing them for their lack of severity. His book, robustly entitled *Degeneration*, caused quite a stir on publication; it was translated into English in 1895, and read by Eliot at Harvard some time between 1908 and 1914. Nordau claimed to hear a 'sound of rending' in the fabric of tradition: 'Things as they are totter and plunge.'[8] Things as they are apparently tottered and plunged most alarmingly in fashionable mansions, where the tireless Nordau was often to be found . . .

The luxurious interiors which . . . upset Benda and Nordau were not all that far from the one described in 'A Game of Chess', with its picture of rape, its jewels pouring from satin cases, its synthetic perfumes which trouble and confuse. Nor was there much difference between the occupants of these various boudoirs.

Society-women had menaced before in Eliot's poetry, in 'Prufrock' and 'Portrait of a Lady'. There they had tried to coax the poet into some kind of intimacy; casual remarks and gestures (settling a pillow, throwing off a shawl, twisting a lilac stem) were hints he could neither ignore nor resolve. It was a world of Proustian codes.

But by the time of *The Waste Land* these women had come to seem a threat to society as well as to the stripling philosopher; their sexuality had acquired a desperate and violent edge. The neophyte now found himself confronted not by an occasional escape of scent, but by a hearty female stench. That last phrase comes from the description of Fresca which Pound edited out of 'The Fire Sermon'. . . .

Eliot describes Fresca awakening from pleasant dreams of love and rape to summon a maid whose hand is coarsened and whose tread is plebeian. The social implications of her sexuality only become evident when it is framed by the plebeian hand and tread. Sexuality, which might have been thought a realm outside or prior to social structure, and perhaps even the ground of a reconstituted subjectivity, proves as schematised an experience as any other. Different classes, that is to say, entertain and abide by different representations of sexuality. In 'A Game of Chess' the behaviour of the woman whose hair spreads in fiery points contrasts sharply with the bluntness and the scarred fertility of the women in the pub.

By 1921 an issue which sharpened the contrast even further – birth control – had become a topic of widespread concern and debate. Two clinics were opened in that year, one by Marie Stopes, the other by the Malthusian League. In October the King's Physician, Lord Dawson of Penn, addressed the Church Congress in Birmingham and caused a great stir by advocating birth control. Next year the Malthusians published the proceedings of a conference on the subject which had attracted a large number of delegates from Britain and from abroad. In July 1923 one of the leading medical journals, the *Practitioner*, produced a special number on birth control. 'The subject of contraceptives,' its editor reported, 'has now become a commonplace of conversation at women's clubs and mixed tea-tables'.

The debate revealed that in one respect at least the nation's sexual conduct differed according to social status. The enlightened and responsible classes used contraceptives, the rest did not. As the *Practitioner* put it, 'limitation is now practised by the classes from which it is desirable that the community should be recruited, and is not practised by the undesirables'. Clearly this had important social and political consequences. 'To attempt,' one contributor said, 'to lower the number of the efficient while the inefficient multiply spells disaster in the future.' Eliot's juxtaposition of a childless and frustrated middle – or upper – class couple with a recklessly fertile working-class woman followed the line of a real social fissure which was asserting itself in terms of sexual conduct.[9]

The debate about contraception revealed the depth of class-division in post-war Britain. Sexual and reproductive behaviour seemed to vary according to social status, taking the form of neurotic inhibition among the bourgeoisie and of reckless breeding among the proletariat. Eliot's juxtaposition of scenes in 'A Game of Chess' reproduced exactly the difference between these two worlds.

He even found a separate idiom for each world, devising modes of speech which would render meticulously the 'social tone' of the people who used them, or had become implicated in them. (His efforts recall Ezra Pound's contemporary interest in novelists who seemed able to catch the tone of minds immured in cliché.) Thus the disorientation one might feel in the lady's antithetical boudoir is rendered by what Donald Davie calls a 'sustained ambiguity' between past participle, past indicative and adjectival participle.[10] The language tells us that we must not doze, but be thrilled.

By contrast the speech of the working-class women in the pub reveals a kind of vacancy. They constantly talk around the subject; or, to be more precise, around the reference item 'it'. We can guess what 'it' refers to in each case, but the women refuse, or are unable, to give 'it' a name. Perhaps they know each other so well (unlike the husband and wife in the previous episode) that they don't need to specify. At any rate their speech defines their 'social tone' and separates them effectively from the clotted luxury of the bourgeois temperament. For all their talking around the point, they recognise what is at issue; whereas the portrayal of the neurotic couple owes more to the indirect representation of sexuality in the novel from Austen to James.

When even such natural processes as sexuality and reproduction are constituted differently for different groups of society, we are faced by a truly formidable schematism. The caricature rites of 'The Burial of the Dead' had failed to restore wholeness and immediacy to this divided society. So Eliot turned to fiercer remedies.

He sought the most ancient remedies: purgation by fire, pilgrimage, quest, initiation, revelation. But he had to bring them home to readers who had grown sceptical of ancient remedies. He had to revive in those readers who did not merely 'snatch a glance' perceptions of wholeness and immediacy (and thus learn for whom he was writing). To that end, he made use of a particular form of what I have called 'external reference', one involving the demonstratives 'this' and 'that' and their respective plurals. These are specifying agents, which serve to identify the individual or sub-class within the class designated by the noun they precede. (If I talk about 'this pencil', I am referring to a particular, identifiable specimen.) As with all reference items, the information they presuppose can be retrieved either from another part of the text or from the situation of its utterance. In *The Waste Land* it is the use of demonstratives to refer outside the text which is the more interesting. For example, when Eliot talks about 'this red rock' and 'that noise', we know he means a particular rock and a particular noise, but the poem does not supply the information needed to iden- tify them. We will have to supply the information ourselves, from our knowledge or imagining of the situation in which the rock and the noise occur.

But poems do not have situations. We know that we will never gain access to the full identity of the rock and the noise. The referential function of the demonstratives cannot be fulfilled. This being the case, their relation to one another within language comes to the fore. In English 'this' and 'that' are ranged along a scale of proximity. The former refers to things which are close (in time or space) to the speaker, which bear some relation to him or her; the latter refers to things which are distant from and bear no relation to the speaker. (I talk about 'this' table if I happen to be leaning on it at the time, and 'that' table if it stands at the far end of the room.) 'This' has associa- tions of intimacy and relatedness built into it, while 'that' tends to suggest distance and strangeness. These associations are so powerful that they survive even where we can not identify the object referred to, as is often the case in *The Waste Land*. It was in such terms that Eliot revived for his readers a perception of wholeness and immediacy.

After the rendering of Marie's 'social tone' in 'The Burial of the Dead', an authoritative voice beckons a prophet in under the shadow of 'this red rock'. The rock is indicated firmly – *this* one, not that un- inspiring lump of sandstone over there – but we learn nothing about it except its colour. For what matters is that it has been identified by the demonstrative as lying close to the speaker. We feel that we are in the vicinity of or the approaches to a source of redeeming knowledge; the closeness matters more than the nature of the object we are close to, because what is intimate is more real. If we obey the associations of relatedness embedded in the demonstrative, we can perceive some- thing which the poem itself will not name. The allusion to Ecclesiastes suggests an end to mortmain, an apocalyptic return to wholeness and immediacy. However, Ecclesiastes also recommends, as Frazer's men- tor Robertson Smith pointed out, 'extreme scepticism towards all religious speculation'.[11] The shrine proves to be empty. There have surely been more encouraging revelations than 'fear in a handful of dust'. . . .

What could a prophet in the desert, an imagination unfettered but unfed, hope to see except 'fear in a handful of dust'? We are in the presence not of truth but of empty religious speculation.

A few lines later we encounter Madame Sosostris, with a snuffle, fortune-telling. The cards she interprets for us seem cryptic enough: drowned sailor, Lady of the Rocks. But worse follows:

> Here is the man with three staves, and here the Wheel,
> And here is the one-eyed merchant, and this card,
> Which is blank, is something he carries on his back,
> Which I am forbidden to see.

'Here', the adverbial equivalent of 'this', establishes an atmosphere of intimacy, a sense of crowding round the source of knowledge. But again all that emerges is an empty speculation, a blank, an icon as unforthcoming as the red rock: 'this card'. Like the voice in the desert, Madame Sosostris can only show us part of what we would like to see: 'something different', 'something he carries on his back'. She really does play her cards close to her chest.

These episodes represent abortive struggles against mortmain, deluded attempts to initiate a purging rite. But they also bring into play a relation between knowledge and intimacy which was to prove crucial to Eliot's quest for ritual immediacy. To know something is to come into its presence, probably alone and probably at the end of a perilous journey. Fragments from the manuscript use the demonstrative to posit a moment of intimate awareness which can be lackadaisical or transforming, indifferent or redemptive. The poem itself had somehow to twist from one kind of intimacy to another, from neurotic to religious ceremonial.

. . . If the first section of the poem sets up small but futile movements in the direction of a saving knowledge, the second puts us back in the cage and slams the door. Not only is its description of social and personal dividedness particularly harsh . . . but its demonstratives posit a place stranger and more sinister than the red rock or the blank card, a place at the far end of the scale of proximity stretching between 'this' and 'that'. We find ourselves in an enclosed room, listening to 'that noise', which may or may not be the wind under the door, but which is in any case nothing. The wind's nothing seems more terrible than the something revealed to us by the voice in the desert or by Madame Sosostris. Knowing what caused the noise would not erase the mark left by the demonstrative 'that', the mark of a distant and hostile exterior.

In the first section of the poem, we edge towards a tantalising but ultimately sterile knowledge; here, we edge away from a threat to the very possibility of knowledge. Such is the span of consciousness allocated to the inhabitants of the waste land, a narrow wavering between credulity and oblivion. The next section of the poem, 'The Fire Sermon', binds these two tendencies into a defensive strategy, a neurotic ceremonial. Tiresias presides over it, a 'mere spectator', Eliot said, although what he sees is in fact 'the substance of the poem'. Tiresias is the authoritative voice sought by earlier poems, the observing eye which utterly possesses the significance of what it observes. . . . He presides over a moment of annihilation and utter night, when a young clerk visits and seduces a typist . . . The clerk leaves, groping his way down unlit stairs. Unlike the protagonists of Eliot's early poems, who used to worry about getting up stairs, he has trouble getting down them. He has already scaled his summit, and what was once anticipated nervously has become predictable. His acts have meaning not for himself but for the observing eye, whose world-weary parenthesis makes out of them a site of intimate if unsavoury knowledge: *this* same divan or bed.

What Tiresias holds to himself, the typist pushes away, thus completing the neurotic ceremony:

> Her brain allows one half-formed thought to pass:
> 'Well now that's done: and I'm glad it's over.'

What was 'this' to him is 'that' to her, already distant and somehow unrelated. What she pushes away from her Tiresias will presumably gather in to himself once more; so the ceremony goes on. In this respect we might compare the episode with Freud's attempts, in *Beyond the Pleasure Principle* (1920), to theorise something he had already noted as a clinical phenomenon, the 'compulsion to repeat'. Freud noted that the recent war had provided all too many examples of traumatic neurosis, in which the patient was brought back repeatedly to the situation of his original accident; since this process was extremely painful, the force which compelled him to it must be stronger than the pleasure principle.

Freud's efforts to define this force led him to a game played by his young grandson. The boy had a wooden reel attached to a piece of string. Holding the end of the string, he would repeatedly throw the reel away from him into his cot, and then draw it back towards him. As he threw it away from him, he would utter a sound which Freud interpreted as 'fort', meaning away or gone; as he pulled it back towards him, he would say 'da', meaning there or present.

According to Freud, the boy was compensating himself for the absence of his mother by 'staging the disappearance and return of the objects within his reach'. He was repeating an unpleasant experience in play so as to master the pain it caused him. 'At the outset he was in a *passive* situation – he was overpowered by the experience; but, by repeating it, unpleasurable though it was, as a game, he took on an *active* part.'[12] The content of the experience remained unpleasant; but by staging it over and over again in play, and in language, he put himself in a different relation to it, although the process was of course compulsive and therefore a rather uncertain kind of mastery. We do not really know whether the child is playing the game, or the game playing the child.

Eliot's poem also engages in a compulsive repetition, a drawing close and pushing away, as Tiresias gathers in what the typist has renounced. The two elements of the earlier poems, observing eye and empirical self, have been replaced by a neurotic ceremony, a play within language between 'this' and 'that'. And the trauma against which the ceremony has been erected is the young clerk, a figure of social and personal division.

The clerk is a petty-bourgeois, caught between the class from which he is trying to escape and the class he wishes to enter. . . . What fascinated Eliot about such people (here an artisan, more often a petty-bourgeois) was the way that uncertainty about their social status had produced an inner division between speech and identity. They hoped to raise themselves by aping bourgeois dress and speech and manners, and so their behaviour was inevitably at odds with their class origins. . . .

Indeed, this whole section of a supremely class-conscious poem belongs to the petty-bourgeoisie. Even the class origins of the girl seduced in a boat on the Thames are patiently explained in a draft version. Her parents were humble people, and conservative in a way unfamiliar either to the rich or to the poor. They owned a small business, an anxious business, but one providing enough for a house in Highbury and three weeks at Bognor. In the minds of those excluded on one side from what the rich know and on the other side from what the working classes know, life is indeed an anxious business. Eliot's ceremony tries to master the anxiety these minds give off by compulsive repetition.

But Eliot could not let matters rest there. He had to find some way of transforming neurotic into religious ceremonial. He had to purge the divisiveness of social structure by stepping beyond into some regenerative margin. . . .

The concluding section of the poem, 'What the Thunder Said', involves a journey to a regenerative margin. But as important as the metaphor is a subtle revision of the terms of neurotic ceremonial. In 'The Fire Sermon', Tiresias had drawn to himself an experience which the typist rejected, endlessly foresuffering what she wishes to forget. But only reverse the terms, and the circuit is broken. For a pilgrim may wish to forget the boredom and terror of the life he is leaving behind, but he can regard them as the means to an end, as something he must endure in order to separate himself from one world and become fit for another. The significance of his actions does not belong to a perceiving eye, but to the shrine he approaches. The menace surrounding Eliot's pilgrims is a phase through which they must pass on their journey to the source of truth:

> What is that sound high in the air
> Murmur of maternal lamentation
> Who are those hordes swarming
> Over endless plains, . . .

The demonstratives 'that' and 'those' pick out a sequence of threats equivalent to 'that noise' in 'A Game of Chess' and 'that' seduction in 'The Fire Sermon'. They are superseded, the moment we arrive at the Perilous Chapel, by a welcoming 'this':

> In this decayed hole among the mountains
> In the faint moonlight, the grass is singing . . .

The chapel seems singularly without amenities, and there is no guarantee that we will catch a glimpse of anything more fruitful than fear in a handful of dust. But now the aura of intimacy and relatedness bestowed by the demonstrative comes as a reward for surviving the boredom and terror of the world. The scale of proximity stretching between 'that' and 'this' has been transformed into a spiritual progress, a route-map of our quest. We are closer to the source than we have ever been before.

It is from the chapel that the thunder speaks. What it says is what Freud's grandson had said: a solemn and emphatic DA. . . .

Eliot's thunder . . . speaks from afar, but echoes in the pilgrim's skull. It introduces into the defensive ceremonies of the poem a relation to others: give, sympathise, control. For arrival at the Perilous Chapel has not only revised those ceremonies, but transcended them. The thunder speaks a foreign word which is also a root-word, a margin which is also a beginning-again.

But it is an anxious business, this rite of passage. What the thunder says, once it has spat out its root-word, sounds remarkably like what has already been said by the voice in the desert and by Madame Sosostris and by Tiresias:

> The awful daring of a moment's surrender
> Which an age of prudence can never retract
> By this, and this only, we have existed . . .

By this and this only: privately, defensively, secretively, under the shadow of a red rock, on the same divan or bed. What we have given is investment in the *this*. Who is to say whether we have taken part in a neurotic or a religious ceremony? The poem ends with the Fisher King, most ritual of mythic figures, but it is not certain that he has been made anew by the voice of the thunder. 'These fragments,' he says, 'I have shored against my ruin.' These fragments, not those.

One might argue that things have changed, to the extent that the poem at last supplies the information needed to identify what the demonstrative refers to. 'These fragments' are quotations from Dante and Nerval and Kyd. Like Madame Sosostris the Fisher King plays his cards close to his chest, but at least we can see what is written on them. And yet quotations cannot be all that a man in such extremity would shore against his ruin. We are free to suppose that he would assemble everything that was most dear to him, all those perceptions which are 'real for us in a sense in which nothing else is real'.[13] Even here the associations of intimacy and relatedness built into the demonstrative outlast, as they do more obviously in other parts of the poem, the identity of what it refers to. The passage from Bradley cited in the notes reinforces this impression:

> My external sensations are no less private to myself than are my thoughts or my feelings. In either case my experience falls within my own circle, a circle closed on the outside; and, with all its elements alike, every sphere is opaque to the others which surround it . . . In brief, regarded as an existence which appears in a soul, the whole world for each is peculiar and private to that soul.

Eliot's thunder was surely meant to break down the opacity of those spheres. But it ended up illuminating from the inside a circle still closed on the outside. Eliot could not find the ritual immediacy that would transform neurotic into religious observance. 'At the outset he was in a *passive* situation – he was overpowered by the experience; but, by repeating it, unpleasurable though it was, as a game, he took on an *active* part.' Did the child play the game, or the game play the child?[14] □

In the final extract of this chapter, Maud Ellmann asks what lurks underneath the masculine game-playing of *The Waste Land*. Like Trotter before her, Ellmann turns to Freud in her analysis of the poem and refers to the child's *'fort/da'* game as a means of illuminating the poem's haunting sense of loss.[15] She locates this sense, as indeed does Freud, as an effect of the First World War. She notes how Freud later observed the same child's game, but that its meaning had become more culturally forceful. The child's casting out and retrieval of his toy bobbin now carries with it a compulsion to repeat that is an attempt to overcome death. This is, according to Ellmann, analogous to the poem:

■ [the child] sent his bobbin to the trenches. 'A year later', Freud writes:

> . . . the same boy whom I had observed at his first game used to take a toy, if he was angry with it, and throw it on the floor, exclaiming: 'Go to the fwont!' He had heard at that time that his absent father was 'at the front,' and was far from regretting his absence . . . (SE XVIII, p. 16).

Like this child, *The Waste Land* is confronting the specific absence that succeeded World War I, and it evinces both the dread and the desire to hear the voices at the 'fwont' again. In fact, the poem can be read as a seance, and its speaker as the medium who tries to raise the dead by quoting them.[16] □

But what fascinates Ellmann is the very act of casting out that is performed by the poem. This makes her essay perhaps the most exciting and challenging reading of the poem to have been written. For, through her examination of what the poem seeks to throw away – or lay waste – she performs a magnificently subtle and authoritative deconstruction of the text and its dual fascination with, and repulsion by, femininity. She notes that 'the poem is enthralled by the femininity that it reviles, bewitched by this odorous and shoreless flesh'. And in so doing, her analysis pushes understanding of the poem's ideological and cultural gestures much further than the rather too complacent dismissal of the poem by feminist critics Sandra Gilbert and Susan Gubar whose point about the poem, though valid, is hardly subtle or liable to open up further investigation of the poem's inscription of femininity. Gilbert and Gubar declare that:

■ . . . whether he celebrates female silence or castigates female cacophony, Eliot transcribes female language in order to transcend it, thus justifying Joyce's claim that *The Waste Land* 'ended the idea of poetry for ladies'.[17] □

It is simply not clear, here, what is meant by transcending female language, nor does this lead to an investigation of why the poem should desire such transcendence. So, whereas Gilbert and Gubar stop at the point where they see *The Waste Land* depicting women as an unfathomable riddle, for Ellmann this is just a starting point for her to 'trace' what she calls 'the poem's suicidal logic':

■ *The Waste Land* is a sphinx without a secret . . . and to force it to confession may . . . be a way of killing it. This poem, which has been so thoroughly explained, is rarely read at all, and one can scarcely see the 'waste' beneath the redevelopments. Most commentators have been so busy tracking its allusions down and patching up its tattered memories that they have overlooked its broken images in search of the totality it might have been. . . .

This is how Freud first undertook interpretation, too, but his patients forced him to revise his method, and his experience may shed a different kind of light upon *The Waste Land*. In *Studies on Hysteria*, Freud and Breuer argue that 'hysterics suffer mainly from reminiscences' (and by this definition, *The Waste Land* is the most hysterical of texts). . . .

Now, *The Waste Land*, like any good sphinx, lures the reader into hermeneutics, too: but there is no secret underneath its huggermuggery. Indeed, Hegel saw the Sphinx as the symbol of the symbolic itself, because it did not know the answer to its own question: and *The Waste Land*, too, is a riddle to itself.[18] Here it is more instructive to be scrupulously superficial than to dig beneath the surface for the poem's buried skeletons or sources. For it is in the silences between the words that meaning flickers, local, evanescent – in the very 'wastes' that stretch across the page. These silences curtail the powers of the author, for they invite the *hypocrite lecteur* to reconstruct their broken sense. Moreover, the speaker cannot be identified with his creator . . . because he has no stable identity at all. The disembodied 'I' glides in and out of stolen texts, as if the speaking subject were merely the quotation of its antecedents. Indeed, this subject is the victim of a general collapse of boundaries. . . .

Let us assume, first of all, that *The Waste Land* is about what it declares – waste. A ceremonial purgation, it inventories all the 'stony rubbish' that it strives to exorcise. The 'waste *land*' could be seen as the thunderous desert where the hooded hordes are swarming towards apocalypse. But it also means 'waste ground', bomb sites or vacant lots . . . where ancient women gather the wreckage of Europe. It means Jerusalem or Alexandria or London – any ravaged centre of a dying world – and it foreshadows the dilapidation of centricity itself. The poem teems with urban waste, butt-ends of the city's days and ways: 'empty bottles, sandwich papers,/Silk handkerchiefs, cardboard boxes, cigarette ends' (177–8). However, it is difficult to draw taxonomies of waste, because the text conflates the city with the body and, by analogy, the social with the personal. Abortions, broken fingernails, carious teeth, and 'female smells' signify the culture's decadence, as well as bodily decrepitude. The self is implicated in the degradation of the race, because the filth without insinuates defilement within.

It is waste *paper*, however, which appals and fascinates the poem, the written detritus which drifts into the text as randomly as picnics sink into the Thames (177–8). . . . Indeed, *The Waste Land* is one of the most abject texts in English literature . . . Waste is what a culture casts away in order to determine what is not itself, and thus to establish its own limits. In the same way, the subject defines the limits of his body through the violent expulsion of its own excess: and ironically, this catharsis *institutes* the excremental. . . .

The word 'abject' literally means 'cast out', though commonly it means downcast in spirits: but 'abjection' may refer to the waste itself, together with the violence of casting it abroad. It is the ambiguity of the 'abject' that distinguishes it from the 'object', which the subject rigorously jettisons (ob-jects). According to Julia Kristeva, the abject emerges when exclusions fail, in the sickening collapse of limits. Rather than disease or filth or putrefaction, the abject is that which 'disturbs identity, system, order': it is the 'in-between, the ambiguous, the composite'.[19] In the 'brown fog' of *The Waste Land*, for example . . . the in-between grows animate: and Madame Sosostris warns us to fear death by water, for sinking banks betoken glutinous distinctions. In fact, the 'horror' of *The Waste Land* lurks in the osmoses, exhalations and porosities, in the dread of *epidemic* rather than the filth itself, for it is this miasma that bespeaks dissolving limits. The corpses signify the 'utmost of objection', in Kristeva's phrase, because they represent 'a border that has encroached upon everything': an outside that irrupts into the inside, and erodes the parameters of life.[20] It is impossible to keep them underground: Stetson's garden is an ossuary, and the dull canals, the garrets, and the alleys are littered with unburied bones.

'Tumbled graves' (387) have overrun the city, for the living have changed places with the dead: 'A crowd flowed over London Bridge, so many,/I had not thought death had undone so many' (62–3). *The Waste Land* does not fear the dead themselves so much as their invasion of the living; for it is the collapse of boundaries that centrally disturbs the text, be they sexual, national, linguistic, or authorial.

Kristeva derives her notion of abjection from Freud's *Totem and Taboo,* which was written ten years before the publication of *The Waste Land* and anticipates its itch for anthropology. Like Eliot, Freud draws analogies between the psychic and the cultural, linking 'civilised' obsessionality to 'savage' rites. In both cases the ritual 'is ostensibly a protection against the prohibited act; but actually . . . a repetition of it' (SE XII 50).[21] *The Waste Land* resembles this obsessive rite, because it surreptitiously repeats the horror that it tries to expiate. In particular, it desecrates tradition. The poem may be seen as an extended 'blasphemy', in Eliot's conception of the term, an affirmation masked as a denial. For the text dismantles Western culture as if destruction were the final mode of veneration. . . .

Take, for instance, the opening words. The line 'April is the cruellest month' blasphemes (in Eliot's sense) against the first lines of *The Canterbury Tales,* which presented April's showers as so sweet. At once a nod to origins and a flagrant declaration of beginninglessness, this allusion grafts the poem to another text, vaunting its parasitic in-betweenness. Only the misquotation marks the change of ownership, but the author's personality dissolves in the citational abyss. . . . As blasphemy, *The Waste Land* is obliged to poach upon the past caught in a perpetual allusion to the texts that it denies.[22] . . . Because [the] lines allude to Chaucer, they invoke the origin of the tradition as well as the juvenescence of the year. But words like 'stirring', 'mixing', and 'feeding' profane beginnings, be they literary or organic, provoking us to ask what 'cruelty' has exchanged them for uniting, engendering, or nourishing. Thus the passage whispers of the words its words deny, and sorrows for the things it cannot say. . . . [It typifies] the way *The Waste Land* differs from itself, forever trembling towards another poem which has already been written, or else has yet to be composed.

This betweenness also overtakes the speaking subject, for the first-person pronoun roams from voice to voice.[23] The 'us' in 'Winter kept us warm' glides into the 'us' of 'Summer surprised us' without alerting 'us', the readers, of any change of name or locus. At last, the 'us' contracts into the couple in the Hofgarten, after having spoken for the human, animal and vegetable worlds. What begins as an editorial 'we' becomes the mark of a migration, which restlessly displaces voice and origin. Throughout the poem, the 'I' slips from persona to persona, weaves in and out of quoted speech, and creeps like a contagion through the *Prothalamion* or Pope or the debased grammar of a London pub, sweeping history into a heap of broken images.

However, Eliot insisted in the Notes to *The Waste Land* that Tiresias should stabilise this drifting subject, and rally the nomadic voices of the text. . . . But what *does* Tiresias see? Blind as he is, the prophet has a single walk-on part, when he spies on the typist and her lover indulging in carbuncular caresses. . . . Eliot emphasises the osmosis of identities more than their reunion in a central consciousness . . . Tiresias's role within the poem is to 'melt' distinctions and confuse personae . . . [In this passage] the seer turns into a peeping Tom, the most ambiguous of spectators. 'Throbbing between two lives', Tiresias could be seen as the very prophet of abjection, personifying all the poem's porous membranes. A revisionary, he foresees what he has already foresuffered, mixing memory and desire, self and other, man and woman, pollution and catharsis. . . .

The typist symptomises this betweenness, too. Her profession parodies the poet's, demoted as he is to the typist or amanuensis of the dead. Too untidy to acknowledge boundaries, she strews her bed with stockings, slippers, camisoles, and stays, and even the bed is a divan by day, in a petit bourgeois disrespect for definition. She resembles the neurotic woman in 'A Game of Chess', who cannot decide to go out or to stay in, as if she were at enmity with their distinction. Eliot himself declares that all the women in *The Waste Land* are one woman, and this is because they represent the very principle of unquency. . . . Yet the misogyny is so ferocious, particularly in the manuscript, that it begins to turn into a blasphemy against itself. For the poem is enthralled by the femininity that it reviles, bewitched by this odorous and shoreless flesh. In fact, woman is the spirit of its own construction, the phantom of its own betweennesses. In 'The Fire Sermon', Eliot personifies his broken images in a woman's bruised, defiled flesh:

'Trams and dusty trees.
Highbury bore me. Richmond and Kew
Undid me. By Richmond I raised my knees
Supine on the floor of a narrow canoe.'

'My feet are at Moorgate, and my heart
Under my feet. After the event
He wept. He promised "a new start".

I made no comment. What should I resent?'

'On Margate Sands.
I can connect
Nothing with nothing.
The broken fingernails of dirty hands.
My people humble people who expect
Nothing.'
          la la

To Carthage then I came

Burning burning burning burning
O Lord Thou pluckest me out
O Lord Thou pluckest

burning

(292–311)

The body and the city melt together, no longer themselves but not yet other. It is as if the metaphor were stuck between the tenor and the vehicle, transfixed in an eternal hesitation. Both the woman and the city have been raped, but the 'he' seems passive in his violence, weeping at his own barbarity. . . . The woman's body crumbles in a synecdochic heap of knees, heart, feet, weirdly disorganised: 'My feet are at Moorgate, and my heart/Under my feet.' But the city which undid her decomposes, too, in a random concatenation of its parts – Highbury, Richmond, Kew, Moorgate – and ends in broken fingernails on Margate Sands.

Itinerant and indeterminate, the 'I' slips from the woman to the city, and then assumes the voice of Conrad's Harlequin in *Heart of Darkness*, who apologises for a humble and exploited race. At last it merges with the 'I' who came to Carthage in St Augustine's *Confessions*. As the last faltering words suggest, it is impossible to 'pluck' the speaking subject out of the conflagration of the poem's idioms. . . .

Here no experience is proper or exclusive to the subject. Moreover, the speaker is possessed by the writings of the dead, and seized in a cacophony beyond control. . . .

In 'Tradition and the Individual Talent' Eliot celebrates the voices of the dead, but he comes to dread their verbal ambush in *The Waste Land*. In the essay, he claimed that 'not only the best, but the most individual poetry' is that which is most haunted by its own precursors. Only thieves can truly be original. For any new creation gains its meaning in relation to the poems of the past, and writing is a voyage to the underworld, to commune with the phantasmal voices of the dead. Eliot published this essay immediately after World War I, in 1919, the same year that Freud was writing *Beyond the Pleasure Principle*. As Middleton has pointed out, they both confront the same material: the unprecedented death toll of the First World War. Like Freud's theory of repetition, Eliot's account of influence attempts to salvage something of a past that had never been so ruthlessly annihilated – however fearsome its reanimation from the grave. Whereas Freud discovers the death drive in the compulsion to repeat, *The Waste Land* stages it in the compulsion to citation.

In 1919 Freud also wrote his famous essay on the 'uncanny', which he defines as 'whatever reminds us of this inner compulsion to repeat.'[24] The *Waste Land* is uncanny in a double sense, for it is haunted by the repetition of the dead – in the form of mimicry, quotation and pastiche – but also by a kind of Hammer horror: bats with baby faces, whisper music, violet light, hooded hordes, witches, death's heads, bones, and zombies (378–81). According to Freud, 'heimlich' literally means 'homely' or familiar, but it develops in the direction of ambivalence until it converges with its opposite, *unheimlich* or uncanny.[25] Thus the very word has grown unhomely and improper to itself. The passage Eliot misquotes from *The White Devil* provides a good example of the double meaning of uncanniness:

'Oh keep the Dog far hence, that's friend to men,
'Or with his nails he'll dig it up again! . . .

Since the passage is purloined from Webster, the very words are ghostly revenants, returning as extravagant and erring spirits. This kind of verbal kleptomania subverts the myth that literary texts are private property, or that the author can enjoy the sole possession of his words. But Eliot writes Dog where Webster wrote Wolf, and friend where Webster wrote foe. Thus he tames the hellhound in the same misprision that domesticates the discourse of the past. Friendly pet and wild beast, the Dog becomes the emblem of the poem's literary necrophilia, and the familiar strangeness of the past that Eliot himself has disinterred.

Quotation means that words cannot be anchored to their authors, and the fortune-tellers in the text personify this loss of origin. For prophecy means that we hear about a thing before it happens. The report precedes the event. The bell echoes before it rings. Tiresias, for instance, has not only foreseen but actually 'foresuffered all', as if he were a living misquotation.[26] A fake herself, Madame Sosostris lives in fear of imitators ('Tell her I bring the horoscope myself'), nervous that her words may go astray ('One must be so careful these days'). This anxiety about originality and theft resurges in the form of Mr Eugenides. A Turkish merchant in London, he also speaks demotic French: and the word 'demotic', Greek in etymology, alludes to Egyptian hieroglyphics. Being a merchant, he is not only the product but the sinister conductor of miscegenation, intermingling verbal, sexual and monetary currencies. Even his pocketful of currants could be heard as 'currents', which dissolve identities and definitions like the 'current under sea' that picks the bones of Phlebas, his Phoenician alter ego. His reappearances suggest that repetition has become a virus, unwholesome as the personages who recur. Indeed, the poem hints that literature is nothing but a plague of echoes: that writing necessarily deserts its author, spreading like an epidemic into other texts. Any set of written signs can fall into bad company, into contexts which pervert their meaning and their genealogy.

The worst company in *The Waste Land*, both socially and rhetorically, is the London pub where Lil is tortured by her crony for her bad teeth and her abortion. Here, the publican's cry, 'HURRY UP PLEASE ITS TIME', becomes as vagrant as a written sign, orphaned from its author. Any British drinker knows its origin, of course, so Eliot does not identify the speaker, but sets the phrase adrift on a semantic odyssey. When it interrupts the dialogue, the two discursive sites contaminate each other . . . the more the publican repeats his cry, the more its meaning strays from his intentions. Instead of closing time, it now connotes perfunctory and brutal sexuality: it means that time is catching up with Lil, in the form of dentures and decay, and rushing her culture to apocalypse. There is no omniscient speaker here to monitor these meanings, no 'pill' to control their pullulation. It is as if the words themselves had been demobbed and grown adulterous. When Ophelia's good-byes creep in, just as the dialogue is closing, the allusion dignifies Lil's slower suicide . . . Yet at the same time, the text degrades Ophelia by suturing her words to Lil's, reducing Shakespeare to graffiti.

In general, the poem's attitude towards Shakespeare and the canon resembles taboos against the dead, with their mixture of veneration and horror (SE XIII 25). As Freud says, 'they are expressions of mourning; but on the other hand they clearly betray – what they seek to conceal – hostility against the dead . . .' (SE XIII 61). But he stresses that it is not the dead themselves so much as their 'infection' which is feared, for they are charged with a kind of 'electricity' (SE XIII 20–2, 41). The taboo arises to defend the living subject from their sly invasions. But strangely enough, the taboo eventually becomes prohibited itself, as if the ban were as infectious as the horrors it forbids. Prohibition spreads like a disease, tainting everything that touches it, 'till at last the whole world lies under an embargo' (SE XIII 27). A similar reversal takes place in *The Waste Land*, where the rituals of purity are perverted into *ersatz* desecrations of themselves. When Mrs Porter and her daughter wash their feet in soda water, the ceremony of innocence is drowned, and the baptismal rite becomes its own defilement.

. . . If writing is in league with death, however, it is also in cahoots with femininity. In *The Waste Land*, the 'hearty female stench' converges with the odour of mortality – and both exude from *writing*, from the violated and putrescent corpse of speech. To use the text's sexology, writing and the stink of femininity have overpowered the priapic realm of voice. . . . Now, the strange thing about smell, as opposed to vision for example, is that the subject smelling actually imbibes the object smelt, endangering their separation and integrity. And it is the fear of such displacements that Eliot's misogyny reveals, a terror deeper even than the dread of incest, which is merely the most scandalous offence to place. In *The Waste Land*, the fall of the father unleashes infinite displacements, be they sexual, linguistic or territorial. Even personal identity dissolves into the babble of miscegenated tongues. As effluvia, the feminine dissolves the limits of the private body, and the boundaries of the self subside into pneumatic anarchy. It is as if the father's impotence entailed the dissolution of identity, imaged as asphyxiation in the body of the feminine.

At the end of the poem, Eliot demolishes the discourse of the West, petitioning the East for solace and recovery. . . . Here at last the poem silences its Western noise with Eastern blessings. But ironically, the effort to defeat its own 'concatenated words' has only made the text more polyglot, stammering its orisons in Babel. It is as if the speaking subject had been 'ruined' by the very fragments he had shored. . . . Because the poem can only abject writing with more writing, it catches the infection that it tries to purge, and implodes like an obsessive ceremonial under the pressure of its own contradictions.[27] □

The following, and final, chapter of this Guide plots the trajectory of this implosion in some of the most recent critical readings of the text. Its essays examine further the ideological consequences of *The Waste Land*'s mixing of memory and desire.

CHAPTER SIX

Cultural Readings: Modernism, Ideology and Desire

THE MOST striking development in recent interpretations of *The Waste Land* is the move away from models of impersonality towards critical methodologies that exploit details from Eliot's biography and new theories about modernism in their attempts to explain the seeming riddle that is the poem. *The Waste Land* is now being read, it would seem, as much for what it conceals as what it reveals. This development has had the effect of reconfiguring the ways in which the master poem of modernity is now read by a postmodern readership facing the end of the millennium. It seems unthinkable, now, to attempt to read the poem without considering, in some way, the almost unbearable mental anguish under which Eliot was suffering at the time of its composition. Far from being seen as the epitome of disinterested rational analysis of the modern condition, *The Waste Land* is finally seen as the product of profound personal and cultural trauma. In many ways this realisation about the poem has helped to smooth out – or at least account for – some of the difficulties that have faced readers and critics of the poem since it was first published. It is broken, fragmentary and obscure because it expresses a troubled mind on the brink of collapse; and its analysis of modernity is likewise despairing. Critical analysis of the poem is now thought of in terms of bringing to light the ideologies of the self and of modernism that the poem tries so scrupulously to hide. It is in this sprouting – so to speak – of the corpses that the poem has tried to bury, that criticism of the poem sees a way forward. Broadly speaking, then, the poem is now read deconstructively as a means of getting beneath the surface of modernity in order to expose the workings of its cultural drives and desires.

In terms of Eliot's biography it is now clear that the poem is his attempt, artistically, to sublimate the mental anxieties and frustrations that resulted from his disastrous first marriage, the boredom of his job at Lloyd's Bank, and the crippling schedule of writing and lecturing that he had undertaken. Published in 1984, Peter Ackroyd's biography of Eliot can be seen to have given the impetus to such reassessments of the impact of Eliot's own life on his poetry. An intensely private man, Eliot had remained resolutely tight-lipped about his personal life. However, Ackroyd's book brought to public (and critical) attention details of Eliot's life that had previously been rumoured, or guessed at, but not substantiated. According to Ackroyd, by the late summer of 1921, while struggling to finish the poem that was to become *The Waste Land*, nursing his sick wife Vivien and trying to keep up with his commitments to the literary journal *The Dial*, he suffered a breakdown that resulted from 'acute mental distress'.[1] But, Ackroyd notes, Eliot's distress was not simply personal. To some extent it was symptomatic of a wider public sense of distress at the state of postwar culture. According to Ackroyd:

■ Eliot's distress was not caused by private matters alone, since he told [Richard] Aldington that public events had provoked in him a mood of despair. The year in which *The Waste Land* was written was one of intense political and economic discontent: the post-war 'boom' had collapsed, there were two million unemployed and the economic chaos was exacerbated by the indecisiveness of the coalition government. Eliot despised democracy, he explained to Aldington in the same letter, and he described in vivid terms the feelings of loathing and repugnance which the contemporary situation induced in him.

It was precisely under the strain of these difficult circumstances that he began consistently to work on the poem . . .[2] □

What readers (especially those *not* of a New Critical persuasion) have long suspected, and what we have seen throughout the poem's critical history – that the poem arises from a severe personal and cultural crisis – is now firmly established as a critical commonplace. The extracts that make up this final chapter all seek to explore further the implications upon reading *The Waste Land* of such knowledge. They are all interested in the light that can be thrown on to modernism's persuasive ideology by Eliot's feelings of despair, loathing and repugnance when faced with 'the contemporary situation'. In short, as we shall see, they all attempt to get to the roots of Eliot's and modernity's hidden prejudices.

Recent examinations of the sort of 'high' or 'aesthetic' modernism represented by Eliot and (most especially) Ezra Pound have shown the ways in which modernism endorses totalitarian politics.[3] In the particular case of Eliot, much recent critical debate has focused on the question of his anti-Semitism and the extent to which this can be seen as a symptom of wider cultural prejudices that haunt modernist ideology. Though Eliot's anti-Semitism and right-wing politics are briefly discussed in Ackroyd's biography, it was Anthony Julius' book *T. S. Eliot: Anti-Semitism and Literary Form* (1995) that brought such matters to the forefront of critical (and public) debate about Eliot's poetry.[4] Julius' book represents the culmination of many of the arguments over the political implications of modernist aesthetics in which academics and critics have been engaged for at least the last two decades.

While his argument about the pervasiveness of anti-Semitic thinking within modernism is vehement, and his emphasising of the inescapable connection between anti-Semitism in poetic practice and in political practice is timely, Julius seems unable to extricate himself from an apparent contradiction that has troubled many recent critiques of modernist poetry, namely the contradiction between condemnation of its political message and endorsement of its aesthetics. He finds himself caught uncomfortably on the horns of a peculiarly modernist dilemma; he loves the poetry but hates the politics:

■ Of Modernism and anti-Semitism, and their connections, one has to ask: what can the history of infamy have to do with the examination of a major twentieth-century literary movement? The one study entails condemnation, the other, endorsement. Approaching anti-Semitism from the perspective of Modernism risks trivialising the horror in contemporary Jewish history. Interpreting Modernism from the perspective of anti-Semitism seems both perverse and reductive. Examining either one by reference to the other would seem to guarantee that justice is done to neither. There are thus books on Eliot that pretend he had nothing to say about Jews. Conversely, there are studies of anti-Semitism in which he will be cited without any acknowledgement that he was a poet or that the quoted passage is itself poetry of a high and challenging order.[5] □

But such a recognition of the dilemma facing a reader of Eliot's poetry does little to resolve such a dilemma. It merely reconfigures it as an unresolved problem of aesthetic value. In Julius' reading, therefore, Eliot's poetry is redeemed (or at least significantly loosened from its collusion with anti-Semitism), as it were, by the fact that it is 'poetry of a high and challenging order'. Curiously, Julius' critique of Eliot reinscribes the contradiction between radicalism and conservatism that has been felt to be central to *The Waste Land* throughout its critical history. Now, more than ever, it seems necessary that for a critical reading of *The*

Waste Land to resolve such apparent contradictions, it needs to be based in a critical practice that can fully acknowledge that one's enjoyment of the poem is part of one's complicity with the political structures it proposes. What is called for, then, in contemporary critiques of the poem, is an examination of the structures of cultural power and the strategies of persuasion by which the poem performs and produces modernism's collusive ideology.

The first major extract of this chapter is taken from Christopher Ricks' book *T.S. Eliot and Prejudice* (1988). This was one of the first major critical works on Eliot to tackle the problem of the complicity of Eliot's poetry with the prejudices – political, social and cultural – of his age. While Ricks' examination of *The Waste Land* may, therefore, be seen to owe much to the opening up of critical assumptions about it that had been performed earlier by critics such as David Craig and Terry Eagleton, it is interested less in developing a radical critique of the poem's political agenda than in examining the very process itself by which poetry comes to have political force. As a result of this, Ricks' reading of the poem can seem rather equivocal. On the one hand it is refreshing in its questioning of the structures of thought *from* which the poem arises, and *with* which critics have sought to explain the poem. In this sense Ricks certainly does attend to the call for a new – broadly deconstructive – criticism of the poem that is fully aware of the ideological gestures of the modernism that it puts into play. On the other hand, however, Ricks' essay is terribly frustrating, with the very intricacy of his argument tending to obscure the force of its own convictions. Ricks' high sophistication may be equal to that of Eliot's, but it has the effect of turning the concept of prejudice, upon which the book's central argument rests, into such a diffuse notion that, in terms of reading the poetry, it is a rather blunt instrument.[6]

Despite this, Ricks' analysis of *The Waste Land* is full of fascinating new insights into the poem. Most interesting is the way in which a consideration of questions of nationality and cultural identity emerges from his examination of the slippages and gaps in the poem between its differing voices and textual fragments. What Ricks' methodology suggests, therefore, is that the poem's radical form as multicultural mosaic is what speaks most clearly of the disruptions and confused hybridity of European culture in the early years of the century. Its prejudices are part and parcel of this many-layered confusion and can be seen to seep out, as it were, via the cracks between the text's constitutive fragments. In effect, then, Ricks re-engages the central problem that has exercised critics of the poem throughout its history – whether or not it has formal coherence – in order to deconstruct the culture from which the text is produced. In Ricks' reading, *The Waste Land* closes on an untranslatable 'shantih' because it realises the limits of both Western culture and its own prejudices. What makes Ricks' analysis of the poem so revealing and suggestive is that he notes so very clearly how the text tries to look beyond its prejudices, but finds them continually re-affirmed by what it never manages fully to articulate. This leads the way for the critical extracts that follow on from Ricks in this chapter. If Ricks charts the poem's desire to say what is unsayable in, and through, its culture, then Frank Lentricchia and Harriet Davidson plot the extent to which the desires of modern culture itself are framed by the poem and our reading of the poem.

■ *The Waste Land* is a congregation of voids. The 'dead sound' of a church clock; the tarot card 'Which is blank'; 'the violet hour' which issues in a 'throbbing between two lives': all of these are fostered by the encompassing vacuum of silence or rather silences. There is the wounded malignant silence of the woman and her hair which 'Glowed into words, then would be savagely still'; and the painful benignant silence that is 'the heart of light, the silence', Heart of Darkness astonishingly flooded with light. There is 'the frosty silence in the gardens'; and the horror which is at once heraldic and animal: 'The jungle crouched, humped in silence.' But perhaps even this last is not the worst. 'There is not even silence in the mountains.' . . .

A relation of the sound of sense to the sense of void is intimated in the opening words of *The Waste Land*, perfectly clear in their meaning but with an elemental simplicity of doubt as to just what word is to be stressed, what exactly is the posture proper to the opening.

> April is the cruellest month, breeding
> Lilacs out of the dead land, mixing
> Memory and desire, stirring
> Dull roots with spring rain.

Manifestly the first five words are a disagreement with – even a courteous rebuke to – something which it is believed that you senti-mentally believe. The speaker reveals a preconception, or a prejudice, as to a preconception or prejudice of yours. But is this fixed upon April or upon the cruelty of months? If you stress 'April', then the meaning is: 'April – and not as you will have thought, November – is the cruellest month'. If you stress 'cruellest', the meaning is: 'April is the cruellest – and not as you will have thought, the kindest – month'. These two intonations are more likely contestants than, for instance, 'April *is* the cruellest month', though this is not impossible: it would convey to a listener an insistence that the grim fact be admitted 'April is, come on, admit that you really know this to be so, despite the usual romanticizing of April – the cruellest month.' Or it would convey someone bringing home this acknowledgement fully to himself: 'April is – I really do have to admit it, odd though this be – the cruellest month.'

The force of this opening, its unforgettability, is in its combination of unmistakable directness with all these lurking possibilities of mistaking its direction. On the one hand, the gist and pith of the opening words are not in doubt; on the other, much might hang upon the exact discrimination of what we are being disagreed with about, or of the prevailing presupposition about our presupposition.

. . . What we are thought to think is related to what we may be expected to know, and often the intonation (and the sound of sense) of a poem may be affected profoundly by some prior piece of knowledge invoked, such as gives a particular dramatic embodiment to the words. . . . Here the sound of sense is the refraction . . . of thoughts in a head, met by a counter-thought. 'April is the cruellest month.'

Or take the opening not of the first but of the last section of *The Waste Land*.

> After the torchlight red on sweaty faces
> After the frosty silence in the gardens
> After the agony in stony places
> The shouting and the crying
> Prison and palace and reverberation
> Of thunder of spring over distant mountains
> He who was living is now dead
> We who were living are now dying
> With a little patience

The first three lines announce their sound of sense, their intonation an incantation. But it is not at first clear, and it is never at last clarified, in exactly what way the ensuing fourth line comes 'after' those three premonitions. Is it: After A, after B, after C: then D? Or is the fourth line too another After, simply no longer needing to reiterate After since by now the word can tacitly govern the lines? After A, after B, after C, [after] D – and so into what would be the same syntactical dubiety of the fifth and sixth lines. The sequence is clear as to each unit of meaning but not as to its articulate energy. Is it a series of lines that stretches out to the crack of doom, the doom finally arrived at as 'He who was living is now dead'? Then the voice, an Atlas, will have to hold up everything from 'After the torchlight' through to the distant words 'distant mountains', only then coming upon the painful thought it has been painfully seeking. Or is the voice to arrive earlier? After that, and that, and that, then this, this, this. What is being asked in the reading is what is being creatively contemplated in the writing, something finally though only equivocally arrived at: patience.

. . . Is 'With a little patience' a retrospect or a prospect? The effect depends upon there being no punctuation supplied such as would placate our impatience and settle the matter: no full stop after 'dying' or after 'patience'. . . .

And to what end, all this? The realization of patience, the incarnating of what it is to possess one's soul in patience. For patience is itself a relation of past to future here in the present. To be patient is to relate a future to a past here and now. . . . Yet patience may save us. For whereas courage presupposes no such relation of past to future, patience does, like its companions endurance, fortitude and perseverance. All of these are virtues especially important to Eliot in their kinship to tradition, the literary and cultural embodiment of a relation of past to future such as is in the best sense living in the present. In patience, retrospect and prospect meet in a re-affirmation, just as retrospect and prospect meet in the play of Eliot's syntax against his line-endings and his punctuation or lack of it – yet not a complete lack of it, since, as Eliot said, 'verse, whatever else it may or may not be, is itself a system of punctuation; the usual marks of punctuation themselves are differently employed'.[7]

. . . The tonal recesses of foreignness echo before even the first line of *The Waste Land*, since the epigraph from Petronius does not simply give us both Latin and Greek, it gives us Latin within which Greek is spoken. How confident can we be of tone within such vistas? There is an instability even in the signal difference of the alphabets, which we see with our own eyes.

Nam Sibyllam quidem Cumis ego ipse oculis meis vidi in ampulla pendere, et cum illi pueri dicerent: Σίβυλλα τί θέλεις: respondebat illa: ἀποθανεῖν θέλω.

He may have seen the Sibyl with his own eyes, but can we hear with our own ears what the boys say and what she replies? So much of the life of tone is efficacy of feeling, and Eliot pointed out that 'it is easier to think in a foreign language than it is to feel in it'; what then of feeling in a foreign language which is ensconced within another foreign language? And both of them, dead languages here, in one of which someone says, but not then in our living language, 'I want to die'.

Or what of the tone within the first foreign words of the poem proper, words which are not only foreign but are about the complications of foreignness and whether a Lithuanian be Russian or German or even perhaps simply Lithuanian?

> . . . we stopped in the colonnade,
> And went on in sunlight, into the Hofgarten,
> And drank coffee, and talked for an hour.
> Bin gar keine Russin, stamm' aus Litauen, echt deutsch.

. . . it is not only that the single line of German gives us so little context, but that the snatch which is all that comes to our ear is not of our tongue. . . . A further kind of wondering is invited by the lines than the one about what had since happened to the woman from Lithuania. Wondering about the tone; not about what her words meant exactly but about what exactly she meant by them. For one marked feature of the foreign eruptions within *The Waste Land* is their initiating themselves as not only foreign but about foreignness: first a Lithuanian speaking German about not being Russian, and then, twenty lines later, someone singing in German about his Irish girl, '*Mein Irisch Kind*'.

What the Lithuanian said is finally overtaken by 'What the Thunder said'. What the Thunder said is massively clear: DA. What the Thunder meant is massively unclear, or rather is categorically clear since the meaning is a consequence of the category to which the listener belongs. DA is heard differently by each group. This bespoken hearing is prejudgement or prejudice pushed to both unanimity and dissent, unanimity within the group and dissent from the other groups. It is the interpretative community raised to divine heights.

The most straightforward elucidation of DA is this:

> Three groups – gods, demons, men – approach the creator Parajapti and each in turn asks him to speak. To each group he answers 'DA'. Each group interprets this reply differently. According to the fable, 'This is what the divine voice, the Thunder, repeats when he says DA, DA, DA: 'Control yourselves; give alms; be compassionate.'[8]

But, bringing this home, Eliot reinterprets this foreign parable of interpretation and its categorial inevitabilities. The re-ordering of the sequence may remind us that here too prejudice is sequential. . . . But what Eliot then puts at the very end, in his final act both of control and of surrender, is the movement into the other word or words of Sanskrit:

> Why then Ile fit you. Hieronymo's mad againe.
> Datta. Dayadhvam. Damyata.
>   Shantih shantih shantih

The very end, and yet not, since after as many as five full-stops within the antepenultimate and penultimate lines, perfect peace asks no punctuation. Here is no formal ending.

Eliot had two tries at explaining what he had effected with 'Shantih', and neither of them will quite do. The note as originally published reads:

> Shantih. Repeated as here, a formal ending to an Upanishad. 'The Peace which passeth understanding' is a feeble translation of the content of this word.

The note as revised in later editions reads: '. . . "The Peace which passeth understanding" is our equivalent to this word.' But neither was quite it. Eliot did well to repudiate the slight to such wording as is a glory of Christianity in English, 'The Peace which passeth understanding'; to call this a feeble translation of the content of the Sanskrit word is not only the wrong kind of surrender but also questionable in itself, for strictly speaking 'The Peace which passeth understanding' is not a translation of the content of the Sanskrit. But in remedying this slight, Eliot played into the hands of those who would accuse him of ostentatious pretension in having recourse to Sanskrit, for if 'The Peace which passeth understanding' really is 'our equivalent to this word', why not simply use our equivalent? The thought of an equivalent is both unavoidable and misguided. What Eliot achieves in the words of the poem, and does not quite find words for in the notes, is something else: the poignant admission that even so perfect a phrase as 'The Peace which passeth understanding' can no longer effect within our culture what 'Shantih' can effect within its culture. There should be no surprise that this word of Sanskrit which – until Eliot gave it such currency – was itself likely in the most literal sense to pass understanding should mean 'The Peace which passeth understanding'.

. . . Though there is a sense in which Eliot is indeed thinking in traditional Christian terms, one of his saddened thoughts is that such thinking and feeling have become enfeebled ('a feeble translation . . .'). The poem's pain is in the acknowledgement that it is only outside our own traditional terms that we can now even conceive of the peace which passeth understanding, while at the same time the fact that this is outside our own culture means that we can do no more than conceive of it, cannot enter into and possess it. . . .

'And the peace of God, which passeth all understanding, shall keep your hearts and minds through Christ Jesus.' But what if, in our Waste Land, our hearts and minds do not any longer keep 'the peace which passeth understanding'?

If such chastened losses and chastening ungainabilities are Eliot's admonitory art here, then Conrad Aiken mistook the poet's purpose:

> Why, again, Datta, Dayadhvam, Damyata? Or Shantih? Do they not say a good deal less for us than 'Give: sympathize: control' or 'Peace'? Of course; but Mr Eliot replies that he wants them not merely to mean those particular things, but also to mean them in a particular way – that is, to be remembered in connexion with a Upanishad. Unfortunately, we have none of us this memory, nor can he give it to us; and in the upshot he gives us only a series of agreeable sounds which might as well have been nonsense.[9]

There can be no doubt that Eliot wants the Sanskrit words to mean in a particular way, but '*remembered* in connexion with a Upanishad' is too uninterested in the difference in the depth of 'remembered'. To remember it as a surface item of information is one thing, but to have it alive within a deeper memory is quite another. Aiken sees fit to remind Eliot that 'Unfortunately, we have none of us this memory, nor can he give it to us' – as if Eliot were so stupid and so out of touch as ever to have supposed otherwise. The inaccessibility, except to merely schooled memory, of 'Shantih' is Eliot's piercing point. 'The Peace which passeth understanding' has passed from our memory; 'Shantih' can never be part of our memory. There is little peace in the thought, but there is much more thought than is suggested by 'only a series of agreeable sounds which might as well have been nonsense'.[10] □

Frank Lentricchia's consideration of the cultural force and impact of *The Waste Land* (from his magnificent reconsideration of the culture of modernism, *Modernist Quartet* (1994)) shares with that of Ricks a sense that the poem is animated by the desire to escape, or go beyond, the limits of its culture. For Ricks, as we have just seen, the poem passes deliberately into a cultural aporia: it tries to speak that which cannot be spoken by its mixing of memory and desire. And for Lentricchia, the poem continually exceeds its desires, it reaches beyond what he terms its 'plan'. In fact,

Lentricchia's essay describes the way in which *The Waste Land* can be seen to have passed through a number of different cultural mediations in its desire to escape from itself, and from the 'loathing and repugnance' which, we were told earlier in this chapter, Eliot felt towards the modern world. The poem mediates, according to Lentricchia, between Eliot's private and public lives by detailing the frustrations of his unhappy marriage while also acting as 'the signature of a lost generation'. It acts out Eliot's frustrations in writing poetry for a culture in which poetry will never pay the rent, while its mythic structure is an attempt to mediate between such everyday economic concerns and truths that are felt to be everlasting. Even the poem's critical history is a narrative of mediation; Lentricchia notes that 'it is hardly possible anymore to read the poem without passing through scholarly mediation', and thereby implies that although the poem necessitates such cultural interventions, it also articulates the desire to escape their necessity. The poem itself, the real pleasure of the text, has been lost, and yet that loss is precisely the message of *The Waste Land*, it is this which assures its 'cultural centrality'.

In Lentricchia's carefully wrought and delicately argued reading of the poem, then, desire is central; the desire to overcome loss, the desire to escape the conditions of modernity that the poem frames: 'the driving desire at work in *The Waste Land*', he notes, is 'to get out of the waste land'. Ultimately, this desire leads to the poem's closing imagery of final escape, apocalypse, and thus mediates between the real world and its imagined conclusion. It is this, Lentricchia argues, which defines *The Waste Land*'s modernity. And it is this which assures Lentricchia's crucial position in the critical history of the poem:

■ Three events set the shape and texture of Eliot's everyday life through the publication of *The Waste Land* in 1922. In 1915, he decided to move to London; in the same year, he met and married (in rapid succession) Vivienne [*sic*] Haigh-Wood; in the month they were married, *Poetry* published 'Prufrock'. Thanks to 'Prufrock', Eliot entered the avant-garde with a splash, as a writer of such originality that, on the basis of this single poem, he was established as the new poet to watch, a tone-setter. But *The Waste Land* brought him out of the alluring literary underground for good, where Pound remained as a writer's writer, to the riveted attention of the literary world at large. *The Waste Land* made Eliot at once the towering poet of modernism and its public face, the figure to whom those who cared (and those who did not care) for modernism would need to pay attention, an awesome image, idolized and detested. Very quickly, *The Waste Land* ceased to be a poem to be read and became a phrase to be intoned, the essence of a perspective and an attitude, the signature of a lost generation: in other words, a cultural event that got beyond Eliot's intention and control. The scandalous success of the poem, the reams of commentary it has spawned, its centrality for the teaching of modern literature, all have had the double effect of making Eliot a major force in world literature while obscuring the specific narrative of his life and poetry. More than any other figure of literary modernism, we have tended to know Eliot – and, consequently, to like him or dislike him – as a reputation.

. . . Eliot's views of what 'literature' ought to be and how it ought to function were influenced in large part by his reading, and they were expressed on numerous celebrated occasions in critical writings that span his career. But these views were also driven by the economically constrained life he felt forced to lead in London – and 'forced' is half right and half wrong. 'Right' because it would be difficult to imagine anyone, with foreknowledge, choosing the misery in which he lived; 'wrong' because Eliot believed that the life we get – he got – was a matter of desire, if not choice: 'everybody gets the kind of life he wants', as he put it to his brother in 1916.

From all manner of sources Eliot knew the romantic claim that poetry was radically different from all other kinds of writing: it presumably resisted utilitarian manipulation, it was autonomous, a unique thing working only for its own ends. Despite declaring himself to be against romanticism on various occasions, he tended to accept these staple propositions of literary theory in the romantic mode, especially in his early career. But the truth of the theory that authentic poetry has no function in the world of profit and loss he learned from experience. It would not feed him and Vivienne or pay the rent, unlike, say, editing, or writing for the popular press, or teaching literature at night to working-class people who taught *him*, to his delight, that they too took a disinterested view of literary experience, they too valued it for itself. The autonomous nature of art, his art in particular, had economic effects in life, his life. Other kinds of writing might pay the rent – Frost and Pound had tried their hand at fiction, because with fiction you might get lucky – but poetry of the high modernist moment, Eliot's poetry certainly, was economically hopeless, which, of course, it was supposed to be (he got the life he wanted).

And so the more his time was eaten up by economically necessary pursuits, the less time he had for writing poems (exactly the life he wanted!), the more deeply special those moments became, because they opened up an alternative space of consciousness, another level of living. . . .

Like Stevens, Pound and Frost, Eliot was a modern American man, with all the problems that the world imposes upon one who chooses to become a poet. Eliot, too, was a full-fledged citizen of the bourgeois world, a modern writer in a sense that Yeats was not. Yeats had fired away at similar social enemies of poetry, but from a position that the American modernists could not assume, with memories of a hospitable aristocratic (Anglo-Irish) past, a real Coole Park become a Coole Park of the mind, a bitter but delicious nostalgia that was poetically productive, a memory which no American could share.

The modern American poets (Stevens is the exception: he would never lift a finger on his own literary behalf) cultivated literary schizophrenia: they pursued poetry as an alternative culture yet worked mightily to make their poetry and themselves, as figures of the poet, important, influential, and, in a word that Eliot never shied away from, *powerful*. In the process of composition, a poem was to put one on another plane of existence beyond the reach of the reason that reigned in the culture of capital. . . .

It is the mind of Europe that Eliot, in 'Gerontion' and *The Waste Land*, surrenders himself to, because he believes it to be more valuable than his private mind, and in so surrendering enters a literary community of long historical duration, as the 'conscious present'. This consciousness attaches epigraphs to its poems (in a language not necessarily English: the mind of *Europe*) and tends to express itself in associative leaps (embodied in the discontinuities of collagelike formations) – leaps that defy logic and chronology because the 'conscious present' is aware of the past all at once, as a totality, not as a linear series of events. Allusion for this kind of consciousness is not a simple literary strategy, a knowledge of the past manipulated in the present by a writer dispassionately distant from the past, but a mode of consciousness whose nature is historical. . . .

The Waste Land is the fullest working-through of the impulses, and the voice of those impulses, driving Eliot's major early work, a poem that needed to be written after 'Prufrock' and 'Gerontion'. Its formal and spiritual inspirations are complex and difficult to discriminate, but nevertheless in rough presence they are clear. James G. Frazer's *The Golden Bough* and Jessie L. Weston's *From Ritual to Romance* are the anthropological sources Eliot names in his notes to the poem, the books that gave him stories of ritual pagan religious practices – hints, as he took them, for literary form and a possible narrative of redemption (personal and collective, a distinction not much admired by Frazer, Weston and Eliot). Frazer and Weston were sources for a deep structural underpinning of *The Waste Land* that, thanks to Eliot and a number of his explicators, have been made too much of (both the sources and the deep structural underpinning). . . .

The basic narrative, its rituals and symbols, provides, Eliot says, 'the plan' of his poem: plot, intention, design, and the attendant values of 'the plan'. Knowledge of the plan is useful if we are going to grasp Eliot's historical consciousness, his playing against the anthropological plan with contemporary characters, situation, and dialogue (the living theater of the plan). The counterpointing and the setting up of diminished and truncated (and sometimes comic) contemporary parallels constitutes 'the mythic method' of the poem, which other writers could learn from Joyce, Eliot thought, and would need to follow, as if *Ulysses* were a scientific model, if they would write in a form appropriate to the modern world, and if they were to control – give order, 'a shape and significance' – to what he called, in the essay on Joyce, 'the immense panorama of futility and anarchy which is contemporary history'. He meant contemporary history viewed and evaluated from the prospect provided by 'the plan' – or at least he should have meant that.

Milton leaned on the Bible and on all those who had read it or had absorbed its myths without necessarily reading it, not having to read it because they lived in the culture of the Bible – these readers comprised his potential readership and gave Milton a chance at cultural centrality and immortality. Eliot, by leaning on still rather obscure texts in anthropology, would appear to have had no chance to make *The Waste Land* a readable text outside the modernist coterie. Nevertheless, *The Waste Land* has achieved a certain diminished centrality by finding a readership of insiders, other poets whose careers were in part formed by negative reactions to the poem or what they thought the poem stood for: Hart Crane, William Carlos Williams; a movement of antiformalist poets in the 1950s and 1960s; and, most crucially, university readers, academic literary critics and the generations of their students who were taught what they needed to know in order to avail themselves of the insider's pleasures; they were taught not only Frazer and Weston but the classic texts of the Western literary tradition, the university being perhaps the last place where those texts may be systematically and rigorously read. As the keeper of what are called canonical texts, the university has become what Eliot would never have approved of for his idea of a healthy society: the cordoned-off preserver of literary culture, the institution that unavoidably puts at the margin what it preserves; the literary department, in other words, as upscale bohemian enclave, site of the last serious readers of the major literature of the West. 'Alienated readers' is understood.

For all those so armed with special decoding devices, the poem, beginning (obviously now) with its title, becomes a radiant series of organic fragments, survivals or traces, in a minor key, of ancient ritual and deep persistent myth. In its first section, 'The Burial of the Dead' (an echo of the Anglican burial service), are found the imagery from the desert, the brown fogs of Dickens and Robert Louis Stevenson, the stony rubbish, the dead tree, and the dry stone which gives no sound of water; the references to the Tarot cards, and particularly the reference to The Hanged Man, figure of a dead God, a Christ-like being who may be reborn, but which the fortune-teller cannot find, and the gruesome but thematic humor of the planted corpse beginning to sprout. In the second section, 'A Game of Chess', are counterpointed scenes of marriage, impotence, and abortion; in 'The Fire Sermon', variations on the theme of infertile love, and again the brown land, the river 'sweating' oil and tar (a startling figure of the perversions of nature, human and otherwise); in the fourth, the ambiguous 'Death by Water', the title itself as reference to a central nature-cult ceremony of rebirth; and, lastly, in 'What the Thunder Said', are the references to Gethsemane, the journey through the desert, the approach to the chapel perilous, and the anticipation of life-renewing rain. With the aid of Frazer and Weston, *The Waste Land* reads as an ironic quest-romance, filtered through a modernist aesthetic of collage whose effect is to deny narrative progression and change and to insist on a nightmare of temporal simultaneity.

The pleasures of knowing the plan, pleasures attendant upon structural understanding and getting the real story – secret allegory, decoding, riddle-solving, secret translation – are never the pleasures of texture, sensuous pleasures of aesthetic encounter, delights of the surface – values of reading *The Waste Land* that have, oddly, receded over time, that familiarity has not enhanced. It is the pleasure of the plan, the primacy of structure, that has been enhanced over time. It is hardly possible anymore to read the poem without passing through scholarly mediation: the explanations of anthropological sources, the fixing of literary sources, echoes, allusions, and their skillful annotation. No university reader can do otherwise, or would think of doing otherwise, or maybe should do otherwise. The cultural centrality of *The Waste Land*, as *the* pessimistic expression of the lost generation, is the centrality that critics and scholars, with Eliot's boost, have made. Yet the plan, though it underlies the poem, does so faintly and obscurely, tactfully so, despite all the academic labor to make the plan 'obvious', an unavoidable structural presence in constant control of the details of the surface. And the elucidated literary allusions and quotations also now sit there 'obviously', as if Eliot had written his poem standing up, notebook in hand, in front of his library shelves, yanking off the proper texts, putting in the telling quotations.

The Waste Land made by scholarship is largely cold and willful – an image of Eliot that the anti-Eliot movement in poetry and criticism, from the fifties through the seventies . . . was happy to seize upon in efforts to write and promote a new antiformal poetry (as though Eliot's work were not a formal oddball) and to promote the reputations of Hart Crane, William Carlos Williams, Wallace Stevens, and the romantic literary tradition, broadly defined, back to Spenser, that the young Eliot at times, and his inheritors in the New Criticism very often, had trashed. The countertrashing of Eliot and the New Critics helped to refocus our vision of literary history, reinstating movements and figures necessarily excluded by Eliot's and his New Critical inheritors' notion of authentic literary tradition. The countertrashing, so richly deserved, was also useful.

In any effort to encounter a more immediate incarnation of *The Waste Land* we might be helped by what Eliot said about Ben Jonson in *The Sacred Wood*: 'Though he was saturated in literature, he never sacrifices the theatrical qualities – theatrical in the most favorable sense – to literature or to the study of character. His work is a titanic show.' *The Waste Land*, quintessence of modernist experiment, a poem loaded with learning and 'literature', is never sacrificed to 'literature'.

By 'theater' and 'theatrical', Eliot intended several things: first, the literary form he thought best suited down through the eras to meet, engage, and capture the life of the writer's times (the historicality of theater); second, a writer's literary self-consciousness of being *in performance* while writing, seeing himself in a dramatic light, in the act of creating himself as a character; third, a music-hall show, a series of entertainments, or the music-hall performer himself, represented for Eliot best by *her*self, Marie Lloyd, the entertainer whose death moved him to cultural mourning in a short essay published in the year of *The Waste Land*, in which he extols her organic genius, that special connection she activated with her audience, whom she led to discover and know itself as contributing, on-site artistic support of her (in several senses) *living* art.

The Waste Land as theater is attested to by Eliot's own recorded performance and by the frequency with which it turns up as a text for readers' theater on college campuses – persuasive testimony to the poem's dramatic character and possibilities, with its five parts functioning as five separate shows, replete with characters from all classes, language 'high' and 'low', jokes, dialogue, playlets, gossip, sex, popular and operatic song (something for everyone) . . . *The Waste Land* is a titanic variety show (a *satura*, a mixture) offering the pleasures of the theater, pleasures independent of deep structure and myth, analytic intellect, or literary knowledge, pleasures one need not be an insider to enjoy and that cannot be excited by attention to 'plan' and 'mythic method'.

One of Eliot's notes in particular, however, throws up an insuperable barrier to the experiencing of such various pleasures. It is the note on Tiresias which states that Tiresias . . ., who makes his initial (overt) appearance in 'The Fire Sermon', is 'the most important personage in the poem, uniting all the rest'. Various figures, Eliot says, 'melt' into one another; 'all the women are one woman, and the two sexes meet in Tiresias. What Tiresias *sees*, in fact, is the substance of the poem.' This note does the same kind of texture-obliterating (melting) work that Eliot's comments on Weston, Frazer, and 'the plan' had already done. Once again we are encouraged to plunge below the surface, so variegated, to a deep structural principle, by definition homogeneous, essential, and reductive. Whether via Weston, or whether via Tiresias-the-unifying-voice, the poem's presumably presiding consciousness, we come to the same place, where all theater and theatricality, all particularity, vanishes into thin air. No music hall that operated on such principles would last for more than a night. We are not entertained; we are bored when all the women are one woman and all the men one man.

The misleading (and self-misled, if Eliot believed it) note on Tiresias is useful if taken to suggest a less reductive principle of reading, the author's helpful hint for encountering his poem's aesthetic (sensuous, vocal) cohesion in the face of a collection of fragments that might seem unifiable only at the level of deep structure (unity apparent to intellect, not ear or eye). The note on Tiresias, so understood, becomes an instrument for the unveiling of *The Waste Land*'s persistent vocal presence, a presiding but not devouring voice that intones the poem's opening lines, a voice authoritative, prophetic, elegiac, moral, and . . . always soul-weary: 'April is the cruellest month.' This voice, so strongly 'written', quickly disappears in 'The Burial of the Dead' into characters like the insomniac Marie, the fortune-teller, Madame Sosostris, and the unnamed joker who madly teases Stetson about his blooming corpse – disappears, that is, into 'speech', the conversational rhythms of contemporary characters; then into the formal dialogues, the diptych that comprises most of 'A Game of Chess'; then into the music, bawdy and stately, that appears in 'The Fire Sermon'; then, transformed, as the voice which sings the formal lyric of 'Death by Water' and drives the incantation of 'What the Thunder Said.'

This persistent voice, this would-be voice-over, this voice that would stay above and outside, giving moral perspective, delivering judgments dour and covert, in effect falls inside, becoming itself frequently a subject of waste when, for example, toward the end of its introduction of the first dialogue in 'A Game of Chess', we suddenly find it inside the suffocating interior it describes, falling from its perch, the safety of the simple past tense, down into the entrapment of the present participle and the room of desiccation: 'Staring forms/ Leaned out, leaning, hushing the room enclosed.' Or, in other telling moments, when we feel the rhythms of the voice-over duplicated as the rhythms of the unnamed man who fails in the hyacinth garden; or when the persistent vocal presence is spoken *to*, made a sexual offer, *made* a character, in effect, by the proposition of Mr Eugenides; or when, in perhaps as telling a moment as we will find in the poem, the voice-over becomes another of the walking urban dead, lured by the mandolin playing in a workers' pub on lower Thames Street, a pub adjacent to the splendid church of Magnus Martyr, adjacent institutions neither of which he can participate in. The mandolin sounds in his mind in tandem with the music of Ariel, heard by Ferdinand in *The Tempest*, Shakespeare's late play of transformation and redemption. This voice-over, this contemporary Ferdinand (searching for his Miranda, in this poem of numerous failures of love), this head full of echoes and memories of rebirth, who will not himself be reborn, does not go into the pub he wants to go into, where, or so he imagines, life is not lived in the mind: pub and church, side by side, an image of the unified, organic community for which Eliot longed. This lyric moment from 'The Fire Sermon' (257–65) is perhaps the most telling in the poem because it incarnates, in a plain-styled diction, the driving desire at work in *The Waste Land* to get out of the waste land. Desire so framed – the passage sits virtually at the center of the poem – is critical desire. The problem is not being able to come to terms with the modern metropolis, whose scene provides the details of the poem's setting, the debilitating context for a shape-changing urban stroller in the financial district, trying to forget the profit and the loss, a consciousness that would preside over the waste land with moral clarity, but more often than not finds itself losing its authority, becoming resident within. Eliot does not find his 'Miranda', that 'something which is more valuable' to which he would sacrifice his 'self'.

But the immediacy of this voice is not the immediacy of sound by itself, cut off from intellect. It is the immediacy of a total sensibility that takes in the London scene all at once as sensuous datum (of mainly repulsive detail) and as object of knowledge. This is a mind that looks at the world and does not think, London is 'like' Dante's *Inferno*; this is a mind that looks at London and sees Dante's *Inferno*; a mind that imagines the sexually indifferent typist and doesn't think, 'In Oliver Goldsmith it would have been different' (Eliot counts on us getting the difference), but more importantly cannot experience the real except through literary mediation; as a literary voice yielding itself constantly to other literary voices; a mind that looks at 'life' and sees 'literature' in action. The experience of voice in this poem is dramatically concrete, like the experience of a playgoer who, through the medium of the actors' voices, gains access to a presiding mind that functions as the 'conscious present', and 'awareness of the past in a way and to an extent which the past's awareness of itself cannot show', a mind not *with* a perception, but *as* a perception, 'not only of the pastness of the past, but of its presence'. But this presiding consciousness, heterogeneous and impure, this 'conscious present', this head full of memories of literature and ancient ritual, is also the conscious past, in a way and to an extent which the past, as past, could never be conscious – that is, as an awareness of the present from the point of view of the past.

The Waste Land is finally a traditional poem, not because it looks like any poem that was written before it (it does not), but because its experiments in form, its splintered negotiations of a poetic consciousness in full flight from subjective stability (escaping its personality), make sense only as they engage and revivify traditional writers in ways that those writers could never have imagined or desired, in a world that those writers did not imagine. *The Waste Land* is not a monument of literary history. It is an image of literary history itself in the act of undergoing difficult transformation, abandoning, as Eliot put it in 'Tradition and the Individual Talent', 'nothing *en route*'.

We can see *The Waste Land* conceived as its anthropological substructure, a 'plan' now not so obscure; or *The Waste Land* as sensuous embodiment and narrative of a voice constantly reincarnating itself in surprising tones, characters, and in other writers; shattering its substantial unity; or, better, *The Waste Land* as some deep-set plan contacted only through particulars of texture. And as one more version, this one suggested by terms from (for young man Eliot) the new art of moving pictures and the newly revolutionized art of painting: 'montage' and 'collage', recently deployed by critics to characterize the poem's surface (that is, 'aesthetic') impact.

In *The Waste Land*, Eliot, a man of his aesthetic times, created a kind of painting in five panels, which must be grasped by the mind's eye all at once, as a spatial form, taken in as if the poem were a single complex image, not a work to be read through time, from beginning to end, but a work to be 'seen' in a glance. This version of the poem can be contacted only by readers of veteran status who know the allusions like the back of their hands, who have read the poem so many times, in frustration and pleasure, that, in effect, they hardly need a text because they have made themselves into viewers. *The Waste Land*, so encountered, becomes the literary equivalent of a work of analytic cubism, a series of layered 'planes' transparent to each other, whose overall effect is the fracturing of the traditional literary unities of time (1922), place (London), and continuing, binding representations of character (many of them sordid and neurasthenic).

Eliot's experiment does not welcome questions about when, where, and who. And it constantly overrides the distinction between real and representation. So that contemporary London (the poem's 'real', the poem's 'present'), Baudelaire's Paris, and the scene of *The Inferno* stand co-presently in 'The Burial of the Dead'; so that lovers from *The Aeneid* and *Hamlet* stand in co-presence, as if they all existed in the same space with contemporary couples in 'A Game of Chess', the panel of couples; so that *The Tempest*, Spenser, and Marvell provide gestures of love side by side with various contemporary enactments of the flesh in 'The Fire Sermon', where Buddha and Saint Augustine speak, side by side. The old unities are replaced by what an active reader must bring together in a reconciling glance: not, finally, the past and present in ironic juxtaposition (though such juxtapositions stud many local textures of the poem), but past and present, 'literary' and 'real', in immediate painterly presence, a wall of pictures, a horror of simultaneity for a consciousness that knows too much and for which freshness of experience is impossible. . . . But the metaphor of spatial form does not quite hold all the way. In the fifth and final section, time leaks ominously out of space, painterly panel becomes narrative, and the fixed and repetitious seem about to undergo change. A key Shakespearean moment ('Those are pearls that were his eyes') is worked and reworked consciously in the poem's voice-over and unconsciously in characters who say it, not because they know Shakespeare (they do not) and enjoy displaying literary sophistication, but because the line must be spoken, because this longing for transformation must be felt. Section five, then, is seen through a veil of hallucinatory rhetoric: Gethsemane, the road to Emmaus, the whirl-wind tour of exploding European capitals, and the approach to the Chapel Perilous, where the grail-quester might ask the right question, so much the better to facilitate redemption of land and impotent king, so that we might live in a new world, forgetting 'the profit and the loss' (Eliot's sole but insistent political gesture, his revulsion from the world of capital). The tone is apocalyptic: some revelation, the much longed-for change is at hand, but what is it that lurks just over the horizon?[11]

Eliot ends the poem in the mode of a desire (half-fearful) expressed just a year before *The Waste Land* appeared by Yeats in 'The Second Coming', a desire revisited several years later by Frost, most notably in 'Once by the Pacific'. 'Someone had better be prepared for rage' is how Frost puts it, and Yeats would have agreed. Eliot is prepared for rage and hopes for salvation. Like Yeats and Frost, he defines his modernity in *The Waste Land* as that intuition of being on the verge of upheaval – the breakup, the smashing, and the sinking of a whole era: not the new, but the verge of the new, for better or for worse. Probably, these writers fear, for worse.[12] □

This sense of the imminent collapse of modern culture reconfirms Lentricchia's opening proposition that *The Waste Land* became a 'cultural event that got beyond Eliot's intention and control'. The final extract of this chapter, Harriet Davidson's 'Improper Desire: Reading *The Waste Land*' (1994), examines how the poem's framing of desire goes beyond Eliot's control and even exceeds the controls of the culture from which it arises. In asserting the operation of desire and control in the poem this provides a fitting conclusion to this Critical Guide: not only does the poem itself end in control ('Damyata') and the desire for peace beyond understanding ('Shantih'), but the operation of desire and control can be seen to be central to critical readings of the poem, indeed to any critical practice.

Davidson's essay is taken from the very useful book *The Cambridge Companion to T. S. Eliot* (1994), a book that brings together much new scholarship on Eliot and sets the benchmark for future Eliot studies. Davidson focuses on the problem that has continually vexed criticism of *The Waste Land*, the sense of 'deep contradiction' in the poem. This contradiction, she argues, is felt most powerfully through the poem's operation of various tropes of desire. The poem desires order and control. It also desires disorder and chaos. Once again, then, the poem is read as both conservative and radical or, in Davidson's terms, its desires are either 'proper' or 'improper'. This means that although Davidson sees the poem surrounded by the 'unruly forces' of the culture from which the poem arises, her reading is unwilling to surrender fully to the implications of its own reading of the desires of the text. For example, the deeply troublesome question of the poem's depiction of women – surely of basic concern to an examination of the text's mobilisation of desire – is rather too easily glossed over. To claim that the poem presents women as both 'objects of' desire *and* 'subjects with' desires is highly unconvincing. It is simply not possible to substantiate the claim that the women in *The Waste Land* 'all bring their own yearnings to [the] poem'. On this point, then, Davidson seems to rely too heavily on the model of contradiction with which she is reading the poem's structuring of desire: if it is passive, then it must also be active. In any case, the women's supposed 'yearnings' are all mediated through the poem's own discursive desires, and can hardly, therefore, be taken to represent real desires of real women. Davidson's reading, then, finally sees the real desires and frustrations – personal and cultural – in which the poem is based, as subject to the poem's desire for aesthetic order and control. But no matter how tense the relationship that it sets up between the proper and the improper, *The Waste Land*'s desires can never, properly speaking, be resolved into such a neat duality. Its fragments trace the operation of desire, not its resolution:

■ *The Waste Land* can be read as a poem about the proper and the improper. Eliot's . . . epigraph . . . contribute[s] to emphasizing what we might call the 'proper' side of this poem, that is, its scholarly apparatus, its respect for tradition, and its recoil from the chaos of life, rather than its 'improper' side – its equally apparent lack of respect for tradition and poetic method and its fascination with mutation, degradation, and fragmentation. Proper means not only respectable or correct, but also in its etymology as 'own' it means belonging to one thing, connecting the proper not only to social propriety, but also to property and the jealous guarding of boundaries. The poem returns again and again to 'improper' sexual desire, temptation, and surrender and their often tragic consequences. The poem also, in its interest in metamorphosis and use of quick juxtapositions, blurs the proper boundaries between things; different characters and voices confusingly mutate into each other. Most obviously, the poem questions the boundaries between poems, liberally appropriating other poets' property as its own. As any reader of *The Waste Land* knows, none of this is done in the spirit of play; the overriding tone of the poem seems to yearn to be rid of improper desires, setting up a deep contradiction within the poem.

This contradiction, along with the poem's lack of thematic clarity and its careful refusal of connections between images, scenes and voices, makes *The Waste Land* particularly open to different interpretations. . . . Early New Critical readings of the poem canonized the poem as the exemplar (even origin) of a kind of high modernism that powerfully depicts and rejects modern life, valorizing myth over history, spatial form over time, an orderly past over a chaotic present, and the transcendence of art over the pain of life – what I would call the proper over the improper. Recent, politically minded critics make similar observations to dismiss the poem as the worst, most conservative side of modernism.[13] These interpretations tend to concur that the barren waste of the poem's title is a metaphor for the chaotic life within the poem and that the enormous longing to escape that life implies that a world of greater propriety, of stability, order, and beauty must exist somewhere, usually in a transcendent realm of the past, of religion, or of the aesthetic imagination.

But the power of the poem, I will argue, comes from its refusal to supply anything to appease the longing for propriety. The poem treats myth, history, art, and religion as subject to the same fragmentation, appropriation, and degradation as modern life – nothing transcends the effects of finitude and change brought on by the regeneration of April. The strong binary oppositions in the poem between desert and water, emptiness and crowdedness, suggest that the barren waste can be read as different from, and in opposition to, the chaotic life in the poem, not as a metaphor for it. In this reading, the empty unchanging desert represents what would happen if our wish to escape the uncertainties of life through absolutes, transcendence, or, like the Sibyl, immortality were to be granted. Sadly, the only alternative to the human world of thwarted and degraded desires, loss, change, and confusion is a barren waste. While the poem provides an emotional and often visceral critique of the state of human life, it equally provides a critique of the desire to transcend and escape that life, and it offers no alternatives beyond that life or the persistence of that desire.

The Waste Land strongly reveals the unruly forces of improper desire in its emotional yearning, in its constant return to sexual tragedy, and in its disorienting juxtapositions and displacements. But the textual history of the poem, from draft, to edited version, to published version with endnotes, tends to tame some of the unruliness of the poem. The manuscript draft of the poem, which is even more various than the final poem, includes three long narrative sections cut in the final version by Pound and by Eliot himself. These cuts excise Eliot's rawer side: scenes of drunkenness, whoring, urinating, defecating, and bigotry are removed from the poem and from Eliot's emerging public persona. And with the removal of the manuscript's comic, narrative opening, the poem foregrounds the life-denying voice, which begins by recoiling from spring: 'April is the cruellest month'.

Perhaps even more important for confusing understanding of the poem are the notes which were not originally attached to it but were added only for the book version. . . . Eliot may not have intended them to be taken so seriously, and may even have been playing an elaborate and highly successful practical joke on the academic profession. . . . Nevertheless, the notes seemed to offer a key to the poem and to promise a full and scientifically accurate explanation which would overcome its fragmentation and suggestiveness. Regretfully or not, Eliot had endorsed a public image of scholarly propriety and encouraged interpretations which tended to erase the improper side of the poem in favor of its proper, pedagogic side. . . .

Knowing the story of the quest for the Grail or the significance of the Tarot does not, of course, hurt when reading *The Waste Land*. . . . In Eliot's own variant on these stories in *The Waste Land*, death is never redeemed by any clear salvation, and barrenness is relieved only by a chaotic multiplicity, which is not only an ironic kind of fertility, but is also the distinctly urban chaos that the young Eliot appreciated as conducive to his work . . . The other lesson of the fertility myths, in which a sacrificial death (often a ritual death by water) is necessary for life to continue, is the connection of life and death. Death is not the only horror, as the Sibyl, incapacitated with age and loneliness after being granted her wish for immortality, well knows. Kurtz's cry of horror at the vision of his wretched life and death is matched by the Sibyl's horror at a sterile, changeless state without life, death, love, or loss.

The Waste Land suggests both horrors. Imagistically, the 'little life with dried tubers' and the dry, unchanging desert contrast throughout the poem with life-giving rain and the drowning sea. The images are supported by two distinct ways of speaking. The lyric voice opening the poem uses highly metaphoric, often symbolic images and speaks in repetitive, stylized syntax, suggesting on the one hand order and propriety, and on the other hand stasis. This voice speaks with authority and finality as it recurs in scenes throughout the poem where the vision of barrenness and revulsion from life is intensely clear and controlled.

This voice contrasts with the babel of many voices speaking in metonymically rendered narrative scenes full of movement and change. These other voices resist categorization, ranging from vivid characters such as Marie, the hyacinth girl, Stetson's friend, Madame Sosostris, the nervous woman, the pub woman, Tiresias, and the Thames daughters, to the non-human voices of the nightingale, the cock, and the thunder, and the voices from literature in the many allusions in the poem. The many abrupt changes and mutations in the voices of the poem often blur the proper boundaries between identities, further increasing the reader's confusion about who is speaking.

Both modes – of sterile propriety and fertile impropriety – cause despair, but neither is repudiated entirely. Much of the drama of this poem comes from the interweaving and crisscrossing of these two modes as desire disrupts order and desire for order sets up paradoxical and unbearable tensions. . . .

'The Burial of the Dead' famously begins with a desire for stasis and anxiety about the change, growth, and sexuality symbolized by April and the spring rain. The slow, repetitive syntax and hanging participles – 'breeding', 'mixing', 'stirring' – seem to freeze and control the movement in the first seven lines. This despairing opening voice is universal and dislocated; it is not in a narrative, nor does it speak to the reader. The clarity and authority of this voice mark it as the voice of propriety, wanting to maintain clear boundaries and rules, and, at its most extreme, hoping to halt forward movement and stop the pro-liferation of possibilities in life or language.

As readers of *The Waste Land*, we tend to privilege this voice because we, too, would like clarity and the stability of a proper mean-ing for this confusing poem. But the desire for stability, the desire to end desire, is always a paradoxical one. If we follow recent psycho-analytic theory, we could say that desire is both caused by the lack of absolutes in human life, the inevitable finitude and change, and *causes* change in its restless search for something to relieve this lack. The reader's interpretation, like any desire for order, is really just another proliferation of possibility, not at all a stabilizing of the poem. In this sense all desire is improper desire, disrupting clarity and stability in favor of change and movement. And the figure of desire, that endless movement from object to object, is metonymy.[14]

Thus, in these opening lines the desire for stasis brings about change. Line eight begins as if to continue the rhythm and tone of the preceding lines, but then the syntax suddenly mutates into a chatty and incidental narrative:

> Summer surprised us, coming over the Starnbergersee
> With a shower of rain; we stopped in the colonnade,
> And went on in sunlight, into the Hofgarten,
> And drank coffee, and talked for an hour.

Now the participle 'coming' is not left hanging to indicate continuing action by the generic 'Summer', but is connected to its object indicating an action of limited duration by a particular 'us'. With the syntactic shift from metaphoric similarity to metonymic contiguity, we have left the angst and symbolic world of the opening lines and entered a realist, fairly neutral narrative world replete with the familiar cultural actions of talking, walking, and drinking coffee. In spite of this simple familiarity, most readers feel anxious when confronted with this new turn in the poem. The clear ideas and syntax established in the opening lines no longer control the poem, and attempts to continue a symbolic reading of these lines founder on the difficulty of turning metonymic details like drinking coffee into metaphoric meaning. Not only the coffee in the Hofgarten, but also the overheard line in German, Madame Sosostris's bad cold, Lil's teeth, the typist's stockings, all seem to function as metonymic details from the culture of the time, and they generate a context and a chain of associations which tend to disperse clear meanings.

The speaker of these lines also seems more particularized than in the opening lines, and in lines thirteen to eighteen the clearly gendered voice of Marie further disrupts the expectation of universality. Her story also ignores the metaphors established at the opening; now snow is associated with memory and desire as she remembers a thrilling sled ride with her cousin. Marie, along with the many other women characters in the poem, is associated in a traditional way with sexual desire, fertility, and generation. But quite untraditionally the poem concerns itself not just with women as objects of desire, but also with women as subjects with desires. Marie, Madame Sosostris, the nervous lady and pub lady of part II, the Thames daughters from part III, all bring their own yearnings to this poem; the female perspective, particular and sexual unlike the ungendered metaphoric voice, insists on the continuation of desire but also shows how often desire leads to frustration, ennui, and violence. The narrative world Eliot gives us as an alternative to the little life of dried tubers is driven by desires, but not often happily. The rather neutral scene in the Hofgarten metonymically moves into the emotionally charged story of Marie which ends abruptly in a scene of loneliness and deadening routine: 'I read, much of the night, and go south in the winter' (I, line 18). Once we enter the everyday world, we also enter the world of loss, unfulfilled desire and, inevitably, death.

The movement from metaphoric enclosure to metonymic movement is repeated twice more in 'The Burial of the Dead' – as the metaphoric voice tries to control the improper desires, and the metonymic voice breaks out of this control. First, the horrifying red rock section (I, lines 19–30) returns to a symbolic mode of commanding finality. But it is interrupted by the German allusion to the great story of improper love, *Tristan und Isolde*, by the narrative of desire and loss in the hyacinth girl passage, and then by the comic realism of Madame Sosostris. Second, the 'Unreal City' passage (I, lines 60–68) returns to a symbolic, static vision of London as a suffocating bell, but here the symbolic enclosure is burst apart by the narrative address to Stetson and then to the reader. The energy of these final lines transgresses a variety of boundaries in their wild historical mixing, grisly violation of the grave, and dense allusiveness. The allusion to Baudelaire in the last line '"You! hypocrite lecteur! – mon semblable, – mon frère!"' (I, line 76) confusingly blurs the narrator's voice with Baudelaire, Stetson, and the reader. We, too, are metonymically drawn into the chain of desire in our search for final meanings in a poem which suggests these meanings but then denies them any stability. . . .

[The] final section returns to a barren waste, an inhuman landscape where repetition suggests a pointless circularity. The continuing force of desire is suggested in lines 346–59 as the imagination tries to break out of the sterility of the desert by thinking 'If there were water . . .' Trying to imagine water, the voice metonymically moves from the rock to 'a pool among the rock' to the 'sound of water' and finally to music once again as these lines culminate in imagining the singing of the hermit thrush in the pine trees and the 'drip drop' of water. This magical metamorphosis abruptly stops as the categorical voice of the desert insists, 'But there is no water'. Still, change cannot be stopped. Immediately after this line, the clarity of the desert dissolves and visions begin to proliferate wildly, from the uncertain vision of 'another one walking beside you' (V, line 362), the unclear 'Murmur of maternal lamentation' (V, line 367), to the city that 'Cracks and reforms and bursts in the violet air' (V, line 372). These visions culminate in the surreal scene of a woman fiddling on her hair, of bats with baby faces, and of upside-down towers. This vision is deeply improper, not respecting conventional metonymical association. And the impropriety is a sign that desire has not been burned away.

Instead, the continuation of desire is announced rather forthrightly in the crow of the cock, the flash of lightning, and the welcome gush of rain:

Only a cock stood on the rooftree
Co co rico co co rico
In a flash of lightning. Then a damp gust
Bringing rain

V, lines 391–94

These lines rewrite the formal strategy of the opening lines; here the participle 'bringing' is attached to its object, giving a sense of release to the sexual and spiritual desire in these lines. Appropriately, the voice of the thunder is neither categorical, proper, nor clear; it is a meaningless syllable, 'DA', which needs to be interpreted, starting another chain of dispersion and obscurity. The thunder is interpreted in the Sanskrit words 'Datta', 'Dayadhvam', 'Damyata', allusions to the fable of the thunder in the Upanishads, a different and perhaps unfamiliar cultural context. The translations of these words into the English imperatives 'give', 'sympathize', and 'control' are further interpreted in the poem in enigmatic lyrics.

Many readers find these three lyrics and the allusive ending of the poem which follows some of the most difficult lines of the poem, and they have been interpreted variously as showing resignation, salvation, or nihilism. The sense of change, variety and movement is strong in these lines, as is the sense of being in a social, cultural world. In the first lyric . . . the voice is conversational, opening out to the reader in the address to 'my friend' and the use of the first person plural words 'we' and 'our':

> *Datta*: what have we given?
> My friend, blood shaking my heart
> The awful daring of a moment's surrender
> Which an age of prudence can never retract
> By this, and this only, we have existed
>
> V, lines 401–5

The surrender to desire, to the shaking heart, *is* life, not the safety of prudence nor the lifeless, 'empty rooms' (V, line 409). In the subsequent lyric . . . both the images of the prison and of the key connect with the Sibyl's lonely prison of immortality; the desire for the key, the clear answer, the end to human troubles, is what ironically 'confirms a prison', while the revivifying 'aethereal rumors' of twilight represent yearning and possibility . . . Most importantly and optimistically, in the third lyric . . . the image of the sailboat both propelled by and controlling the wind and water combines the force of desire and control. In this image order and control are linked to the continuation of desire in the boat's movement across the water.

At the end of the poem, the desire for order and the surrender to the chaotic desires of life remain in tension. The speaker sits by the sea, turning his back on the 'arid plain' of the desert. Still he asks, 'Shall I at least set my lands in order?'. . . indicating the continuation of a quest for order and meaning. But the speaker is answered by a series of allusions which are neither properly 'my lands' nor in any discernible order. The lines themselves speak of disintegration and disorder, madness and desire. And the variety of voices here, speaking in different languages and different tones, indicates a world rich with possibility as well as confusion, with salvation as well as loss. The ending is deeply improper, not respecting boundaries between poems, between cultures, or between voices. The impropriety suggests the disrupting power of desire in *The Waste Land*. The passionate and para-doxical desire to end desires leads only to the continuation of life in all its variousness, confusions, tragedies, and improper desires.[15] □

Davidson ends on a note that has sounded throughout the critical history of *The Waste Land* in that she envisions it as a text that is, finally, resolv-able into a single meaning, however contradictory. Here, the text's desires are transgressed by a desire to assert that modernism has a stabil-ity and coherence that, simply, is present in neither the poem itself, nor the culture it articulates. Perhaps the poem's lesson is that we should think, as Peter Nicholls has pointed out, not of modernism but of mod-ernisms.[16] Davidson's essay misses this important point. It can thus be seen, however, to sum up the desire for unity and coherence that runs pretty consistently through critical readings of modernity and of *The Waste Land*. Davidson's essay also, perhaps, helps suggest something that has been apparent throughout this Guide: that *The Waste Land*'s force is due in large part to its ability to resist critical assimilation. Its intricate and intriguing poetic tracings continually slip away from the grasp of its interpreters and frustrate the desires of its readers. In this sense it is most modern, for it constantly renews the challenges it poses to its readers.

NOTES

INTRODUCTION

1 See Richard Ellmann, *James Joyce, New and Revised Edition* (1959; rev. ed. Oxford: Oxford University Press, 1983), p.538; and Peter Ackroyd, *T.S. Eliot* (London: Hamish Hamilton, 1984).

2 See, for example: Frederick R. Karl's massively sprawling *Modern and Modernism: The Sovereignty of the Artist 1885–1925* (New York: Atheneum, 1985); Peter Nicholls' recent and quite brilliant reassessment of modernism, *Modernisms: A Literary Guide* (London: Macmillan, 1995); the indispensable *Modernism 1890–1930*, edited by Malcolm Bradbury and James McFarlane (1976; rpt Harmondsworth: Penguin Books, 1983); and Peter Faulkner's brief survey, *Modernism* (1977; rpt London and New York: Methuen, 1982).

3 In her essay 'Mr Bennett and Mrs Brown' (1924); see Virginia Woolf, *Collected Essays*, Volume I (London: Hogarth Press, 1966), p.320.

4 Bradbury and McFarlane, p.57.

5 Ezra Pound, 'Cavalcanti', in *Literary Essays*, ed. and intro. T.S. Eliot (1954; rpt London: Faber and Faber, 1985), p.154.

6 James Joyce, *Ulysses*, ed. Jeri Johnson (1922; Oxford: Oxford University Press, 1993), p.34.

7 T.S. Eliot, '*Ulysses*, Order and Myth', *The Dial* (November 1923), pp.480–83.

8 'Tradition and the Individual Talent' (1919) in T.S. Eliot, *Selected Essays* (1932; rev. ed. London: Faber and Faber, 1980), pp.13–22.

9 'Hamlet' (1919), in *Selected Essays*, p.145.

10 Quoted as an epigraph to *The Waste Land: A Facsimile and Transcript of the Original Drafts including the Annotations of Ezra Pound*, ed. Valerie Eliot (San Diego: Harcourt Brace Jovanovich, 1971), no page number.

CHAPTER ONE

1 See Gareth Reeves, *T.S. Eliot's 'The Waste Land'*, Critical Studies of Key Texts Series (London: Harvester Wheatsheaf, 1994), p.14. Another indicator of *The Waste Land's* fame, and power to shock, is its appearance in a passage detailing undergraduate life at Oxford in the 1920s in Evelyn Waugh's novel *Brideshead Revisited*. Anthony Blanche, 'the "aesthete" *par excellence*, a byword of iniquity from Cherwell Edge to Somerville', intones, through a megaphone, passages of the poem from the balcony of Sebastian Flyte's rooms in Christ Church college to passers-by on their way to the river. See Evelyn Waugh, *Brideshead Revisited: The Sacred and Profane Memories of Captain Charles Ryder* (1945; rpt London: Methuen, 1989), p.41.

2 Charles Powell, *Manchester Guardian* (31 October 1923). Quoted in *T.S. Eliot, The Waste Land: A Casebook*, ed., C.B. Cox and Arnold P. Hinchliffe (London: Macmillan, 1968), p.29.

3 Gilbert Seldes, 'T.S. Eliot', *Nation*, 115 (6 December 1922), pp.614–16.

4 Seldes, p.616.

5 Anonymous, 'Review of *The Waste Land* and notice of the first issue of the *Criterion*', *Times Literary Supplement*, no. 1084 (26 October 1922), p.690.

6 Louis Untermeyer, 'Disillusion vs. Dogma', *Freeman*, 6 (7 January 1923), p.453.

7 Untermeyer, p.453.

8 Untermeyer, p.453.

9 Edmund Wilson, 'The Poetry of Drouth', *The Dial*, 73 (December 1922), p.612.

10 Wilson, p.611.

11 Wilson, pp.615–16.

12 F.L. Lucas, 'Review: *The Waste Land*', *New Statesman*, 22 (3 November 1923), p.116.

13 Lucas, p.117.

14 Lucas, p.117.

15 Squire's comments about *The Waste Land* appear in a longer review of con-

temporary poetry. See J.C. Squire, 'Poetry', *London Mercury*, 8 (October 1923), pp.655–66.

16 Gorham B. Munson, 'The Esotericism of T.S. Eliot', *1924*, no. 1 (1 July 1924), p.4.

17 Munson, p.6.

18 Munson, p.9.

19 For an interesting discussion of the conflict between European and American sensibilities in Eliot's poetry see Richard Gray, 'The problem of literary nationality: the case of T.S. Eliot', in *American Poetry of the Twentieth Century* (London: Longman, 1990), pp.336–46.

20 Elinor Wylie, 'Mr Eliot's Slug Horn', *New York Evening Post Literary Review* (20 January 1923), p.396.

21 Edgell Rickword, 'A Fragmentary Poem', *Times Literary Supplement*, no.1131 (20 September 1923), p.616. This review was originally published anonymously; see R.L Houghton, 'The Waste Land Revisited', *Cambridge Quarterly*, 18–1 (1989), p.34, and Graham Clarke, ed., *T.S. Eliot: Critical Assessments. Volume II: Early Poems and* The Waste Land (London: Helm, 1990), p.106.

22 Conrad Aiken, 'Prefatory Note' to 'An Anatomy of Melancholy', in *A Reviewer's ABC* (New York: Meridian Books, Inc., 1958), p.176.

23 By Edmund Wilson, see the extract from his review, p.19 of this Guide.

24 Conrad Aiken, 'An Anatomy of Melancholy', *The New Republic* (7 February 1923); rpt in *A Reviewer's ABC* (New York: Meridian Books, Inc., 1958), pp.54–58.

25 For a discussion of Richards' place in the development of the study of literature, and the particular cultural assumptions that his critical practice endorses, see Terry Eagleton, *Literary Theory: An Introduction* (Oxford: Basil Blackwell, 1983), pp.15, 44–46.

26 I.A. Richards, *The Principles of Literary Criticism*, 2nd ed. (London: Routledge and Kegan Paul, 1926), pp.289–95.

CHAPTER TWO

1 See '*Ulysses*, Order and Myth', pp.9–10 of this Guide.

2 Maud Bodkin, *Archetypal Patterns in Poetry: Psychological Studies of Imagination* (London: Oxford University Press, 1934), p.1.

3 Edmund Wilson, *Axel's Castle: A Study in the Imaginative Literature of 1870–1930* (New York: Charles Scribner's Sons, 1931), pp.9–10, 24.

4 The poem actually has 433 lines.

5 Edmund Wilson, *Axel's Castle*, pp.89–97.

6 F.R. Leavis, *New Bearings in English Poetry: a study of the contemporary situation* (London: Chatto and Windus, 1932), p.70.

7 See Terry Eagleton, *Criticism and Ideology: A Study in Marxist Literary Theory* (1976; rpt London: Verso, 1978), pp.145–47 (which appears in chapter four of this Guide).

8 Leavis, p.25.

9 Leavis, p.16.

10 Leavis, pp.70–87.

11 See René Wellek and Austin Warren, *Theory of Literature* (1949; rev. ed. Harmondsworth: Penguin, 1980) who summarise Jung's thesis about the individual and collective unconscious as follows: 'Beneath the individual "unconscious" – the blocked-off residue of our past, particularly our childhood and infancy – lies the "collective unconscious" – the blocked-off memory of our racial past, even our pre-humanity' (p.84).

12 [Bodkin's note] H.R. Williamson, *The Poetry of T.S. Eliot* (Hodder and Stoughton, 1932), p.146.

13 Bodkin, pp.307–14.

CHAPTER THREE

1 For an excellent synopsis of 'New Criticism', see Catherine Belsey, *Critical Practice* (London: Methuen, 1980), pp.15–20.

2 See Cleanth Brooks, *The Well Wrought*

Urn: Studies in the Structure of Poetry (1949; rev. ed. London: Dobson, 1968). Brooks takes the phrase from John Donne's poem 'The Canonization' (1633), see Herbert J.C. Grierson, ed., Donne: Poetical Works (1929; rpt Oxford: Oxford University Press, 1979), p. 15.

3 Terry Eagleton, Literary Theory: An Introduction (Oxford: Basil Blackwell, 1983), p. 47.

4 Belsey, Critical Practice, p. 15.

5 An effect noted by Eagleton, Literary Theory, p. 46.

6 Eagleton, Literary Theory, p. 50.

7 A point made by Karl Shapiro in the essay 'T.S. Eliot: The Death of Literary Judgement', in his In Defense of Ignorance (New York, 1960), pp. 35–60. This essay is reproduced in Graham Clarke, ed., T.S. Eliot: Critical Assessments. Volume II: Early Poems and The Waste Land (London: Helm, 1990), pp. 263–77.

8 [Matthiessen's note] Weston, p. 36.

9. [Matthiessen's note] Weston, p. 21.

10 The revisions are largely, we now know, those of Ezra Pound.

11 The quotation is from Eliot's essay 'Ulysses, Order and Myth', The Dial (November, 1923), pp. 480–83.

12 F.O. Matthiessen, The Achievement of T.S. Eliot: An Essay on the Nature of Poetry (1935; rpt New York and London: Oxford University Press, 1958), pp. 34–55.

13 Cleanth Brooks, 'The Waste Land: Critique of the Myth', in Modern Poetry and the Tradition (Chapel Hill: University of North Carolina Press, 1939), pp. 137–64.

14 Brooks, 'The Waste Land: Critique of the Myth', pp. 165–70.

15 Eliot, Complete Poems and Plays (London: Faber and Faber, 1969), p. 78.

16 Hugh Kenner, 'The Mind of Europe', in The Invisible Poet: T.S. Eliot (1959; rpt London: Methuen, 1965), pp. 125–56.

17 Pearce therefore follows the ideas of R.W.B. Lewis that are set out in his ground-breaking account of American culture and ideology The American Adam: Innocence, Tragedy and Tradition in the Nineteenth Century (Chicago and London: The University of Chicago Press, 1955).

18 Roy Harvey Pearce, The Continuity of American Poetry (Princeton: Princeton University Press, 1961), p. 109.

19 Pearce, pp. 301–309.

CHAPTER FOUR

1 Michael North, The Political Aesthetic of Yeats, Eliot and Pound (Cambridge: Cambridge University Press, 1991), p. 106.

2 North, p. 106.

3 Terry Eagleton, Criticism and Ideology: A Study in Marxist Literary Theory (1976; rpt London: Verso, 1978), p. 149.

4 See Louis Althusser, 'Ideology and Ideological State Apparatuses', in Lenin and Philosophy and Other Essays, trans. Ben Brewster (London: New Left Books, 1971), pp. 121–73.

5 See Althusser, p. 155. Quoted in Fredric Jameson, 'Postmodernism, or The Cultural Logic of Late Capitalism', New Left Review, 146 (1984), p. 90.

6 For useful discussions of Althusser's notion of ideology see Catherine Belsey, Critical Practice (London: Methuen, 1980), pp. 56–63; and Terry Eagleton, Literary Theory: An Introduction (Oxford: Basil Blackwell, 1983), pp. 171–73.

7 [Craig's note] T.S. Eliot, 'Thoughts after Lambeth', in Selected Essays (1951 edn), p. 368.

8 [Craig's note] New Bearings in English Poetry (1950 edn), pp. 90–91.

9 [Craig's note] New Bearings, p. 112.

10 [Craig's note] New Bearings, p. 104.

11 David Craig, 'The Defeatism of The Waste Land', Critical Quarterly, 2 (1960), pp. 241–52.

12 Pierre Macherey, A Theory of Literary Production, trans. Geoffrey Wall (London: Routledge and Kegan Paul, 1978), p. 85.

13 [Eagleton's note] The Use of Poetry and the Use of Criticism (London: 1933), p. 108.

14 [Eagleton's note] *Eliot in Perspective* (London: 1970), p. 22.

15 [Eagleton's note] In a somewhat parallel way, the doctrine of the 'objective correlative' pivots on an arbitrary projection of subjective experience into formulae which are then merely asserted to be the 'objective', consistently identifiable codes for that experience.

16 [Eagleton's note] See *The Idea of a Christian Society* (London: 1939) and *Notes Towards the Definition of Culture* (1948). It is symptomatic of Eliot's political acumen that the regressive social utopianism of the former volume should be offered to the world on the very eve of the Second World War.

17 Terry Eagleton, *Criticism and Ideology: A Study in Marxist Literary Theory* (1976; rpt London: Verso, 1978), pp. 145–50.

18 [North's note] T. S. Eliot, *The Waste Land: A Facsimile*, ed. Valerie Eliot (New York: Harcourt Brace Jovanovich, 1971), p. 31. See Ronald Bush, T. S. Eliot: *A Study in Character and Style* (New York: Oxford University Press, 1984), pp. 56 and 69.

19 [North's note] Michael Levenson, *A Genealogy of Modernism* (Cambridge: Cambridge University Press, 1984), p. 191.

20 [North's note] *The Education of Henry Adams* (Boston: Houghton Mifflin, 1918), p. 445.

21 [North's note] Stephen Spender, 'Writers and Politics', *Partisan Review* 34 (Summer 1967), p. 378. A. L. Morton, 'T. S. Eliot – A Personal View', *Zeitschrift für Anglistik und Amerikanistik* 14 (1966), pp. 284, 291. For a detailed discussion of the debate in the 1930s on obscurity in poetry, see Valentine Cunningham, *British Writers of the Thirties* (Oxford: Oxford University Press, 1988), pp. 298–304.

22 [North's note] Robert Graves, *Contemporary Techniques of Poetry* (London: Hogarth, 1925), pp. 6, 10.

23 [North's note] Theodor Adorno, 'Reconciliation under Duress', in *Aesthetics and Politics*, by Ernst Bloch et al (London: NLB, 1977), p. 166. In the same essay Adorno defends Eliot, along with Joyce, against Lukács's criticism (p. 162).

24 North, pp. 94–105.

CHAPTER FIVE

1 Jonathan Culler, *On Deconstruction: Theory and Criticism after Structuralism* (London: Routledge & Kegan Paul, 1983), p. 86.

2 Frank Kermode, 'A Babylonish Dialect', *Sewanee Review*, 74–1 (1966), p. 233.

3 Kermode, pp. 231–5.

4 [Nevo's note] Jacques Derrida, *L'écriture et la Différence* (Paris, 1967), p. 34. In English, *Writing and Difference*, trans. and introd. Alan Bass (Chicago, 1978).

5 [Nevo's note] Josué V. Harari, ed., *Textual Strategies* (Ithaca, NY, 1979), p. 37.

6 Ruth Nevo, '*The Waste Land*': Ur-Text of Deconstruction', *New Literary History*, 13–3 (Spring 1982), pp. 453–61.

7 [Trotter's note] Julien Benda, *Belphégor*, trans. S. J. I. Lawson (New York, 1929), p. 84.

8 [Trotter's note] Max Nordau, *Degeneration* (1895), pp. 5–6.

9 [Trotter's note] *Practitioner* (July 1923) pp. 2, 4, 24.

10 [Trotter's note] Donald Davie, *The Poet in the Imaginary Museum* (Manchester 1977), p. 101.

11 [Trotter's note] Robertson Smith, *Lectures on the Religion of the Semites*, revised edition (1894) p. 23.

12 [Trotter's note] Sigmund Freud, *Beyond the Pleasure Principle*, Standard Edition vol. 18 (1955) pp. 15, 16.

13 The quotation here is from F. H. Bradley, *Appearance and Reality* (1893), pp. 224–25.

14 David Trotter, *The Making of the Reader: Language and Subjectivity in Modern American, English and Irish Poetry*

(London: Macmillan, 1984), pp. 38–56.

15 In his book *Literary Theory: An Introduction* (Oxford: Basil Blackwell, 1983), pp. 185–86, Terry Eagleton describes Freud's *'fort/da'* game. As 'the first glimmerings of narrative', he maintains that '*Fort-da* is perhaps the shortest story we can imagine: an object is lost, and then recovered'.

16 Maud Ellmann, '*The Waste Land*: A Sphinx without a Secret', in *The Poetics of Impersonality: T. S. Eliot and Ezra Pound* (Brighton: The Harvester Press, 1987), pp. 108–9.

17 Sandra M. Gilbert and Susan Gubar, 'Sexual Linguistics: Gender, Language and Sexuality', in Catherine Belsey and Jane Moore, eds, *The Feminist Reader: Essays in Gender and the Politics of Literary Criticism* (London: Macmillan, 1989), p. 84. The quotation from Joyce is taken from Richard Ellmann (Maud's father, uncannily), *James Joyce* (New York: Oxford University Press, 1959), p. 510. A further feminist examination of *The Waste Land* and of modernity is Sandra M. Gilbert's 'Costumes of the Mind: Transvestism as Metaphor in Modern Literature', *Critical Inquiry*, 7 (Winter 1980), pp. 391–417.

18 [Ellmann's note] See Hegel's *Aesthetics: Lectures on Fine Art*, trans. T. M. Knox (Oxford: Clarendon, 1975), pp. 360–61.

19 [Ellmann's note] Julia Kristeva, *Powers of Horror: An Essay on Abjection*, trans. Leon S. Roudiez (New York: Columbia University Press, 1982), p. 4; see also p. 9.

20 [Ellmann's note] *Powers of Horror*, pp. 4, 3.

21 Ellmann refers to The Standard Edition of *The Complete Psychological Works of Sigmund Freud*, trans. James Strachey (London: Hogarth, 1953–1974).

22 [Ellmann's note] Thus it could be said that writing *engenders* blasphemy, just as law is the prerequisite to crime.

23 [Ellmann's note] Alick West pointed this out long ago: see *Crisis and Criticism* (London: Lawrence and Wishart, 1937), pp. 5–6, 28.

24 [Ellmann's note] 'The "Uncanny"', SE XVII 238.

25. [Ellmann's note] Ibid., pp. 222–6.

26 [Ellmann's note] Even in *The Odyssey*, his prophecies make action a redundancy, for the deed becomes the mere mimesis of the word.

27 Maud Ellmann, pp. 91–107.

CHAPTER SIX

1 Peter Ackroyd, *T.S. Eliot* (London: Hamish Hamilton, 1984), p. 113.

2 Ackroyd, pp. 109–10. The letter Ackroyd refers to is from Eliot to Richard Aldington and is dated 7 April 1921.

3 See, for example, Michael North, 'Introduction', *The Political Aesthetic of Yeats, Eliot and Pound* (Cambridge: Cambridge University Press, 1991), pp. 1–20; Peter Nicholls, *Ezra Pound: Politics, Economics and Writing* (London: Macmillan, 1984); and Nick Selby, 'Fascist Language in *The Adams Cantos* of Ezra Pound', *Journal of American Studies of Turkey*, 2 (1995), pp. 61–72.

4 Ackroyd, passim, esp., pp. 305–6. Anthony Julius, *T.S. Eliot: Anti-Semitism and Literary Form* (Cambridge: Cambridge University Press, 1995).

5 Julius, p. 38.

6 Julius, p. 10, makes a similar point about Ricks' concept of prejudice. He notes that, 'It tends to . . . trivialize the subject [of anti-Semitism] . . . because representing anti-Semitism as a prejudice reduces it to a contingency of personality, when it is in reality a component of our culture.'

7 [Ricks' note] *Times Literary Supplement*, 27 September 1928.

8 [Ricks' note] B. C. Southam, *A Student's Guide to the Selected Poems of T. S. Eliot* (1968), p. 90.

9 Aiken's 1923 essay on *The Waste Land* from which Ricks quotes here is

extracted in chapter one above.

10 Christopher Ricks, *T.S. Eliot and Prejudice* (London: Faber and Faber, 1988), pp. 174–98.

11 Lentricchia refers here to W. B. Yeats' poem 'The Second Coming' (1921): 'Surely some revelation is at hand;/ Surely the Second Coming is at hand. . . . / [But] what rough beast, its hour come round at last,/Slouches towards Bethlehem to be born?' W. B. Yeats, *Collected Poems* (1933; rev. ed. London: Macmillan, 1983), p. 211.

12 Frank Lentricchia, *Modernist Quartet* (Cambridge: Cambridge University Press, 1994), pp. 248–77.

13 [Davidson's note] See, for instance, Terry Eagleton, *Criticism and Ideology* (1976; London: Verso, 1978), pp. 45–51;

also Sandra M. Gilbert, 'Costumes of the Mind: Transvestism as Metaphor in Modern Literature', *Critical Inquiry* 7 (1980): pp. 400–4.

14 [Davidson's note] See Jacques Lacan's discussion of metonymy and desire in 'The Agency of the Letter in the Unconscious, or Reason Since Freud', *Ecrits: A Selection* (New York: W. W. Norton and Co., 1977), pp. 146–75.

15 Harriet Davidson, 'Improper Desire: Reading *The Waste Land*', in A. David Moody, ed., *The Cambridge Companion to T. S. Eliot* (Cambridge: Cambridge University Press, 1994), pp. 121–31.

16 See Peter Nicholls, *Modernisms: A Literary Guide* (London: Macmillan, 1995).

BIBLIOGRAPHY

Peter Ackroyd, *T. S. Eliot* (London: Hamish Hamilton, 1984).

Conrad Aiken, 'An Anatomy of Melancholy', *The New Republic* (7 February 1923); rpt in *A Reviewer's ABC* (New York: Meridian Books, 1958), pp. 54–58.

Louis Althusser, 'Ideology and Ideological State Apparatuses', in *Lenin and Philosophy and Other Essays*, trans. Ben Brewster (London: New Left Books, 1971), pp. 121–73.

Anonymous, 'Review of *The Waste Land* and notice of the first issue of the *Criterion*', *Times Literary Supplement*, no. 1084 (26 October 1922), p. 690.

Catherine Belsey, *Critical Practice* (London: Methuen, 1980).

Catherine Belsey and Jane Moore, eds., *The Feminist Reader: Essays in Gender and the Politics of Literary Criticism* (London: Macmillan, 1989).

Maud Bodkin, *Archetypal Patterns in Poetry: Psychological Studies of Imagination* (London: Oxford University Press, 1934).

Malcolm Bradbury and James McFarlane, eds., *Modernism 1890–1930* (1976; rpt Harmondsworth: Penguin Books, 1983).

Cleanth Brooks, '*The Waste Land*: Critique of the Myth', in *Modern Poetry and the Tradition* (Chapel Hill: University of North Carolina Press, 1939), pp. 137–64.

—— *The Well Wrought Urn: Studies in the Structure of Poetry* (1949; rev. ed. London: Dobson, 1968).

Ronald Bush, *T. S. Eliot: A Study in Character and Style* (New York: Oxford University Press, 1984).

Graham Clarke, ed., *T. S. Eliot: Critical Assessments. Volume II: Early Poems and 'The Waste Land'* (London: Helm, 1990).

C. B. Cox and Arnold P. Hinchliffe, eds., *T. S. Eliot, 'The Waste Land': A Casebook* (London: Macmillan, 1968).

David Craig, 'The Defeatism of *The Waste Land*', *Critical Quarterly*, 2 (1960), pp. 241–52.

Jonathan Culler, *On Deconstruction: Theory and Criticism after Structuralism* (London: Routledge & Kegan Paul, 1983).

Valentine Cunningham, *British Writers of the Thirties* (Oxford: Oxford University Press, 1988).

Harriet Davidson, 'Improper Desire: Reading *The Waste Land*', in A. David Moody, ed., *The Cambridge Companion to T. S. Eliot* (Cambridge: Cambridge University Press, 1994), pp. 121–31.

John Donne, *Donne: Poetical Works*, ed. Herbert J. C. Grierson (1929; rpt Oxford: Oxford University Press, 1979).

Terry Eagleton, *Criticism and Ideology: A Study in Marxist Literary Theory* (1976; rpt London: Verso, 1978)

—— *Literary Theory: An Introduction* (Oxford: Basil Blackwell, 1983).

T. S. Eliot, '*Ulysses*, Order and Myth', *The Dial* (November 1923), pp. 480–83

—— *Selected Essays* (1932; rev. ed. London: Faber and Faber, 1980)

—— *Complete Poems and Plays* (London: Faber and Faber, 1969)

—— '*The Waste Land*': *A Facsimile and Transcript of the Original Drafts including the Annotations of Ezra Pound*, ed. Valerie Eliot (San Diego: Harcourt Brace Jovanovich, 1971).

Richard Ellmann, *James Joyce. New and Revised Edition* (1959; rev. ed. Oxford: Oxford University Press, 1983).

Maud Ellmann, *The Poetics of Impersonality: T. S. Eliot and Ezra Pound* (Brighton: The Harvester Press, 1987).

Peter Faulkner, *Modernism* (1977; rpt London and New York: Methuen, 1982).

Sigmund Freud, *The Standard Edition of The Complete Psychological Works of Sigmund Freud*, trans. James Strachey (London: Hogarth, 1953–1974).

Sandra M. Gilbert, 'Costumes of the Mind: Transvestism as Metaphor in Modern Literature', *Critical Inquiry*, 7 (Winter 1980), pp. 391–417.

Sandra M. Gilbert and Susan Gubar, 'Sexual Linguistics: Gender, Language and Sexuality', in Catherine Belsey and Jane Moore, eds., *The Feminist Reader: Essays in Gender and the Politics of Literary Criticism* (London: Macmillan, 1989), pp. 81–99.

Robert Graves, *Contemporary Techniques of Poetry* (London: Hogarth, 1925).

Richard Gray, 'The problem of literary nationality: the case of T. S. Eliot', in *American Poetry of the Twentieth Century* (London: Longman, 1990), pp. 336–46.

R. L. Houghton, '*The Waste Land* Revisited', *Cambridge Quarterly*, 18–1 (1989), 32–62.

Fredric Jameson, 'Postmodernism, or The Cultural Logic of Late Capitalism', *New Left Review*, 146 (1984).

James Joyce, *Ulysses*, ed. Jeri Johnson (1922; Oxford: Oxford University Press, 1993).

Anthony Julius, *T. S. Eliot: Anti-Semitism and Literary Form* (Cambridge: Cambridge University Press, 1995).

Frederick R. Karl, *Modern and Modernism: The Sovereignty of the Artist 1885–1925* (New York: Atheneum, 1985).

Hugh Kenner, *The Invisible Poet: T. S. Eliot* (1959; rpt London: Methuen, 1965).

Frank Kermode, 'A Babylonish Dialect', *Sewanee Review*, 74–1 (1966), pp. 225–37.

Julia Kristeva, *Powers of Horror: An Essay on Abjection*, trans. Leon S. Roudiez (New York: Columbia University Press, 1982).

F. R. Leavis, *New Bearings in English Poetry: a study of the contemporary situation* (London: Chatto and Windus, 1932).

Frank Lentricchia, *Modernist Quartet* (Cambridge: Cambridge University Press, 1994).

Michael Levenson, *A Genealogy of Modernism* (Cambridge: Cambridge University Press, 1984).

R. W. B. Lewis, *The American Adam: Innocence, Tragedy and Tradition in the Nineteenth Century* (Chicago and London: The University of Chicago Press, 1955).

F. L. Lucas, 'Review: *The Waste Land*', *New Statesman*, 22 (3 November 1923), pp. 116–18.

Pierre Macherey, *A Theory of Literary Production*, trans. Geoffrey Wall (London: Routledge and Kegan Paul, 1978).

F. O. Matthiessen, *The Achievement of T. S. Eliot: An Essay on the Nature of Poetry* (1935; rpt New York and London: Oxford University Press, 1958).

Gorham B. Munson, 'The Esotericism of T. S. Eliot', *1924*, no. 1 (1 July 1924), pp. 3–10.

Peter Nicholls, *Ezra Pound: Politics, Economics and Writing* (London: Macmillan, 1984).

—— *Modernisms: A Literary Guide* (London: Macmillan, 1995).

Ruth Nevo, '*The Waste Land*: Ur-Text of Deconstruction', *New Literary History*, 13–3 (Spring 1982), pp. 453–61.

Michael North, *The Political Aesthetic of Yeats, Eliot and Pound* (Cambridge: Cambridge University Press, 1991).

Roy Harvey Pearce, *The Continuity of American Poetry* (Princeton: Princeton University Press, 1961).

Gareth Reeves, *T. S. Eliot's 'The Waste Land'*, Critical Studies of Key Texts Series (London: Harvester Wheatsheaf, 1994).

I. A. Richards, *The Principles of Literary Criticism*, 2nd edn (London: Routledge and Kegan Paul, 1926).

Christopher Ricks, *T. S. Eliot and Prejudice* (London: Faber and Faber, 1988).

Edgell Rickword, 'A Fragmentary Poem', *Times Literary Supplement*, no. 1131 (20 September 1923), p. 616.

Nick Selby, 'Fascist Language in *The Adams Cantos* of Ezra Pound', *Journal of American Studies of Turkey*, 2 (1995), pp. 61–72.

Gilbert Seldes, 'T. S. Eliot', *Nation*, 115 (6 December 1922), pp. 614–16.

Karl Shapiro, 'T. S. Eliot: The Death of Literary Judgement', in *In Defense of Ignorance* (New York, 1960).

J. C. Squire, 'Poetry', *London Mercury*, 8 (October 1923), pp. 655–66.

David Trotter, *The Making of the Reader: Language and Subjectivity in Modern American, English and Irish Poetry* (London: Macmillan, 1984).

Louis Untermeyer, 'Disillusion vs. Dogma', *Freeman*, 6 (7 January 1923), p. 453.

Evelyn Waugh, *Brideshead Revisited: The Sacred and Profane Memories of Captain Charles Ryder* (1945; rpt London: Methuen, 1989).

René Wellek and Austin Warren, *Theory of Literature* (1949; rev. edn Harmondsworth: Penguin, 1980).

H. R. Williamson, *The Poetry of T. S. Eliot* (London: Hodder and Stoughton, 1932).

Edmund Wilson, 'The Poetry of Drouth', *The Dial*, 73 (December 1922), pp.611–16

—— *Axel's Castle: A Study in the Imaginative Literature of 1870–1930* (New York: Charles Scribner's Sons, 1931).

Virginia Woolf, *Collected Essays*, Volume I (London: Hogarth Press, 1966).

Elinor Wylie, 'Mr Eliot's Slug Horn', *New York Evening Post Literary Review* (20 January 1923), p.396.

W.B. Yeats, *Collected Poems* (1933; rev. edn London: Macmillan, 1983).

ACKNOWLEDGEMENTS

The editor and publishers wish to thank the following for their permission to reprint copyright material: Cambridge University Press (for material from *T.S. Eliot, Anti-Semitism, and Literary Form*, 'Improper Desire: Reading *The Waste Land*', and *Modernist Quartet*); Oxford University Press (for material from *Archetypal Patterns in Poetry: Psychological Studies of Imagination* and *The Achievement of T.S. Eliot: An Essay on the Nature of Poetry*); University of North Carolina Press (for material from *Modern Poetry and the Tradition*); *Critical Quarterly* (for material from 'The Defeatism of *The Waste Land*'); Verso (for material from *Criticism and Ideology: A Study in Marxist Literary Theory*); The Harvester Press (for material from *The Poetics of Impersonality: T.S. Eliot and Ezra Pound*); Methuen (for material from *The Invisible Poet: T.S. Eliot*); Chatto and Windus (for material from *New Bearings in English Poetry: a Study of the Contemporary Situation*); *New Literary History* (for material from '*The Waste Land*: Ur-Text of Deconstruction'); Princeton University Press (for material from *The Continuity of American Poetry*); Routledge (for material from *The Principles of Literary Criticism*); Faber (for material from *T.S. Eliot and Prejudice*); Macmillan (for material from *The Making of the Reader: Language and Subjectivity in Modern American, English and Irish Poetry*); Charles Scribner's Sons (for material from *Axel's Castle: A Study in the Imaginative Literature of 1870–1930*).

There are instances where we have been unable to trace or contact copyright holders before our printing deadline. If notified, the publisher will be pleased to acknowledge the use of copyright material.

Nick Selby is Lecturer in American Studies at the University of Wales, Swansea. He has published on Walt Whitman, Allen Ginsberg and the Beats, sexuality and 1950s American culture, as well as on Ezra Pound and modernism. He is currently writing a book on American poetics and culture that examines (among others) the work of Ezra Pound, Gary Snyder and Jorie Graham. He is the editor of the Icon Critical Guide to *Moby-Dick*.

INDEX